Sex Ed Is in Session

An Adult Guide to Connecting
with Young People About Life's Tough Topics

Mary Jo Podgurski, RNC, EdD

ONE IDEA PRESS PITTSBURGH

Printed in the United States
ONE IDEA PRESS
Pittsburgh, PA
OneIdeaPress.com

Copyright © 2019 by Mary Jo Podgurski, RNC, EdD
**Sex Ed Is in Session: An Adult Guide to Connecting
with Young People About Life's Tough Topics**

Published by One Idea Press
Pittsburgh, PA

This edition copyright © One Idea Press 2019

ISBN: 978-1-944134-26-6

Printed in the United States of America

For information, special sales, premium, custom, and corporate purchases, please contact One Idea Press at hello@oneideapress.com.

Contents

Teach With Your Heart | 1

Narratore | 5

Sex Lady | 11

Never Give It Up for a Sofa | 23

Milk Money | 31

Toolkit for Connection | 41

A Napkin Sex Question | 49

Portable Body Parts & Bodies | 59

Consent | 75

Privilege | 85

Change | 97

Please Don't Make Me Say What My Daddy Did... | 103

Nude Pics, Phones, & Social Media | 113

Hockey | 119

Fear | 127

Silence and Truth | 137

Snow and Ice | 145

Sex on the Road | 151

Lessons Learned | 161

Trauma | 171

Words Matter | 179

Labels | 189

Perfect | 195

Me, Too | 203

Pain and Healing | 211

Forgiveness | 217

Boom Shaka Laka Laka | 227

Faith | 233

Mentoring | 241

Ethics, Morals, & Integrity | 247

Grief | 261

Cancer is Just a Word | 269

Thirty Years | 279

Level Sixty-Seven | 283

Closing | 287

A Final Gift | 291

Dedication

For the young people I've served since 1970,
no matter your age,
you inspire me.

For my parents, A. Delphine and John Cirelli,
you were my first teachers.
You gave me confidence, a passion for learning,
a deep sense of worthiness, and your faith.
Grazie, Mama and Papa.

For la mia famiglia,
I do nothing without the cushion of your love and support.

"A true teacher is someone who helps you discover the teacher in yourself."
-Thich Nhat Hanh

*"Do not be daunted by the enormity of the world's grief. Do justly, now.
Love mercy, now. Walk humbly, now. You are not obligated to complete the
work, but neither are you free to abandon it."*
-from *Talmud*

*"Do the best you can until you know better.
Then when you know better, do better."*
-Maya Angelou

"All grownups were once children, but only a few of them remember it."
-Antoine De St. Exupery

"Good teaching is ¼ preparation and ¾ theatre."
-Gail Godwin

*"Do all the good you can, by all the means you can, in all the ways you can,
in all the places you can, at all the times you can, to all the people you can,
as long as ever you can."*
-John Wesley

Introduction

by ANASTASIA HIGGINBOTHAM,
artist and author of the book series for children *Ordinary Terrible Things*

"Articulate the obvious," writes The Sex Lady, and so I will.

Kindness is often mistaken, consciously and not, for weakness. Gentleness and softness are, too. People who want to help people, who love openly, who take us into their direct care and even into their home, especially when we are strung out and in trouble, who invite us to disrupt their sleep with our woes and emergencies—we tend to worry about these people. We worry they are leaving themselves open to being used or taken for all that they are worth—*all that they are worth!*

But what if each of us were taken for all that we are worth?
And what if by "taken," I really mean *received?*

"Each person is a person of worth," writes Mary Jo Podgurski, who leads with kindness and follows through with gentleness; who helps people, loves openly, takes us into her direct care when we are in trouble, responds to texts from teens in the middle of the nights, and still has boundaries enough to keep her emotional and energetic cupboards full!

She is a registered nurse, doctor of education, certified sexuality educator, childbirth educator, lactation consultant, doula, preventer of bullying, newspaper advice columnist, parent, partner, breast cancer survivor, and the prodigious author and creator of the *Nonnie Series*, which includes books on race, gender, sex, consent, puberty, pregnancy and birth, death, disability, fear, and trauma. This book is her gift to adults who want to reach young people. In these pages, Mary Jo offers steps to connection, as always, holding nothing back. She gives herself completely.

"Each person is a person of worth," I say again, because it's worth repeating, and because it's one thing to say it, but Mary Jo has been living this truth all her day-to-day life, starting early in childhood. Mary Jo's parents, especially her papa, gifted her with compassion and an unshakable moral core, which guided Mary Jo to become the responsible and caring human he always trusted her to be. She has carried this example forward through her vocation and avocation, forever intertwined, into all the areas where she wields influence and authority with humility and grace.

As the Director of Washington Health System Teen Outreach, Founder and President of the Academy for Adolescent Health, Inc., and and adjunct professor at Washington and Jefferson College, Mary Jo Podgurski has had a profound impact on her community and well beyond. She is the mentor and first employer to hundreds of young people who have experienced their own worth as peer educators and trainers on Mary Jo's teaching team. For countless more young people, she was and is the only adult whom they knew they could ask any question as well as give, and get, an honest answer.

But first, she was a beginner—a child, a student, a trainee, a newbie. In this book, we get to see that, too.

I love the people who admit when they're wrong, who can acknowledge when they've acted in a way they would now call small or uninformed, and who take time to grieve not knowing what they didn't know. I love the people who see a moment like this as a chance to learn deeply from a mistake. I love them because they give me courage to do the same, and it's what makes growth and learning possible.

Who better to teach teenagers about sex – which is basically teaching them about themselves – than someone who *knows* she doesn't know it all? Better to find out what a teenager already knows. Better to trust and invite them to share what they think is wise and fair and true. Better to draw them close with care and openness and understanding than to scare them away by waving our own fears (or our closed fists) in front of their curious, confused faces.

I also love the people who have the audacity to be right, who sense and discern the right thing to do and then do it, even when it may get them fired or reviled or run straight out of town. This book has plenty of moments that leave me cheering and awestruck, thinking, *So that's what one does in a situation like that!*

I read this book and marvel at the kindness, gentleness, and softness that has guided this fiery young, and then grown, and then *grand*-mother - this Nonnie who has been family to so many. I enjoyed the recollections and revelations of an expert in women's healthcare and all people's sexuality, who embraces the whole person exactly as they are—just like Mr. Rogers, all the while keenly aware of the society, family, pressures, and inequities into which each person is born.

"I don't give up on young people," writes Mary Jo, and I believe her. But there are many more people she doesn't give up on. For example, a doctor with an abusive bedside manner, a mother who would rather not disrupt "normal childhood pecking orders," a vice principal who misses the whole beautiful point of a lesson outside on the lawn, and all the people who were "raised in a different time," are frightened by change, and don't know what they don't know. In essence, she gives up on exactly *none* of us, including herself, thank goodness.

Each person is a person of worth.

The sign of a great teacher is the joy that pours out of them when they are learning. It makes us want to learn, too.

This book is an outpouring of joy that comes from a lifetime of learning. It makes me want to live, too.

CHAPTER ONE

Teach With Your Heart

I teach.

Teaching takes training and practice and humility and courage and long hours of preparation and passion and commitment and resilience and an intense desire to connect with young people. Above all else, teaching takes heart. To me, it is a vocation and a calling—not a job. To me, it is pure joy.

A teen once told me she spoke with me because I didn't have any edges. She said, "I know if I stumble, you'll catch me, and I can sink into you."

I can think of few greater compliments.

Professionally, I'm known as Dr. Mary Jo, but in my community, I'm often called The Sex Lady! My staff and I have taught sex ed to over a quarter million young people over the last thirty years. I thought I knew how to teach when I began, but even now I'm learning how little I know. My students teach me. Through their courage, I find my own. I've learned knowledge is important, but not as vital as teaching with your heart.

My approach to sex ed is Mr. Rogers meets Dr. Ruth. Mr. Rogers connected with children and told them just being themselves was enough; I connect with teens and young people and teach them they are worthy just by virtue of being born. Dr. Ruth is famous for her honesty and transparency regarding sex. Likewise, I answer all questions without judgment, respecting youth culture and offering medically accurate information. Since the mid-seventies, I've also been available to young people 24/7, 365 days a year.

As another teen told me, "I call you because I know you'll really be there. The shit doesn't hit the fan just between nine and five."

I Believe...

My philosophy sets me apart from some educators because I teach with my heart. Sexual health is about connection, about diversity and inclusion, about social and racial justice, and about the kind of empowerment where adults are not afraid to surrender power and give young people time to find their own.

Our society is doing a lousy job teaching sex. Only twenty-four states and the District of Columbia mandate sex education, and only thirteen of those states mandate the education be medically accurate. We need to do better. This book is my way of expanding my teaching beyond my classroom. If you are an adult who cares about children, it is your guide.

A well-worn educator mantra tells us young people only care what adults say when they know we care. I agree. Teachers can make a choice to love their students. I choose to see the best in them. In turn, young people know and strive for their best.

I was raised to care by parents who taught me through example, action, and metaphors. I was blessed to be born to them.

I have stories to tell. I write these words because they matter. The messages my parents taught me matter. The young people I've served since I was a young pediatric nurse at Children's Hospital of Pittsburgh in 1970 matter. The stories contained here are my gift to you. My parents' wisdom flows through my words and my actions, but I am my own person. I came of age during the civil rights and women's movements. My awareness of social and racial justice was honed when I became the first sexuality educator in our community, as I taught diverse young people who were too often invisible. I saw them then. I see them now.

The young people I serve are important to me. I told them I planned to write a book about my teaching. One said, "Like a memoir?"

I said, "Not exactly. More like essays about how to teach and connect with young people."

She laughed, "Don't write it, Mary Jo. Just take out a full-page ad in the newspaper saying, 'Mary Jo is writing about our town. For $20, your kid's name won't be in the book.' Parents all over town will think, 'Um… my kid had her in school. It's only twenty bucks. Maybe I should pay.'"

I grinned, then grew solemn. Young people confide in me because they know I'd never violate their trust. The names in this book are all changed unless an individual requested to be identified; each young person is protected. I told my young entrepreneur I could never share a confidence.

She said, "I know, but think of it. You've taught everyone in town. What a great fundraiser it would be." She looked around our teen center, "We could use a new game system!"

The stories in this book speak my truth. Like many before me, I speak truth to power, but words are not enough. One must act. My actions are the ground on which I stand. Life is a gift, and seeing life through the lens with which my parents blessed me and through the lens of the young people I've served is worthy of a story. A few stories!

Steps to Connection

My stories are practical guides to reaching young people.

I offer you steps to connection: each step will take you closer to forging bonds with life-long positive consequences. Each step offers advice for talking about sexuality and life.

Life is an unpredictable work of art, where joy should be embraced and savored, like my grandmother's tomato sauce, and grief should be honored and respected in the memory of loved ones no longer with us. I've spent my life immersed in three of life's greatest adventures. The first two are birth and death—there's no dichotomy for me since they complement one another. The third is sexuality—a mirror reflecting the essence of who we are as humans.

Teaching creates a sacred space, where the facilitator inspires and models connections by reaching out with heart and spirit.

There are thirty-four more chapters in this book. Each chapter can be read alone; each offers one more step to connection for adults seeking to reach young people. I offer you thirty-four steps to enhance that connection. Each step empowers adults to reach young people; each brings an adult closer to moving aside and offering young people a chance to find their own power.

Even a long journey begins with first steps.

Open your heart and come with me.

May these words bring you joy.

CHAPTER TWO

Narratore

I'm a storyteller, like my mama before me. I was taught the word "storyteller" translates as "narratore" in Italian, although the word may be more Americanized than Italian after all these years. When I finally visited Italy as an adult, I confidently rattled off the old country Italian my grandmother (my nonna) taught me. Most of the words were corrupted by time's passage and my family's assimilation into America, and my translator's bemused expression shocked me.

My parents purposefully avoided teaching me their native tongue (my papa was a fourteen-year-old immigrant from the small town of Cercemaggiore, near Naples, Italy, and my mama was first generation American). I was raised to be American, not Italian, while simultaneously taught to fiercely protect my heritage and traditions. As a curious teen, I often sat at my nonna's side, asking her to name objects in Italian, pointing to things to avoid saying words in English. I began to sense her language was more *Medigan* (American) than Italian when I motioned to the ceiling above us and Nonna shrugged and responded with, "Un ceil-ing."

My family wasn't financially well off, but we were rich in wisdom and love. My parents gave me a thirst for knowledge, the foundation to learning respect for all people, and my faith. I am the person I am because of them.

My First Teachers

My mama was my primary educator. Forced to leave school after eighth grade and raise her younger siblings when her mother died, she was a frustrated teacher all her life. I was her pupil. I was told she had a huge rose garden before my birth, full of county fair prize-winning flowers. When I saw a black and white photo of her roses as a child, I asked why she no longer grew them. She replied, "I have one rose to nourish." She used the library, her church, other people, and our community to teach me—she never stopped until her death.

Mama read scripture daily and bragged she'd read the Bible in its entirety three times cover to cover. She never limited my search for knowledge. Indeed, the summer between my third and fourth grades in school, she fought the local library to give me access to the adult section. She won. Bolstered by her confidence in me, I read all the books in the Classic Series. I can see their covers: uniform, changing only by title and jacket color. *Les Misérables, War and Peace, David Copperfield, Pride and Prejudice, Jane Eyre, The Hunchback of Notre Dame.* I read them all. I realize now how much of those books' contents were above my limited life experience, but I slogged through them, triumphant in accomplishing what I was told was too much for me.

My papa was my spiritual guide, not only in matters of faith but also in life. His compassion permeated his days. I learned by his example. He was a rock, a solid man of integrity and character who was decades ahead of his time in civil rights and the pursuit of social justice.

Papa was ahead of his time in sexual health as well. As an immigrant, he possessed a European mindset about bodies and sexuality, although he was so chaste I never saw him nude until he was dying, and, even then, he insisted on covering up. It was his open-mindedness that set him apart.

Papa taught me bodies were perfect as they are, declaring me "beautiful" every chance he got, asking me to spin anytime I had a new outfit so he could clap. His humor was earthy, his approach to sexuality kind and empathic. He loved music, although he preferred Perry Como to my favorite songwriters from the sixties. I remember singing along to "It's My Party (and I'll cry if I want to...)" and "Judy's Turn to Cry" as a tween. Papa didn't like those songs. He said they sounded sad and he never wanted me to feel about boys the way the girls in those songs did. (I never did.) But when "You Don't Own Me" was released in 1963 and I played it on my tiny record player, he liked it. I can picture him in my bedroom doorway, listening to the lyrics, nodding in approval, and then encouraging me to sing the song. Before he comes across as too progressive, though, let me share that he really, really disliked The Doors' "Light my Fire," which he told me was about sex. I argued it was not. Now I know he was correct. To his credit, he never made me turn off the song. Long before I knew I'd teach sexuality, I was instructed in how to facilitate discussion about sex with a thirteen-year-old by using everyday moments and making them teachable. He talked with me, not at me. He heard me and respected me.

It was Papa who gently offered me reassurance during puberty. ("It gets better. This, too, shall pass.") It was him who took me aside and talked with me about sex before I drove to see my fiancé at his college. It was him who beamed in my hospital room when our first child was born, grinning from ear to ear, his deep dimples flitting in and out of his cheeks, and then announcing that he and my mama needed to leave because "Mary Jo's body just did an amazing and really hard thing. It needs to heal."

Teaching Doesn't Happen in a Vacuum

Each person is influenced by the circles in their lives - their families, their communities, their friends and work colleagues, their country, their faith or belief system – all of which create an individual's culture. When traveling, I try to be aware of culture. An action like shaking hands in a Western culture may be too much in an Eastern one. One learns by stepping back with humility and listening to hear what matters to people.

Teachers are only one circle of influence in a young person's life, as they should be. *La mia famiglia* - my family – was key to my character growing up. I was taught how much family loyalty mattered. My family mentored me into adulthood.

What happens when children are invisible in their own families?

How do children grow in self-worth if they're not validated at home?

The sad answer is if they don't feel validated in their first circle, their self-esteem may be low. They may not believe themselves worthy. Studies show severe, long-term neglect may be more traumatic than abuse.

Teachers are often called on to fill in for emotionally absent parents. Watching teens create their own kin or tribe is one of my favorite teacher experiences. I look at friend groups and see the *why* behind friend choices.

The words of one teacher can inspire and encourage. They can last a lifetime. A quote from author and Harvard scholar Clint Smith affirms teachers as powerful forces in their students' lives: "…one of the only reasons I'm a writer is because I had a teacher in third grade who looked at my poem about clouds and said, 'You can be a writer when you grow up.' It stayed with me forever. Teachers, don't underestimate what your words can do for your students."

The opposite can be true, sadly. Teachers can cause real emotional harm. I once overhead a principal screaming at a sixteen-year-old, "You're just taking up space here. You're no better than your father and your brother. You should just drop out. You'll never amount to anything."

I couldn't believe my ears. Sadly, I've had teens and parents tell me similarly negative tales. A parent told me her child was told – in front of an entire class – that he was the only child in that teacher's long career that he hated!

Dr. James Longo, my education department chair at the college where I'm an adjunct, tells me that people go into education for one of two reasons: because they are truly committed to reaching children and young people and making a positive influence in their lives, or because they're secretly bullies and an entire classroom of children are perfect humans to bully.

My family's culture modeled acceptance and dignity and compassion and empathy. How lucky I was to learn how to respect all people as a child!

Each encounter with a young person is a cross cultural experience.

Here's my first step:

Step #1: Honor Culture and Each Young Person's Worth

Acknowledge young people's cultures.

Honor their heritage and beliefs.

Hear their stories—each of us has a story.

Make a difference in children's lives.

Respect and accept their identities without trying to "fix" or change them.

CHAPTER THREE

Sex Lady

I doubt my parents ever understood I was a Sex Lady. Their love for me was unconditional and accepting, but sex wasn't a normal part of daily conversation with their only daughter. As a child growing up in an Italian Catholic household, where the concept of sexuality was alternately enticing, exciting, and real, yet vaguely forbidden and not to be discussed, becoming a sexologist wasn't on my radar, even when I graduated as a nurse and put my feet on the path leading to my life's work.

I didn't begin as a Sex Lady, but my life experiences gave me a foundation for teaching with my heart. As a twenty-three-year-old nurse at Memorial Sloan Kettering Cancer Center in New York City, I encountered my own mortality through the deaths of my young patients on the pediatric-adolescent unit. Our unit averaged ten deaths a week. Assignments were made as primary and secondary patients. We were responsible not only for our children's treatment and chemo protocol, but also for the little things that improved their lives: how did they like their hamburgers prepared? What songs made them relax? Did they like to talk or prefer silence? What were the best books to distract them from pain?

When they entered end stage and died, each of them touched my soul. I remember their faces, their spirits, and what gave them joy. Their resilience nurtures me even now.

You see, I fell in love with my young patients. A newlywed in a new city with a wonderful partner who supports me with patience and care, even forty-six years later, I was then childless. My natural tendency to connect deeply with others, conceived in my family and nurtured at Children's Hospital, blossomed at Sloan.

Imagine this: A family goes through one of the most difficult journeys in life—watching a child die. The sound of that child's breathing - ragged, moist, stopping and starting so that everyone in the room holds their own breath until the little one releases another halting breath – is the background for a grief that defies description. Keeping the child comfortable was my primary role, but I held sobbing parents and siblings, brought snacks, malts, and soda pop to families, and spent a lot of time holding space.

Holding space is a term I learned at Sloan. To hold space is to be there, to offer the gift of your presence without judgement, to accept, and to remain. Holding space allows people to be vulnerable and show their fear. It means one does not take away power by trying to fix another person's problems, or overwhelm others by offering more information than they can handle. When one holds space, there is no place for shaming people by implying they should do better or know more. The hospital rooms of dying children and teens became sacred spaces.

When my young patients died, it was my honor to wash and care for them after death. I whispered soft words to the child. It hurt when these young ones died. I always spoke to my patients as I worked, as I did when they were alive. "I'm going to wash your hair now. I hope that's okay with you," I'd say. I'd carefully cover body parts as I washed away fluids and blood and perspiration, just as I did when the young patient lived. When the children were small enough, I couldn't bear putting them on a gurney, so I carried them downstairs to the morgue in my arms.

In this intense environment, building on my parents' foundation, I began to realize the role of empathy and caring – of heart – in my work. Joy became a daily goal for me. I'd witnessed too many little ones die to take my life for granted. I learned mindfulness and added it to the deep spirituality Papa taught me. Soon, I was meditating twice a day. I've loved this routine since then.

Birth & Teen Pregnancy

When we moved to Pennsylvania, I sought out birth and became a Lamaze certified childbirth educator. I thought I was finished with death. I loved growing into a birth advocate. My work focused on life, it encouraged informed choices, and it reinforced my love of teaching. Ironically, my role as a childbirth educator brought me to sexuality education.

Early on, I realized teen parents didn't always fit into a traditional childbirth class. Even unhappy couples typically act loving during a six-week class about birth. I decided to teach a special class for adolescents. It was the seventies. I made myself available 24/7, and I didn't charge. I always fed the young people in my classes. Teens responded enthusiastically. They said I was "free" and "funny" and I gave them "food" – the "Three Fs" – and I didn't freak out if they said "the F word." My classes became very popular.

One evening, during the last trimester of my first pregnancy, I received a call from the parent of a pregnant teen. *Would I teach her?* Of course, I said. Class was on Tuesdays at 6 p.m. at my home. I started giving directions when she stopped me. Her daughter was in foster care. *Could I do a home visit?* I had little experience with home visiting, but I reasoned it was possible. After all, I had a portable rainbow-colored 3D knitted uterus!

When I entered the foster home, I was directed to the young mom's bedroom. I hadn't yet completed my master's work in counseling, but I didn't need a graduate degree to know this child was depressed. All the blinds were drawn. She sat in the dark.

I took a breath and said, "Hi. I'm Mary Jo, and I'm going to help you get ready for the birth of your baby."

She didn't turn around. Her, "Who the fuck do you think you are?" didn't shock me.

I simply responded, "I think I'm Mary Jo, and I'm going to help you get ready for the birth of your baby."

She almost smiled, then she covered her head with a blanket. She didn't speak again during that first meeting. In our second class, she shifted the blanket aside slightly to look at me, but was silent. She was twelve. Pregnant at eleven, she was a hold-over fifth grader. She was the most streetwise young person I've ever met.

I already knew not to assume, but my adult thinking reasoned the conception was a sexual assualt. I was incorrect. Madi wasn't "in love" with the sixteen-year-old father of her baby, but, in time, she shared she'd initiated sex with him. She never named him. I knew little then about adolescent sexuality. I knew less about a person's long-term reactions to child sexual abuse. I didn't realize many children do not have the language or the safety to disclose abuse. I naively didn't know how abuse can remove a young person's ownership of their own body, so sex may become something one uses to pacify a partner or to disassociate from pain. It took Madi two years to disclose her childhood abuse to me, but when she did, I affirmed her worth. She was my best teacher.

I'd only met with Madi twice when she called to say she was in labor. My home phone rang at 10:30 p.m. and she opened with, "Ain't nobody going with me." I ascertained her water had broken. I asked if she wanted me to meet her at the hospital. She said, "Who gives a fuck?"

I told my Rich I was going to the hospital and would return by midnight. Nineteen hours later, Madi's baby was born.

First Lessons

During those long hours, I learned life-changing lessons.

Rubbing Madi's back, giving her ice chips, placing a cool cloth on her forehead, holding the basin when she threw up, and breathing with her taught me I had a passion for doula work. Doulas comfort and offer care during labor, birth, and postpartum (after birth). Some see their clients prenatally (before birth) as well. At 3 a.m., a doula from the next labor room shared techniques to help Madi's pain, like squeezing her hips (honestly, it helps), helping her walk (to lower the baby's station or position in the pelvis), and rocking with her standing, as she leaned into my chest. I can still hear the sound she made in transition, right before the second pushing stage of labor – a jumble of words, sounds, moans, and pop music – that she breathed into my neck as we rocked. Later, official doula training prepared me to serve hundreds of teens through labor. Madi was my first. I've never charged a young parent. I never will.

Madi's birth experience was my first real lesson in privilege, when I realized how protected I'd been in my own life. I began to grasp the concept of socioeconomic and white privilege, even though Madi was white. In fact, the assumption pregnant teens are people of color continues to upset me. In my community, most of the young parents we serve are white.

I'm still learning about privilege. As a doula for teens, I've heard young women of color degraded during labor, sometimes boldly and other times in disparaging words thrown about in nurses' lounges. A tired, cranky nurse once said, "Stop whining. I bet you didn't complain when you spread your legs and made this baby," to a sixteen-year-old biracial teen. A white male obstetrician once told me, "Black girls don't need episiotomies. They're wider down there."

Madi showed me a new respect for extreme depths of resiliency. There were no epidurals available then at the hospital where Madi gave birth. A twelve-year-old body is young. Her baby was nine pounds, six ounces. Madi buried her head in my shoulder for the last two hours of labor. My scrub suit was soaked with her tears, yet she pushed with all her strength.

16 ❀ SEX ED IS IN SESSION

One lesson I learned was planted in my heart and would become stronger over time: young people crave their parents' love, even when they're abandoned by them. Madi's mother never came to the hospital. Estranged from her daughter after Madi's stepfather was sent to prison for sexual abuse, she didn't offer support, yet Madi longed for her presence.

I learned how much courage a child could have.

I also decided I didn't want to give birth myself, although, at thirty-four weeks, I was at a point of no return.

Madi chose adoption. "I need my kid to find a better life than mine." She decided she couldn't go through with "giving up my baby" if she saw the baby, or even knew the child's sex. Before ultrasounds were common, the first shout in a delivery room was, "It's a boy," or, "It's a girl." I alerted the delivery room staff to be silent and respect this brave young mom's wishes. Ultimately, the only sound was the mom's sobs and her newborn's cries. The baby was swiftly whisked away. Madi asked me for a soda. After making sure she was comfortable, I gladly left the room. I wanted out of there more than I wanted to go home, get off my feet, and rest.

The nursery was between the soda machine and the labor suite. Rows and rows of newborns greeted me. I looked for Madi's infant. The little one was easy to find, hidden away from the others, as if isolation and marginalization were pre-determined. I stared in awe at this beautiful, healthy baby. The tiny, perfect fingers and toes, the head of thick hair, the slightly swollen nose, the bright dark blue eyes peering at me without tears. I was overwhelmed. Then it hit me: no one had welcomed this new little one to life. I scooped the newborn up in my arms, sank into a rocking chair, and began to hum. My own baby kicked in utero. I began to cry, and I don't cry easily. The other nurses asked if I was okay. I responded, "No," and kept rocking and crying. I wasn't okay.

Like many pregnant people in the seventies, I had plans for our baby's birth. I hoped to welcome our newborn with a LaBoyer gentle birth, with lights dimmed and soft music playing. I planned to put the baby to breast immediately.

I knew I'd sing one of the Italian lullabies my mama and nonna sang to me. I thought I'd baptize the baby right away, since, as my Mama often said, you never know when there could be a nuclear attack. I made these plans a reality when my own babies were born. What about this amazing twelve-year-old? What about her baby? We both gave life.

The contrast between my life and the life of that young mother still tugs at my heart in my memories. I was on a pedestal in my family. My papa called three times a day to see if I wanted Bing cherries or juicy oranges or fat peaches. I was treasured and honored and loved because I was giving life. Yet this young woman, whose courage and sense of purpose were infinitely higher than mine, this child who gave life no differently than I would, was treated like dirt under society's feet. Madi was judged. Teachers and nursing staff who were unaware of her abuse history called her promiscuous and talked about out of control kids. She was labeled, she was vilified, and her needs were ignored.

A Call to Action

When I returned home, bleary-eyed and exhausted, I told Rich I was going to talk with teens about sex. I wanted to teach. *No, I needed to teach.* As he has all my life, my partner only nodded. I'm sure he thought I was too weary to make sense. I doubt he knew the depth of my resolve. He made me my favorite tea, pulled down the bed covers, closed the blinds, and put on the soft music I loved. He kissed me gently and suggested I nap. When he left, I rose, gathering pen and paper, writing furiously. *How could I teach? Where would I teach? What would I teach?*

The last answer was the easiest. I would teach sexuality. I would teach young people about their bodies without shaming them or their genitals. Madi didn't even know her vulva contained three openings: the urethra for urine, the vagina for sexual pleasure and birthing, and the anus for expelling stool. She thought she could lose a tampon inside her vagina (not possible). Madi had no idea where a clitoris was in her own body, or its purpose in sexual pleasure. None of this was okay. I was determined to teach the truth.

I knew even then I wanted to teach much more than how the body works and anatomy. I knew I didn't want to teach with fear and shame. The list of what I didn't know was long, but I didn't know what I didn't know, so I moved forward boldly!

I began as a volunteer with pregnant and parenting teens in five local school districts, only finally receiving funding for that aspect of our outreach in 1996. I'd meet with young parents during their study halls or lunch. I prepared them for birth, and I helped them find a parenting style that fit their culture. I worked with both teen mothers and fathers. I became very busy.

Sex Ed

In 1987, while still a volunteer, I was having coffee with a wonderful guidance counselor at one of my schools when she asked me, "Why don't you teach the rest of the kids not to have babies?"

I'd taught teens about sexuality since I began volunteering with young parents. I started a sibling program in 1981 to prepare children to be big brothers and sisters. I began a very popular puberty class called *What's Up as You Grow Up* for parents and youth in 1984. That day in school, I didn't hesitate. With the confidence of one who has no idea what was next, I said I would.

I wasn't sure where I was going, I just knew I had to try. My local hospital, The Washington Hospital, joined with me to form a school-business partnership and I began teaching in Trinity School District on October 11, 1988. It was a Tuesday. I know the date because I recorded my anxiety in my journal on Sunday, October 9th—*would I find the right words to connect with young people?* I was grateful I didn't need to teach Monday!

On the evening of October 11th, after teaching ninth graders for the first time, I wrote, "I love this! Can work be this much fun?"

Since then, my staff and I have taught comprehensive sexuality education to young people in forty-eight schools in five counties. At first, we operated without an office building; we met at a local restaurant weekly to discuss assignments and tasks. We often said our kitchen tables were our offices. In 1997, I rented a small office in a local building. Within six months, we'd expanded into six rooms on the same floor. I wasn't happy there. We offered teen programs in a non-teen friendly space. I knew that had to change. I rented the former Department of Health building in 2000 and purchased it in 2001 in a leap of faith. Today, it is full of life and seven youth programs—a garden created annually by our professional team and our teen peer educators brightens the front lawn. I opened the Common Ground Teen Center a few blocks away in 2008. It is run by a paid staff of young people and reflects their needs and dreams.

The teen pregnancy rate in our target population (15-17-year-olds) was 39/1000 in 1989, one year after our first classes were taught in one school district. In 2012, when we trained schools to do their own sex ed, the rate was 12/1000.

In the seventies, I made a pledge to serve ALL young people. *All young people.* This pledge continues to guide me.

I also made a second promise in 1988 and I've never broken it. The day I don't look forward to teaching young people with joy is the day I'll stop. I don't expect that day to ever come.

I never planned to be a Sex Lady. The title, like "ally," must be gifted to a person. One cannot declare oneself an ally—it is only earned when one's actions and commitment and the grace to move aside and step back to support others is real. Allies aren't saviors, they don't take the microphone. When a group calls someone an ally or an accomplice, it is so. The title cannot be self-proclaimed. Sex Lady is similar. My students gave me the name, and I'm sure it will part of my eulogy. I'll be honored if it is.

What IS Sexuality Education?

Close your eyes and remember. Who taught you sex ed? Did you learn about how babies are made from friends or family? Did your school even offer sex ed? Did you attend sex ed classes where the focus was on fear and shame? Were you included in the class, or were you invisible? Was the class presented in a heteronormative way, as if all students were straight? Was the class taught by a certified sexuality educator, committed to reaching all young people with a message of sexual health, or by a reluctant health teacher and/or gym coach assigned to teach reproduction and scare students into abstinence?

Did you receive a mixed message like the one from Coach Carr in the movie *Mean Girls*: "Don't have sex, because you will get pregnant and die! Don't have sex in the missionary position, don't have sex standing up, just don't do it, okay, promise? Okay, now, everybody take some rubbers."

If there are young people in your life, what messages do you want them to remember about sex ed when they're adults?

Would you teach?

1. Bodies are beautifully and wonderfully made.
2. Sexuality is an integral part of one's identity, but does not alone define personhood.
3. Consent conversations are an integral part of sexual connection and must begin in childhood.
4. Healthy relationships take effort.
5. Gender isn't about body parts. Gender and sexual identity must be respected.
6. Love and lust aren't the same.
7. We are sexual all our lives, even if we are not sexually involved.
8. Sexual pleasure is normal, and masturbation is healthy.
9. Young people can be their own self-advocates.
10. Each person is worthy.

Remember Step #1? Begin by acknowledging youth culture. Honor young people by honoring their humanity and their uniqueness. Mr. Rogers' message may sound simple, and, in many ways, it was. *I like you just the way you are.* There is true power in affirming worthiness.

When I teach about sexuality, I affirm a similar simple truth: young people are worthy, just the way they are.

Sex Ed Communities

Sex ed classes need to be communities where we respect rules. Regardless of difference, we are all human. No one is invisible. Set the stage for safe learning by articulating the obvious. No one knows how you feel if you don't speak the truth. Affirm young people's worth by clearly stating what may be obvious to you. If genuine, your sincere words won't be awkward or sound flat. Young people will beam!

"I appreciate you volunteering today. You really made the day work."

"I've noticed the way you jump up and welcome new people to the teen center. I value your kindness."

"It's fun to see you interact with others. Thank you."

"Your voice is wise. I'd like you to facilitate our next panel for adults."

"You're the first to take out the garbage at the end of the night. Your maturity is showing!"

Young people are worthy of respect. Respect means no one in class is put down or ignored. Everyone is seen and heard.

How can we expect young people to learn respect if they are not respected?

Step #2: Respect Young People

Offer genuine respect for their worth.

Information on sexual health is a human right.

Articulate the obvious.

All people are worthy.

CHAPTER FOUR

Never Give It Up for a Sofa

My generation's parents dodged questions about sex, even at home. Consider media representations of sexuality in the fifties. Television was new and black and white. On the popular comedy show *I Love Lucy*, Lucy slept in a separate bed from her husband Desi, and the word "pregnancy" was avoided throughout her real life and TV birth. Instead, her pregnancy was referred to as being "in a family way." Movies routinely cut to fireplaces when couples began kissing. Most people were white. Everyone was straight.

Periods!

My parents, for all their openness, followed the norm. My mama handed me a book about periods when I was ten, averted her eyes and said, "If you have any questions, come to me." If you can call that sex ed, it's all I had before my periods began.

The title of the book was *You're a Woman Now*. A young woman in a pink gown was on the cover. I perused it. It was beyond boring. I reasoned becoming a woman involved a dress. In heavy denial, I put the book in my dresser drawer and decided this simply would not happen to me.

When I started menstruating, I was only in fifth grade, not quite eleven. I used half a roll of toilet paper trying to make it go away. I was mortified. I was shocked. I did find the courage to tell my mother, who promptly announced to my father, "Mary Jo is a woman now." I remember most how upset I was when she told me I would not be able to jump rope with my friends, ever again. *I was a woman now, remember?* Women, apparently, did not jump rope.

Mama was an intelligent woman, but she was deeply superstitious. The start of my period led to a long list of bizarre rules beyond avoidance of jumping rope. Washing one's hair while menstruating was unhealthy. Eating chocolate would give me cramps. My aunt was angry with my mom for telling me about menstrual cramps, as if abdominal pain was a mind over matter phenomenon. What I didn't know, evidently, could not hurt me. It goes without saying I should stay away from boys while on my period. Mama never explained why. Perhaps she thought conception was more likely during menses (it's not).

The toughest part of menstruation under my mother's tutelage dealt with feminine hygiene products. Mama didn't trust them. She was certain they contained fatal chemicals. Instead, she cut white rags into strips and showed me how to pin them to the inside of my panties. You may have heard the term "on the rag." Well, in my childhood home, I was literally on the rag. Every month, Mama would boil the soiled rags on the basement stove, in a special pot reserved for this unsavory activity. The smell of Clorox still brings me back to those unpleasant days.

I was beyond embarrassed. I purchased my first box of sanitary napkins with money from my eleventh birthday. Papa was in on the deception. I continued using the rags at home but took pads to school.

Mama was terrified of tampons. Her knowledge of anatomy was weak. Like Madi, she genuinely thought a tampon could get lost inside the body. Most importantly, she was certain inserting a tampon would take my virginity. Mind you, she never explained what virginity meant. She just issued an intense admonition to avoid tampons.

I used my first tampon in my dorm, my first year of nursing school. My roommate discovered I'd never used one, to my chagrin. In the communal bathroom, during my next menstrual cycle, I heard noises outside the stall. Six tampons suddenly descended on my head, accompanied by a chant from my roommate, "Put it in, Mary Jo. Put it in." I was angry for days, until we talked it out.

Sofas?

Mama's final sex ed happened the night before my wedding. She came to my bedroom and hovered at the doorway. She looked so uneasy. I tried to reassure her I was just fine. She sighed, "Right. You're a nurse, after all. You know about bodies." I smiled. She turned to leave, then spun back. "One piece of advice," she said. "Never give it up for a sofa."

Puzzled, I called her back. "What?" I had no other words.

She shrugged, "You know how my friend Sally always has new living room furniture?" I nodded. Mama said, "When she wants something new, she makes her husband sleep on the couch until he buys it."

Wow. I understood her message. Don't use sex as a manipulative device in a relationship.

Dishwashing and Communication

After that brief exchange, I didn't discuss sex with my mother for nearly two decades, until the day she brought up the topic. She was as old as I am now. We were washing and drying dishes. Mama wisely saw dishwashing as akin to a toddler's parallel play. Without making eye contact, one could discuss something uncomfortable with a little less tension. She asked me, apropos of nothing, if I believed in reincarnation. I wasn't surprised. My mother never questioned her faith, to my knowledge, but she loved exploring the belief systems of others. I responded, "No." I'd studied Buddhism and read of Hindu belief, but I thought we only were given one life to live.

Mama sighed. "I think you're right," she said.

I waited. Several more dishes were washed and dried and put away.

"It's a shame," she said. "I'd like to come back as a man. I'd like to know what it feels like for them."

I swallowed hard. Was this my chance to open this door with this woman I admired so much? I took a deep, cleansing breath. "Mama," I said, striving for a confident tone, "lots of women enjoy sex as much as men."

She stopped mid-plate. Suds ran down her arms. She turned to me, peering intently, then asked, "Do you?"

A second deep breath, in and out. I said, "Yeah, Ma. I do."

A huge grin split her face. She beamed. "Good for you, honey," she crowed. "Good for you!"

I often wonder what the early years of their marriage were like. She knew so little, was so protected, and was thrust into a mother's role when only a child. Papa's distance from his own father – they never really connected emotionally after being apart for eight years while my grandfather was in America - and Papa's place as eldest in his family left him with few male mentors. They were a true love match. I guess they figured it out!

As an adult, I realized they used code to flirt with each other when I was a child. Ten years into me teaching sexuality, a routine they often used clicked in my poor head. Papa would go through the garage and shower in the basement after work. The scent of his Old Spice aftershave preceded him up the stairs. Mama would be cooking at the stove. I'd be doing homework at the kitchen table. He'd come up behind her and put his arms around her. "How's your sister today?" he'd ask, his voice husky. "She misses your brother," she'd respond, smiling. He had a brother, she had many sisters. I didn't catch on for two decades! When I confronted them, demanding they admit they were talking about sex, they just laughed!

Informed Choice

Two years before we lost my Papa, I learned a little more.

My father was diagnosed with prostate cancer and underwent surgery. About two months post-op, I was visiting him on his porch while Rich stayed inside with our kids. I wanted time alone with him, reasoning he had no one else with whom to share anxiety or ask questions. He told me he couldn't maintain an erection; he wasn't transparent, he simply mumbled something about his stuff not working right. It hit me like brick on my heart: the surgeon hadn't told Papa erectile dysfunction was a possible side effect of the surgery. I chastised myself. *Why hadn't I prepared him?* He read the look on my face and patted my hand gently, reassuring me. It was okay, he said. Not to worry.

Just then, my mother emerged from the kitchen. She was deeply affected by Alzheimer's by then and was having a one-sided conversation with someone else no one could hear. My papa looked at her with such love in his eyes! His voice was sad as he whispered, "It's a shame, really. When we were first married, she didn't always like it, but now that she's *testa vuota* (empty headed), she likes it a lot!"

Sex in a healthy relationship is about connection (with or without sofas). I was happy my parents' relationship stood the test of time. I was also angry the surgeon didn't respect my father enough to be honest with him about outcomes. Perhaps the doctor didn't think sex would be important to an eighty-two-year-old. He didn't give Papa enough information to make an informed choice before the surgery.

We are sexual beings throughout the lifespan, even if we aren't sexually involved with a partner.

Partners

If a person wants a partner, that choice is huge. Not all relationships are life-long. My parents told me I shouldn't go out with someone with whom I wouldn't consider spending my life. I thought they worried too much.

When parents watch their teen children select first partners, they often are anxious. The words "puppy love" and "temporary" and "you're too young to know what love is" may be judgments thrown at young people. Love is an emotion, a feeling. I cannot negate another person's feeling. Love can be mature (where a partner is often other-directed, considers everyone's wellbeing in a relationship, and is supportive of the other person's dreams) or immature (where a partner encourages falsehood, is ego-driven, and appears unworried about the other person's future).

When teaching seniors, a young man asked me if I thought it was okay to be involved with a ninth grader. I said I needed more information. *What type of relationship was it? How old was the person? Was he aware statutory rape in our state is when one person is under sixteen – the age of consent – and the other person is four years older? Aside from legality, was the relationship mature?*

He replied by shrugging. "She's fifteen. It's cool. Plus, I love her," he said, cocky, oozing confidence. His audience of peers grinned.

I nodded. "Then, if you're sexually involved and have penis-vagina sex..."

"I am," he interrupted, "we do," he said, causing smirking all around.

I continued as if he'd not spoken, "...then you've discussed birth control and protection."

"We're careful," he protested.

"How careful?" I asked. I looked around the room, making eye contact. I pulled the class in. "Because if you love her as a person, you know what an unplanned pregnancy at fifteen can do to her life. If you love her as a person, you want her future to be glorious. If you love her as a person, and don't take responsibility for protection – with her - I believe you love an orgasm more than you love your partner."

Relationships based on mutual respect are mature.

Papa died in June of 1996, Mama in October. Alzheimer's stole Mama's selfhood ten years before she died, but Papa cared for her and loved her without pause. She forgot him the moment he died, refusing to go to his funeral. Beside her bed, however, I kept a picture of them, taken right after their wedding. They were young and beautiful. When Mama woke, she'd look at that picture and grin.

"Now that's a good-looking man," she'd say.

I'm sure she would've chosen him again.

Our sexuality is part of what makes us human.

Step #3: Avoid Judgment

Too often, adults had little to no sex ed growing up.

Too often, adults believe young people won't have sexual thoughts and desires if they're kept ignorant of sexual information.

Too often, adults think sex ed makes young people sexual.

We are all sexual, from birth through death, even if we don't have sexual experiences.

Reaching young people means accepting their sexuality and our own.

CHAPTER FIVE

Milk Money

❋

My colleagues in sexuality often wonder how
our own children's reactions to sex are affected by our work. We quip about doing
research to ascertain how sexuality educators' kids develop their sexual selves.

I have no research, but the anecdotes I've accumulated over the years
while raising our three children to adulthood point to a positive result. Our adult
children have healthy relationships with partners who complement them and share
their lives. As they grew up, though, I often pondered: *How did it feel to be the child
of the primary sex educator in the community?*

I wrote my master's thesis when our youngest, Nate, was breastfeeding!
When he graduated high school, I started my doctoral journey. Nate was my
companion and was more involved in peer education than his sisters. He never
knew a time when I wasn't a Sex Lady. At ten, he asked me if I'd teach him in
school. I explained I would, but only if he preferred me. I could easily assign
another sexuality educator to his school. "No," he said. "I want you to teach my
friends." He told me he wanted to be the SLS – the Sex Lady's Son.

Learning Through Storytelling

One of my favorite stories about our own children's reactions to my work happened when our daughter, Amy, left for college. I missed her acutely. She was just fine. I fussed until our family went to visit her at Penn State's main campus over Labor Day weekend of her freshman year. She'd been at school less than two weeks.

The same week Amy left for college, Nate asked me about sex. He already knew more about sexuality than the average second grader. I was open with all our kids. I taught childbirth classes in our home. There were anatomically correct posters, knitted uteruses, and a life-sized pelvis in my teaching room. When he asked me, "What is that sex stuff you teach? How do babies get made?" on the way to baseball practice that summer, I wasn't surprised. I pulled over and answered him. I gave him short, developmentally appropriate answers – less is more – but honest ones. He listened intently, only asking, "Did you and Dad do that three times?" I took a deep breath, reached for courage, and said, "More than three times." He gave me a look that said, *You don't get anything right*, and we moved on.

The day we drove to central Pennsylvania and State College was a glorious late summer day, full of sunshine, bright gold and brilliant red changing leaves, and warmth. My Rich is a golfer. The three-hour trip was tense as we drove past one golf course after another. Let's just say we got there, but there wasn't a lot of conversation. Our son Nate was eight, our daughter Lisa was thirteen. They both read in the backseat, but no one was happy. Except me. I was overjoyed!

When we arrived at State College, I realized Amy had Blue Band practice from 9 to 11:30 a.m., 1 to 4 p.m., and 6 to 9 p.m. Picture this: watching an entire band of musicians, majorettes, and the color guard marching on an empty field, over and over, while my disgruntled husband and bored children glared at me.

After taking Amy and her friends to the pre-requisite college *my-parents-are-here* lunch, I was faced with three hours of time and no plans. The movies, I thought! We'll go to the movies. There were two movies playing in the single movie theatre at the time: *Natural Born Killers* and *Milk Money*.

I knew *Natural Born Killers* wasn't a good choice. Nate was into Power Rangers at the time and would morph into an action figure at a moment's notice. I didn't want him watching such a violent movie. I selected *Milk Money*. I knew nothing of the plot.

Ten minutes into the film, I realized it wasn't a good choice for an eight-year-old. *Milk Money* is about a self-described hooker, played by Melanie Griffith. The main characters are pre-pubescent boys who are fascinated with all things sexual and save their milk money to approach her and ask to see her breasts. One of the opening scenes shows a diaphragm, as the inquisitive children wonder what it is.

I whispered to my husband, "We should leave."

His response? "We paid six dollars for these seats." We stayed.

As we left, I asked Nate if he had any questions. He was quiet a moment, then shrugged. "Nah," he said, and we all gathered with Amy for dinner. That evening, after consideration, he asked me, "What's a hooker?" When I discussed conception with Nate the week before, I hadn't explained the commercial aspects of sex.

I responded succinctly, "'Hooker' is a slang word for a sex worker. Hooker isn't a very nice word. A sex worker is someone who makes money from sex."

Two days later, Nate and I were in the parking lot of our hometown grocery store. As we walked to our van, an eighth grader from one of my schools saw me. He gave me a big hug and said, "Hey, Sex Lady, how was your summer? When will you be at school?"

We reached our van and began to load groceries in the back among baseball equipment, cheerleading gear, and my suitcases of school props and games. My eight-year-old glanced at me with the look children give when they "get it"—when the lightbulb goes off in their heads and something makes sense. Says my boy, "I know what you do when you go to work, Mom. You're a sex worker, right?"

I answered truthfully, "No, honey. I teach. I don't make that kind of money."

Starting Sexuality Education

Some may criticize my willingness to answer my child's questions, but parents are their little ones first educators, even if they are silent. Silence is a loud message that screams, "Don't come to me!"

One of the parent questions I continually receive deals with timing: when is the "right time" to give "the talk?" In my opinion, holding one talk about sexual health at what is allegedly the "right time" isn't the best choice for parents.

We begin teaching our children about sexuality when they're babies. When we put babies to breast after birth or swaddle them close while singing a lullaby or reading a book, we teach them touch is important to life. Touch is how many people connect; eventually, touch may become sexual, but the foundation for connecting with others starts in those early days of life. In truth, it begins moments after birth.

When we do skin-to-skin contact with newborns for attachment and to enhance the transfer of healthy bacteria to the infant, we teach about sensuality, which is an integral piece of our sexuality. When we are positive and affirming when ten-month-olds discover their penis or clitoris, we teach their bodies are amazing.

When we model healthy relationships with a romantic or sexual partner, we teach sexuality. When we use respectful language for all people, avoiding offensive slang terms for people who are different from us, we teach a foundation of healthy sexuality and mutual respect. When we begin consent conversations as preschoolers are tickled, stopping if they say "no," even if they're laughing, we teach sexuality. When we help our toddlers *own* their "no," we teach.

When we name body parts correctly, saying *penis, scrotum, testicles, vulva, vagina, clitoris, anus,* not *peebug, weewee, butterfly* or *cookie,* we teach these body parts are normal and okay—we teach sexuality. Just as noses and eyes are different, genitals are also uniquely made for each person. Most of the anxiety and angst I've seen from fifth and sixth graders stems from fear of being different and the terror that their particular difference is horribly wrong.

Most importantly, when we respond to questions right away, avoiding the words, "I'll tell you when you're older," we teach and respect each child. If a child is old enough to formulate a question, the question should be answered, but less is more.

I didn't show my eight-year-old diagrams of genitals and describe fallopian tubes and menstruation and spermatogenesis when he asked about sex. I simply talked about sperm and eggs and the way they unite. I was open, I was honest, I used gender inclusive language and talked about people with uteruses and people with testicles.

Some research says children are ready to learn about conception early, at least by the age of six. Each child is different. Let children lead you.

Saying as little as possible while answering honestly is a great way to validate a child's question. Here are some hints:

- Keep your words developmentally accurate.

- Caring parents know their own children. Let your child lead you.

- Watch body language.

- Stop when your child appears disinterested.

- End by affirming your willingness to continue the discussion.

- If you don't know an answer, admit it. Questions about sex are no different from questions about anything else. How does the garbage truck smoosh up the trash? Why are we stopped so long in traffic? Where do the strawberries we buy at the store come from? How do airplanes work? We respond because we love our children's curiosity.

No one panics when math is taught. No one says, "Oh dear, they might add!" Our cultural fear of sexuality leads us to create walls between our children and us. If we bring up the topic of sex when our kids hit puberty, our discomfort may show. At the least, in today's age, they will already be exposed to online information – and misinformation!

What if a Parent is Uncomfortable?

"How do I bring this up?"

"What if I'm uncomfortable?'

"What if I can't find the words?"

"Should I talk about condoms?"

"What if I don't want my child to have sex until marriage? How do I handle that?"

"I'm divorced. How do I teach my child about healthy relationships when I failed at mine?"

"I think my kid might be gay. What do I say or do? I don't want to encourage this…"

These and many other questions echo in my memories of the last forty-plus years. I suggest parents remind themselves of their unconditional love for their children. Babies are priorities with parents; they'd not survive without adult care. Teens need just as much care and commitment, and they also need independence and a chance to develop autonomy and find their identities. It's all about developmental stages.

As our three children grew to adulthood, I often told my Rich they were in a "critical developmental stage." When they all were grown and finished with college and married, he turned to me with a knowing grin and said, "Are we finished now? Are the critical stages finally done?"

Answering Tough Questions

With respect, and acknowledging each person parents differently, here are my hints for those questions:

"How do I bring this up?" If a parent starts early, it's easier. Sexuality will be a matter of fact, safe topic in your family. If not, it's never too late. Be up front. Say something like, "I think you know a lot about sex and growing up. I'd like to be the adult you come to when you're confused or just want someone to talk with who won't judge you. Let's talk about what you know and what I think you know. You might teach me a few things!"

"What if I'm uncomfortable?" Say so! It's okay to say, "No one ever talked about sex with me when I was young. I'm kind of uncomfortable talking about it, but you mean so much to me and I want to be an adult in your life you can talk with about anything. I won't judge you, please don't judge me as I try to do this right!"

"What if I can't find the words?" Let children guide you. Start the conversation. Wait for the right moment. Start another day if things fall flat. Use movies, TV shows, stories in the news, what's happening in your community, and family anecdotes to teach. Parents don't need to do this alone. Read books, go to classes together, explore science centers and museums.

"I'm divorced. How do I teach my child about healthy relationships when I failed at mine?" No parent is perfect. Articulate the obvious. "I didn't expect my relationship to fail, but it did. Failure is one of the ways humans learn. Good things came from the relationship, like you. I'd like to help you make fewer mistakes, but I will be here if you stumble. Let's talk about what you want in a relationship."

"What if I don't want my child to have sex until marriage? How do I handle that?" In my experience, fear and shame are unhealthy ways to promote these values or teach about sex. The primary reasons I've found for teens delaying sexual involvement are personal to the teens. Religious faith can lead teens to wait; the faith must be genuinely theirs, not their parents'. Goal setting with long-term dreams can also cause teens to pause and take fewer risks. Once more, these motivations must be inner-driven.

Be aware of example. Telling a young person not to drink or get high won't work well if parents do either. Expecting teens to have a strong moral stand on sexuality isn't as effective if parents do not model this behavior. Bottom line, I've seen way too many teens sneak and lie to parents. Be open-minded as a child grows, and hear their side.

"I think my kid might be gay. What do I say or do? I don't want to encourage this…" Being gay is part of a person's identity. Parents neither create a child's sexual or gender identity, nor do they have the power to change it. Encourage the child's self-worth. Honor the whole child. Be open and accepting. When a child comes out, the best thing a parent can do is accept. Speak your support and follow it with actions. "I love you exactly as you are," said with heart and truth can help an LGBTQIA (lesbian, gay, bisexual, transgender, questioning/queer, intersex, asexual/aromantic/agender, and more) young person feel secure and lower chances of depression. Studies show parental support for an LGBTQIA young person can literally safe a life.

"Should I talk about condoms?" Values are conveyed by example more than by words. If a parent doesn't want to talk about condoms and birth control in an age-appropriate way, I think examining the reason for this hesitancy is important. Data strongly suggests children who know about prevention are no more likely to grow up taking sexual risks. In fact, knowledge and skills like communication, decision-making, problem-solving, and refusal skills enhance a young person's ability to lower risks. Condoms don't cause pregnancy and they may save a life. Again, listen to your young person. Ask open-ended questions: "What have you heard about condoms?" and, "What do you know about birth control?" and, "Why would someone need or want to use prevention items if they're sexually involved?"

It's Okay to Start Over!

As part of my childbirth classes, I always offered my home number for questions when the class ended. Many people called me, usually to ask if I thought they were in labor. One of the parents in my class laughingly tells me she asked questions longer than anyone else (she did not). We see one another on Facebook now and she never fails to be complimentary. Being available wasn't a big deal to me then, being there for young people now isn't a problem. I see it as part of teaching with heart.

I do remember this mom's question when her child was five, though. A very conscientious, involved parent, she worried her son would ask her about condoms long before he was old enough to use them. He had older cousins, and she was wise enough to know most "sex ed" happens within groups of kids or on a school bus. She called and we discussed her approach. Less is more, so she decided she'd simply say, "Condoms are used by adults." Her son was, after all, only five. If he wanted more, we practiced how to ease his curiosity without offering more information than he could handle.

She called again right after he started first grade. Condoms were discussed on the school bus. She was driving down the road with her boy and his younger sister when his voice piped up from the back seat, "Hey, Mom. What's a condom?"

I suppressed laughter during her call, respecting her angst, but her response – shared to me with deep concern – still makes me chuckle. She said, "I had all of our conversations in my mind. I knew at five it was okay for him to ask, and his sister is only fourteen months younger, so I thought, *I'll just tell him what we practiced.* Then, an ice cream shop appeared ahead. I completed dodged the question and said, 'Who wants ice cream?'" I reassured her, no harm done. Later, she brought up the topic of condoms. Her boy nodded and went on to describe in detail a playground interaction where a condom was found.

It's okay to not find the right words. It's okay to start a conversation over. It's okay to say, "I didn't know exactly what to say yesterday, but I'm ready to talk today." It's okay to try. Young people are forgiving of technique and respond to adults who care.

Mixed Messages

Teach about mixed messages. Many parents teach their younger drivers the dangers of drinking and driving. Some parents add to the lesson with reassurance and a promise. Saying, "If you drink at a party, even though you know you've broken our family's rules on drinking, I don't want you to drive home drunk. Don't get into a car with a driver who's high or who has been drinking either. Call me and I'll pick you up, no questions asked, no consequences. I want you alive."

If taught carefully, condom and birth control information is no different. Young people are sexual. That doesn't mean they're doing sexual things, but it might. Love them unconditionally and protect them.

Kids are ready when they're ready. We don't teach calculus first. We start with basic math. Sexuality is like any other topic, despite its sensitive nature in our culture. Start small. It all works out. If a child isn't ready for the information, they'll get bored and tune a parent out.

The greatest gift an adult can give a young person is unconditional love. Acceptance is interwoven within that love.

Step #4: Less is More

Do respond to all questions.

Respond to all questions with as simple an answer as possible.

Remember, silence is a response.

Example speaks louder than words.

Remember Emerson said, "What you do speaks so loudly, I cannot hear what you say."

Model values you want children to adopt as their own.

CHAPTER SIX

Toolkit for Connection

When I go to a school to teach, I often look

like I'm leaving for an airport. I wheel a packed suitcase behind me. Inside are my portable body parts, my Opinion Hat and Curiosity Bag, my Power and Guideline Cards, Koosh balls, timers, whistles, stickers, pens and pencils, prizes, internal and external condoms, IUDs, sticky notes, stuffed microbes representing STIs, and at least six original games linked to the lesson I'm teaching.

Power Cards

I created my Power Cards to give my students a voice, even if they want to remain silent. The cards are laminated and spiraled together to create a 6x9 inch flip book. Each student receives a book. I also disperse identical 3x5 inch cards throughout the classroom.

There are six cards in each pack: *I Pass, Boring, Too Gross, Too Much, One Speaker,* and *Great, Keep Going!* A young person may hold up an *I Pass* card to indicate a desire to sit out an activity. Raising the *Boring* card signals the class isn't interesting—it takes real courage for an educator to put this card in the hands of sixth graders. A student can show the *Too Gross* card when the topic is disgusting from a young person's point of view. This card is typically only used by my adult staff! The *Too Much* card is waved if a topic is more than a young person wants to discuss—if I see even a corner of this card, I change the subject to football, "How about them Steelers?" The *One Speaker* card helps me reinforce respectful discussion and gives permission for their voices to be heard without interruption. Students police themselves with this card the most, making sure each speaker takes turns and shares airtime. *Great, Keep Going!* is an affirmation to encourage class discussion.

Guidelines

I've also created and printed Guideline Cards. I set the stage for learning by creating a community where my students mutually agree on our promises to one another—these are our guidelines. We begin with the guidelines I've chosen and add to them through open discussion. My current guidelines are: *Respect, Confidentiality, Power of Words, No Judging, Laugh?!, No Names,* and *Curiosity.*

Once more, I have large 8x10 cards on rings as a visual reinforcement of our contract. Smaller 5x7 cards are distributed throughout the room, so my students can take charge of these promises to one another and to me. People learn through visual, auditory, and kinesthetic (by experience) ways. I cover them all.

The key Guideline Card is *Respect.* I model my conviction that each person is a person of worth. I articulate the obvious. Are there any groups of people who deserve less respect than another? No, not in my spaces. All are respected. We don't need to agree with everyone, but we do need to offer dignity and respect to each human.

I teach about *Confidentiality,* carefully explaining mandated reporting—that I must, by law, reveal abuse or danger to a child—while simultaneously promising to alert a young person to my need to speak with anyone else about their words. I talk with them before telling others. I've not broken that promise. I do not intend to ever break it.

Here's an example of how confidentially is handled by me and my professional team. Twenty-five plus years ago, a fifteen-year-old named Sara told me she was pregnant, then asked me to keep her secret until the Memorial Day holiday ended. It was the last school day before the holiday break. She shared the chance of her parents drinking over the holiday were high and she wanted to wait for a better time. I agreed. That afternoon, her best friend came to see me. She told me Sara was an insulin-dependent diabetic. Diabetes doesn't prevent a healthy pregnancy, but what I deemed typical and safe suddenly became a pregnancy needing medical supervision. I called Sara to the office and told her we needed to find a trusted adult in her family for support. After cussing at me with enthusiasm, she thought of an aunt she could trust. I stayed with her at school until her aunt arrived and arranged for prenatal care. Sara wasn't happy with my decision, but I still protected her. Respect for young people means honoring their need to know about their own lives and making informed choices.

The other guidelines help me set the stage for learning. *Power of Words* covers the reality that some words are hurtful. The poem "Sticks and stones will break my bones, but names will never hurt me" is a lie. Names hurt. I take the time to call out words – without saying them – that are not okay in our class. No racist words, no homophobic ones, no words that demean or put down disabled individuals. Young people react well to this guideline, and introducing it before class begins creates a safer space. *Power of Words* also allows me time to clarify. I will respond to all questions, honoring without judging any slang terms for body parts, then instructing in the correct word.

No Judging is obvious, although I do share how much people love to judge and am honest about trying hard to avoid judging others, even though it can be challenging. *Laugh?!* is followed by both a question mark and an exclamation point. Teaching sex ed means loving laughter. Students share that their health teachers won't let them laugh when discussing reproduction (as if making babies is all there is to sexuality). I disagree. I love hearing laughter in my classes and at our teen center. People laugh for many reasons: nervousness, a sense of camaraderie, or because something is just plain funny. I love easing tension. The question mark after the word *Laugh* is to clarify that we do not laugh AT one another, only WITH each other.

The *No Names* Guideline Card reminds my students to avoid gossip and real names when they share stories. I tell them to use Barbie and Ken or Buzz Lightyear and Woody. I encourage *Curiosity*.

I created an Opinion Hat – a ball cap printed with the words *Teen Outreach Opinion Hat* on its brim. I put it on when I'm asked for an opinion, to differentiate fact versus opinion. I ask for a definition of opinion first: *what do my students believe is an opinion?* Lately, the term "fake news" often comes up. I don't talk politics with my students, but I do explain that perspective makes one resource more credible than another to different individuals. I personally read my news from all types of viewpoints. I avoid opinions in general, but if I have one, the Opinion Hat goes on my head!

Power Objects

Koosh balls are used as power objects in my classes. When a young person says something wise, I toss a Koosh ball. Soft, safe, and fun to hold, it is a coveted object. When the next wise statement is offered, that student throws the Koosh ball to the next speaker. I often have three or four Koosh balls in play.

A decade ago, I delivered a keynote in the South where over eight-hundred professionals were in the audience. I realized I'd forgotten my Koosh ball when I unpacked my suitcase. I tried to explain how I used the balls, but the concept was challenging without a visual. I moved on.

After my presentation, a participant approached me. "You seem like a good woman," she began. A "but" was coming! I thought of the character Ned Stark's line in *Game of Thrones*, "Everything before the word 'but' is bullshit!" "I don't know what it's like up North," she continued, "but down South, we don't think it's polite to talk about koochie quite so much." To clarify, "koochie" is one of many slang terms for a vulva and vagina. What did she think I was throwing at teens? Small body parts?

Wheeling my suitcase makes me stand out. Over the years, teachers and administrations have added "wheels" and "squeaky" (I bought WD-40 after that name) to the Sex Lady title. In general, I am received with warmth. Most teachers are thrilled they don't need to cover my topics!

Seeing Good in All Young People

I'm often warned about certain students as I enter a classroom. A teacher will take me aside and whisper, "Third row, second seat. Watch out for that kid. He's bad news."

I'm nearly always warned about young men. They're typically outgoing, loud, and ready to test me. I love these students the most. A feisty young man walked into my class as a ninth grader and asked boldly, "What the fuck is this class about?"

I silenced the class and said, "You need to be a peer educator with me."

Stunned, he stared at me. "Me?" he said with disdain. "Why me?"

"Because," I explained, "you've got courage. You knew you could get in trouble for saying the F-word, yet you opened with it. You made eye contact with me and dared me to yell at you. I think you're not only brave, I think you could be one of the best peer educators I've ever trained."

He proved me right.

He took on my challenge and trained as a peer educator. His personality was vibrant and charismatic. He drew people in. Every time I put his name on the list to travel to the middle school with me or to teach at a professional conference, the principal tried to remove it. "He's a bad kid," I'd hear.

I don't get this mindset. I don't understand adults who label young people, telling them they won't succeed or don't have what it takes to follow their dreams. I've heard adults say, "Set a more realistic goal. Becoming an attorney (or doctor, or psychologist) is too hard. So many years of school. Why not try community college?"

Adults should be cheerleaders for young people. We support. We encourage. We model. We teach lessons are learned from failure. We honor dreams. We respect choices. We believe in young people, we love them, and we don't give up.

For four years, this young man persevered. His outgoing personality and resilient spirit made him fun to be around. After a year, he declared, "This role model shit is cramping my style. I can't get any!"

He had his ups and downs, but he never faltered in his commitment to peer education. He's in his mid-thirties now, a successful teacher, and an excellent father. He recently texted me to thank me for his time with peer ed. He said I saved him. I gently told him no. He saved himself.

My conversation with this young man reminded me of an exercise I use with young people called *The Boat*. I use an illustration of a boat or ask the young person to draw one. We then create a story to go with the boat. The boat represents their lives. Young people draw themselves as a figure on the boat, placing the figure wherever they see themselves. *Are they in front or back? Topside or below? Do they change position as the journey moves on? How and why?*

We talk about who is on the boat, who steers it, its destination. Adding a storm or rough seas, we discuss what they'll need to withstand the waves. *A lifeboat? A fellow traveler to help maintain balance? What are their life preservers? Education? A job? The cultivation of a skill? Short-term goals? Long-term goals? Problem-solving skills? Conflict resolution? Anger management? Who are their lifeguards? Parents? Friends? Teachers? Coaches? Faith leaders? Does their course change? How do they adjust to the change? Do they sometimes not want to steer their boat? What happens if they fall overboard?*

The young, successful man's words were generous. I reminded him of *The Boat* activity. I told him he was his own captain, he had steered his boat to safety.

He countered with, "I am my own captain. You taught me that. But you were the wind in my sails."

I told him he sounded like a song title, and we both laughed.

Teaching with your heart means stepping back. You may never know if a connection makes a lasting impression in a young person's mind. You keep connecting anyway. My goal is to no longer be needed, not because I want to move on to another young person. I love when connection continues, but my goal is to help young people find their own course and steer their own boat.

One of the teen mothers I served is now a master's prepared educator, running her own program for teen parents. A former peer educator served four deployments in Iraq and Afghanistan and is career Army with a rank of Captain. Our peer ed alumni are successful in business, in medicine, and in law. They're counselors and educators and parents. They stay in touch.

When two people connect, they can teach each other.

Connection can be life-long.
Look for the good in each young person. It's there.

Step #5: Create a Safe, Brave Space for Learning

Set the stage with guidelines. Call them promises, agreements, or a contract, but start each session with them.

Allow young people a voice in their creation.

If you see a student for only ten minutes, devote the first minute to guidelines.

First impressions happen quickly – in seconds.

Make your first impression your openness, your caring, your acceptance.

CHAPTER SEVEN

A Napkin Sex Question

Writing About Sex Weekly

In 2005, I started writing a weekly advice column for young people in our local newspaper, the Observer-Reporter. It's called *Ask Mary Jo.* I've written through breast cancer and treatment, four surgeries, and the births of five grandchildren. I've missed one column. In my first teaching trip to China in 2008, I was unable to get internet access the first week. Writing the column is a labor of love and I pray I can continue.

In the beginning, my editor worried I wouldn't have enough questions for a weekly column. I decided to use real questions, not ones created to teach a point. I'd written responses to columns for adults in the past, and often the organizations who hired me gave me canned questions for which they wanted responses. I wanted my column to be fresh and real. The truth is, I doubt I'll ever run out of questions and topics. As of this writing, nearly fourteen years and 728 columns later, I continue to respond to at least ten questions weekly. At times, I receive six to eight questions a day.

The initial questions were typically sexual, but, over time, their range became broad. I've responded to health questions, nutrition concerns, grief and loss, abandonment, and a ton of relationship concerns.

In 2006, I added a unique component to my column. Having started peer education in 1995 - my staff and I have trained over 15,000 young people to teach other teens since then - I created the *Ask Mary Jo Peer Educator Advisory Board*. My pattern is to select a question by Sunday of each week and write my response. Our peer educators give me their responses by Tuesday, and I submit the column each Wednesday. My earliest meetings with the Board were learning experiences for me. I'd not expected young people to show such wisdom and compassion. These peer educators reinforced that each encounter with a young person is a cross-cultural experience. I can no more understand their life experiences than they can understand mine. Just as visiting another country requires one to step back, listen to hear, and develop empathy, connecting with young people requires adult humility. Teens are insightful, but too often adults don't hear their messages. I love writing the column.

Ironically, the only area in which the column was censored was female masturbation. Since I respond privately to all questions and obtain permission for inclusion in the column, no query goes unanswered. All published questions are anonymous. After my second year, I removed gender and simply state the age of the questioner. However, I was told not to respond to many questions on female masturbation over the years. Male masturbation was acceptable. The patriarchy behind that decision inspires a conversation for another story, but even the male masturbatory question received negative press in the form of a letter to the editor, scathingly attacking me for corrupting the souls of boys by telling them to sin. One positive letter to the editor defended me. I didn't engage in any way.

I mention self-pleasure (a less clinical way to describe masturbation) because it's crucial to this story. Over time, adults began writing to me. Parents and grandparents regularly seek out advice.

Adults Question, Too

One day, in the tenth year of *Ask Mary Jo*, I was at my favorite salon, having my grey hair colored. I know, I know. I should be courageous enough to let it become natural. Every year, I discuss this with my stylist, and every year, I put it off. Someday, I say, I'll find the courage. At this appointment, a white-haired woman approached me, describing herself as a fan of my column. I thanked her. She then asked, "Do you respond to questions from grown-ups, too?" I assured her I did. She smiled, we parted ways.

A few moments later, I sat under a revolving device created to hasten the effect of the hair color. A paper napkin was suddenly dangled in front of my eyes. Stunned, I looked up. The white-haired woman was holding it. Her hand shook minutely, she avoided my eyes.

The napkin read, "Is it a sin to mastturbb-ate?"

I stifled a laugh. The spelling and the hyphen amused me, but I immediately realized the seriousness of this question from her point of view. I moved out from under the hair dryer and motioned her to have a seat. "Thanks for asking me," I said, projecting acceptance. "What a great question."

She took a deep breath and shared. Her husband had died after a long battle with cancer and she lived alone. She was a person of faith, and worried she was committing a sin by exploring her body. She blushed as she explained she didn't want to stop.

I shared I was a sexologist, not a theologian. I said her body was beautifully and wonderfully made, and her body parts were good. I smiled and said pleasure was seen by many as a God-given gift, and, in my opinion, self-pleasure or masturbation was normal. Many people enjoyed it, and it eased tension. She gave me a tentative smile and agreed. It helped her relax, she said. I gave her my phone number, explaining I was not only certified as a sexuality educator, but also as a sexuality counselor. I invited her to call anytime. She called six hours later.

After a long, pleasant conversation, she asked if I would come to her home for tea and talk with her friends. I packed my clitoral model, plastic body parts, and posters. Sitting in her kitchen with five of her friends, all of whom were over seventy-five, I was struck by the lack of knowledge these women endured all their lives, through marriages and childbirth. Their questions were basic and covered information familiar to most middle schoolers.

I remembered teaching my first childbirth class in 1975 to my mama, hoping to practice with a safe audience before teaching professionally. I recalled her first question to me when I finished teaching, "Do other women know this about their bodies?"

Sadness clutched at me. Denying women information about their own bodies and shaming them about their body parts isn't uncommon, but my experience in that sweet lady's kitchen reinforced the need for education. A few months later, I created a program called *Sexuality, Intimacy and Aging* and began presenting it at our local wellness center. The first class was attended by thirteen people over seventy-five. One male participant spoke longingly about his deceased wife. He missed her voice, her face, her smell, her presence. The women in the class looked at him with interest. He proceeded to repeat the same story at least ten times in the first hour, their interest waned.

Affirming Young People's Questions & Concerns

Adult questions reinforced the need for sexuality education across the lifespan, but my primary questioners are young people. I once answered the question, "How big should my penis be?" in my column. Porn viewing on cell phones or tablets is increasingly popular, and the question is a common one and came from a fifth grader. Viewing *gifted* men's penises worried him. What if he fell short?

My column runs on Thursdays. The week I confirmed penis size as uniquely different, stating clearly that size does not make a man, I reported to teach at a rural school. The secretary - a shy, private person - motioned me to her desk. "You said 'penis' in the newspaper," she whispered, her face scrunched as if she'd eaten a lemon.

"I did," I responded. "Why are you whispering?"

She looked furtively around the office, "Why did you say 'penis' in the newspaper?" Her face flushed, her breath quickened.

"I had a great question and a good answer," I explained, modulating my tone as I would to a frightened toddler. "I told the boy his penis was as big as it should be. Isn't that a good response?"

The secretary sighed, admitting it was. "Why didn't you change the word to something else?" she queried, a little calmer.

I pondered how she wanted me to change the word penis! I collect old sex ed books, and in one from 1905, the penis is only referred to as the "*male reproductive organ!*"

I smiled. "I did change the word," I said smoothly. "The actual question was 'How big should my dick be?'"

She gasped and nearly swallowed her tongue.

Imagine if I'd discussed the clitoris!

Babies, Genitals, and Touch

We often give two different messages to our children based on their sexual body parts. If you've given a nine or ten-month old baby a bath, you know genital touching is normal. Babies also put their fingers in their ears (and your mouth as you feed them a bottle or nurse them). They're exploring. In her book *The Magic Years,* Selma Fraiberg calls small children scientists. In *When Sex is the Subject: Attitudes and Answers for Young Children,* my friend and colleague Pam Wilson talks about removing our adult glasses when considering sexuality from a child's perspective.

What are those two different messages, you may ask? Ah, yes. Sadly, we use unique tones to speak, based on our babies assumed gender and their sexual body parts. Most parents seek to distract their babies from their genitals; maybe that's why rubber duckies were invented! The words are often the same: "Don't touch!" The music behind the words, the tone we use to give messages – another pearl of wisdom from Pam – is often worlds apart for different children when the same words are used. Children with a penis are told to "not touch" in a tone that conveys acceptance, sometimes accompanied by giggling. "Look, honey," a woman may say to a partner. "He's tugging so much. Will he pull it off?" Laugher ensues.

A baby with a clitoris is given the same message, but the tone is firm and full of command. "Don't touch," is a credo, a manifesto, a commandment. Female sexuality is complicated. It has dark ramifications in many cultures where girls are property or bartered about as goods. In America, we still assign blame to women. In all these years, I still see teen moms who are scorned, while teen dads are often not identified. Double standards rule. Slut-shaming is real and pervasive.

What if a parent or trusted adult simply said, "Those are your genitals." (I'd name penis/testicles or vulva/vagina.) "They're your body parts. They belong to you. They're okay. It feels good to touch them. No one can touch them unless you say they can." Will little ones understand all those words? In time.

We take great care to protect our children from physical danger. We tell toddlers to look both ways before crossing the street. We repeat important messages. *The stove is hot. Water from a tap may also be hot. Stay away from the grill. You must be in a carseat or wear a seatbelt when you're older.* Why do we avoid lessons about body autonomy and consent?

Testing!

One of my newest sex educators recently taught a group of sixth graders for the first time. As children of this age often are, they were very excited about class. One of the boys shouted out, "Do you masturbate?"

My brave staff educator gave a quick and appropriate response by respectfully telling the student he'd asked a personal question. As part of our guidelines, we don't answer personal questions and we don't ask young people personal questions. She did well. I've given that response in the past. The student was probably testing her—although, I'm equally sure he needed/wanted answers to questions about masturbation.

I've used such a question in the past as a bridge to discussing pleasure. Pleasure is often left out of sexuality education, as if we're afraid to connect sex with bodies feeling good. I've turned the question around by stating my staff person's response – we don't respond to personal questions - and then adding, "An interesting question. You're asking about sexual pleasure and I'm a woman. Are you saying all people – not just boys your age and men – are interested in pleasure?"

Where Our Cultural Fear of Sexuality Begins

I own a set 1905 sex ed books where the word "pleasure" is absent, and masturbation is referred to as "self-pollution." There are two companion volumes, one for young women of fifteen years and up and one for young men of fifteen years and up.

The book for young women never mentions masturbation, nor does it explain conception (how babies are made). It talks about how wheat and corn and barley reproduce, then gives tips for being a good wife. Did you know hanging clothes on a line to dry removes a backache? Or that washing dishes eases headaches? No sex, not even periods, are discussed in this book entitled *What a Young Woman Needs to Know about Sex.*

What a Young Man Needs to Know about Sex does a similar review of plant biology. There are three chapters – three whole chapters, mind you – devoted to the great and horrible sin of self-pollution, however. Young men are chastised to avoid touching their "male parts" during their weekly bath(!). They were instructed to wash their bodies and vigorously splash cold water on those "parts" and let them air dry to avoid stimulation. They were also admonished to abstain from sliding down banisters for the same reason.

Lest these young men ignore their prohibitions, the authors added several pages about the consequences of the dreaded act of self-pollution. Would they go blind, get hairy palms, or go insane? Their fate was far more final: the book clearly states self-pollution will result in death! The young men were told they will not be able to predict which act of self-pollution will be fatal. I picture boys in 1905, clutching their Sears Roebuck catalog underwear sections, deciding if pleasure was worth the risk!

Many people in the early 1900s believed masturbatory activity led to mental illness. Both John Harvey Kellogg (inventor of Kellogg's corn flakes) and Sylvester Graham (for whom the graham cracker is named) felt people's diets contributed to their sexual urges. They both wrote about the evils of "self-abuse" and promoted an "anti-masturbation diet," consisting of whole grains. For some people, sadly, nothing has changed.

I'm continually frustrated by medically inaccurate statements from our elected officials. In my opinion, our entire body of elected officials needs basic anatomy, sexuality, and embryology education. People need to stop promoting and voting for bills that are impossible to reinforce and which also deny science. This seems like willful ignorance. Political beliefs cannot change the way bodies work. I volunteer to teach them all! Send me in!

Privacy and respect for the body are key messages.

Step #6: Teach Pleasure is a Normal Part of Being Human

Babies will touch their genitals. Never shame.

Gently explain these body parts are good and belong to them.

Explain touching another person's genitals is never okay without permission.

Take time to go over diaper changes and doctor visits as exceptions to that rule.

As the child grows, offer them privacy, especially during puberty.

CHAPTER EIGHT
Portable Body Parts & Bodies

I've gone through eight uteruses in my lifetime and a dozen pelvises. I even ran over a plastic pelvis once while backing down my driveway. I purchased fifty styrofoam penises in Germany in 2001, and I recently acquired a 3D clitoris. I own two vulva puppets, and bought a visual aid used in France from SIDA (the French AIDS Education Organization) that includes five brightly colored wooden penises on a circular disc. I call it my penis cozy. How many people can claim such ownership?

I began purchasing portable body parts when I started teaching childbirth education. My first knitted uterus was a life-sized one holding a fetus, placenta, and umbilical cord. It was rainbow colored. My current uterus is blue striped. I also own a pocket size uterus, complete with fetus, amniotic membrane, and placenta. I used these DIY body parts in my early days as an educator, but my first big financial splurges were quality visual aids. Posters are nice, but nothing enhances childbirth preparation more than a life-sized uterus.

I taught sibling classes for the first time in 1980, when my second pregnancy made my first child a sibling. Low on funds, I sewed ten multi-cultural babies to use in class. Their bodies were great—their faces, not so much. I can sew, but my artistic talents are weak. Once again, as soon as I could afford to do so, I purchased real baby dolls. After a few years, I splurged on dolls with the ability to cry, whose heads flopped and needed support. Interestingly, the children in my sibling classes never seemed to mind how much the babies appeared life-like. Once those dolls were given blankets and I distributed them to each child for diapering and swaddling, my small students were somber, handling the dolls with great care, as if they were live infants. They were practicing for the real event!

Recently a former middle and high school student tagged me on social media and shared a picture of the certificate I gave her during the sibling class she attended in 1994! Complete with her fingerprint (I made a big deal of these little ones "graduations" as big sibs), the certificate was old and wrinkled, but she'd saved it! She was cleaning out boxes and found it. She wrote to me, ecstatic, saying, "I thought you only influenced my life when I was older. Now I see you've always been there! Thank you!" It was so nice to be remembered. I didn't tell her that I'd also taught her parents childbirth when they were expecting her!

Pelvises are important for childbirth education, and a wise instructor will practice second stage labor (the pushing part) and expulsion (the birth) before using the pelvis in front of a class of anxious parents-to-be. A fetal head stuck in a pelvis can be frightening to expectant parents. *What if the head doesn't fit?* Demonstrations need to ease anxiety, not add to it.

Normalizing Body Parts

When I began teaching sexuality in 1981, I purchased a different kind of pelvis: a plastic model capable of being divided in half so internal organs could be viewed. I ordered it online. I thought the vagina was ridiculously portrayed. This amazing body part is more like potential space than a gaping channel; I discovered using a balloon to explain the vaginal walls worked nicely. The sides of a balloon touch, just as the strong vaginal walls do, yet both can be stretched as needed. Putting air into the balloon and then releasing it shows the elasticity of mucous membranes. Again, practice was vital. Can you imagine the faces of students watching a vaginal balloon break? It never happened to me, but I lived in dread.

Ordering body parts and receiving them at home was an educational experience for our children. When I began teaching breastfeeding classes in 1991, I purchased breast models in two types of skin tone. Both models used an extra flap of material to demonstrate milk ducts. The educator simply pulled back the material to reveal a colorful diagram of the inside of the breast. Our son opened the box before I could. He lifted out one of the breasts and examined it. The flap was accessed by a thin piece of dental floss-like material that ended with a small plastic circle. He held the breast by the circle and said, "Is this so you can attach it to the van's rear-view mirror in case someone in town doesn't know what you do?"

I eventually hired and trained a team of sexuality educators, primarily registered nurses, to teach in our community. My staff and I regularly carted body parts to and from school. One day, I was observing one of my nurse-educators teach for her quarterly review. When I arrived, she admitted she'd forgotten her plastic model. Her tone was casual and matter-of-fact as she asked, "Do you have your vulva and vagina with you?" Before I could respond with, "They're in the car," a male teacher walked past and laughed. "Only the Sex Lady," he said, grinning.

Anatomical models leave a lot to be desired. A real penis, testicles, vas deferens, scrotum, seminal vesicle, and prostate gland look nothing like the varying colored body parts available for educational use. Ditto the vulva, vagina, uterus, cervix, and clitoris. Don't even get me started on the bladder!

Sadly, not knowing the medical names of genitalia is even common among adults in our nation. How many adults know the word "vulva?"

Curiosity

Sexuality educators know a lose-lose situation when they see one. There's a reason we don't respond to personal questions. No matter how many young people ask me about my personal sex life, I'll never respond. I don't ask them. They don't ask me.

Why are personal sex questions lose-lose? No matter what you say, it's wrong. Unlike some sex educators, I've been married with children since before I started teaching. An assumption of heterosexuality is common, but I see no need to address my personal orientation. My personal sex life doesn't matter to their education. I also believe it is unethical to share.

It's complicated. Suppose a teen asks me if I had sex before marriage. Let's say I respond with "no." I've given two implicit messages with the potential to break teacher-student connection: 1. I've opened the door to further personal questions: "Why did you wait?" or, "Was it good to wait?" and 2. I've immediately alienated myself from any teen who's sexually involved. *Why should they speak with me? What about young sexual abuse survivors? Have I made them feel less worthy?*

Let's say I respond with a "yes." Then my students will follow with questions like, "How old were you?" and, "What kind of sex?" Trust me. Some young people are that bold. Once more, I've given two implicit messages with the potential to break teacher-student connection: 1. The question thing (see above), with the added risk of questions becoming explicit, and 2. I've set a standard of my choice as a model for the correct choice. Educators model empathy, compassion, respect, and integrity. We use medically accurate information to teach. We don't impose our own choices on our students.

I do answer all non-personal questions when I teach. In time, I learned to do so with care. I was unprepared for a question the very first week I taught, shouted out to me by a ninth grader who looked so sweet and innocent my inexperienced self was floored. I answered poorly.

My new student's question, on the first day I met his class, and my fourth day as a sexuality educator, was this: "Suppose my girl gives me a blowjob and I cum. Then we tongue. Then I go down on her. Can she get pregnant?"

Flustered, I responded, "Yes," and the bell rang. A teacher can be in the midst of the greatest wisdom of all history, but when the bell rings, students leave. This day, I was grateful the class ended. I sank into a chair, pondering my shock. *I was prepared for anything, right?* I also realized my answer was probably incorrect. Even if semen transferred during this long process, sperm most likely would not survive.

I had a dilemma. I was certain young people needed answers to their questions. I wanted to prevent a question being blurted out without my control. I had to create safety for all students, assure anonymity, and screen questions with care. *How to do so?*

My Curiosity Bag

I created the Curiosity Bag. I knew colleagues who used question boxes or jars, but I wanted something portable that could be passed around the class. I printed large blue bags embossed with our logo, *One Kid at a Time*, and the words *Curiosity Bag* across the front in large font. I selected the word *curiosity* with care. Teaching young parents taught me students could be educationally scarred. I knew asking a question could be perceived as a lack of knowledge on a young person's part, making a student reticent, unwilling to admit that lack of knowledge. I needed questions. I didn't know what my students didn't know, and, as the poet R.D. Laing eloquently says in the poem at the end of this book, my students may not know how to tell me. Peer pressure to perform in class is real. I stressed curiosity to give my students an out—anyone can be curious, and curiosity only means a person is thinking, not ill-informed.

I started bringing small sticky notes with me to class. My Curiosity Bag was always with me, and the notes were available. Every other session, I distributed blank notes and instructed my students to each take one. If they were curious about something, they should write the topic anonymously - no names. If not, they should still write. They could write *Nothing today*, or *I'm not curious today*, or *No questions*.

This technique worked famously. Questions filled my bag. Young faces beamed. Kids appeared relieved. I used different colored sticky notes for different classes, and the notes could easily be folded onto themselves so the words were invisible. They even stuck and stayed closed, so no student could inadvertently see the writing. For a while, I opened the notes in front of my students, but I quickly realized they self-identified, often with words, but nearly always with body language. To protect them, I expanded upon my idea. I didn't answer the notes the day they were written. Instead, I took them home after school, read them, and typed a list for the next session. Then, I wove the answers into my class as seamlessly as possible. I explained all of this to my students, who received the activity well. It worked.

A common middle school question in my Curiosity Bag is "What does it mean to pop a cherry?" I explain that "cherry" is often used as slang for the hymen and remind my students that female bodies do not pop like champagne. I then have a wonderful opportunity to discuss myths about the hymen. Despite popular belief, first vaginal penetration doesn't *break* anything. The hymen, or vaginal corona, is a small thin tissue inside the vagina, shaped a little like a doughnut with a hole. It may be absent, it may be a thin, elastic membrane, or, rarely, it may be thick and dense. Some of the hymen can stretch or tear from normal activities like sports or exercise. Hymens have no purpose. None. The myth that they keep fecal matter out of the vagina is ridiculous. Each hymen has a hole, or the flow from a menstrual period couldn't leave the body. Rarely, a hymen has no opening. This is a medical condition called imperforate hymen and requires surgery to correct. Penetration doesn't necessarily change a hymen. Studies have shown no difference between many hymens without penetration and after. Bleeding at first penetration isn't true for every person, although some studies report 50% of people with vaginas report some bleeding, often just spotting (a small amount of blood, like a spot).

Recently, rapper and actor T.I. created a backlash when he shared he accompanied his daughter (now eighteen) to a yearly gynecologist visit to check her hymen for a "virginity test." There is no virginity test. There's no way to check for first sexual experience, especially since the first experience may not involve vaginal penetration, and the presence or absence of a hymen means nothing. Forcing a young person to face such an exam is a clear violation, in my opinion. Her personhood is doubted and her worth devalued.

A hymen discussion often leads to myths about virginity. I no longer define the word. Many young people ask questions like, "If two women only have sex with each other, are they always virgins?" and, "What kind of sex makes a person not a virgin?" and, "What if a person is raped? Still a virgin?" I've facilitated open discussions on the idea of virginity, and I listen as young people sort through their awareness and opinions on the concept.

Counseling young sexual abuse survivors reinforced the need for education surrounding hymens and the social concept of virginity. Picture the angst of a twelve-year-old girl who was repeatedly raped by her father. Imagine her trauma, her pain, and her confusion. What does she ask me? *Am I still a virgin?* When I reassure her that her the sexual experiences that matter are the ones where she gives consent, that hymens are useless, that her body has physically healed, the relief on her face is heartbreaking. Why do we socially stigmatize people for no reason?

The myth of an intact hymen – a hymen that isn't torn or stretched – is non-medical. Using such a criterion for a woman's worth is historically based on ownership. Sexual assault and sexual abuse are real, and survivors face harsh judgment in an often victim-blaming culture, so acceptance of a person's worth as human is key. Everyone experiences first-times for sexual acts. In my opinion, these experiences are personal and not determined by the absence or presence of a hymen.

Challenge Questions

Since 2010, there's been a proliferation of smart phones. Parents who tell me they have blockers on their home computers are giving their children hand-held mini-computers. All it takes is one person in the back of the bus with internet access and curiosity and an entire group of children see sexual things most adults would choose to censor. Coincidentally, around 2010, I noticed questions from sixth graders in my Curiosity Bag once asked in the past by my tenth graders! These questions change every year. I am no longer startled.

I realized how much I needed to protect the children who weren't developmentally ready for some information. At the same time, I needed to respond to all concerns. *Why else was I there?* I was a trusted adult who could give them what they were afraid to ask others.

I devised a plan. Most school class periods are forty-two or forty-four minutes long. I've taught long enough to understand class time frames. In fact, my activities automatically come to completion moments before the bell. I realized my students weren't aware of my competence. I decided to play a little game of deception. When I received a question I knew could be controversial, the next session I'd say, "Oh, my. The period is almost over. The bell will ring in a minute. I don't think I answered all your notes. If I missed yours, please come and see me after class. I'll write you a pass to your next class if you need one."

They always stay. Sometimes they're so excited about an answer, they begin talking while other students linger, and I think that's okay. Those who remain are usually the questioner's friends and know the topic in advance. They, too, want answers. I call these notes my Challenge Questions.

One of my most interesting Challenge Questions dealt with squirting, or female ejaculation. A sixth grade boy asked it. His actual question was, "Why do women squirt?"

Full disclosure. I didn't know about female ejaculation until I was an adult. Online access changes things. After class, my student remained and said, "You didn't get to my note."

I said, "I'm sorry. I'm so glad you stayed to talk with me. What was it?"

He responded, "It was about squirting."

I said, "What do you want to know?"

He scrunched up his face, "Do all women do it? It's gross."

I assured him female ejaculation wasn't common. Some research shows it occurs in less than seven percent of women. He seemed relieved. I kept him in conversation a few minutes more, talking about the Steelers and his interests. Football is religion in my community. Weaving in online access, I asked, "Do you watch whatever you want online?

"Yep," he said. "No one cares."

I hesitated, seeking wisdom, "Tell me about your family. Do you have brothers or sisters?'

I was lucky. He shared he had an older brother and a younger sister. "You know my brother," he added, proud. "He was a peer educator with you before he went to college."

Ah, excellent. I connected him to his brother in an instant. They even resembled each other. I asked, "Does Ryan know you're watching this stuff online?

He shrugged, a little uneasy.

"Will you tell him? I'd like him to guide you through what you're viewing."

He shuffled from one foot to the other. I asked, "What if I text him and ask him to spend time with you when he's home on break?"

"He's home next week," he said, obviously excited about seeing his brother.

"I think an adult in your life needs to help you sort things out. Sex is everywhere online, but it's not always easy to understand. Would it be okay if I talked with Ryan?"

He looked relieved, "Yeah, that's okay. Just don't tell my dad."

I agreed. He gave me a huge grin and left. That evening, I texted Ryan and asked him to mentor his young brother. A sharp young man, he understood immediately. Knowledge is power, but processing knowledge requires guidance.

That's my job.

Body Image

When we talk about bodies, we need to consider how young people feel about their own. When do we first develop body images, both negative and positive?

I've never really been thin. In American culture, body size can lead to negative body images, lack of self-worth, poor confidence, and genuine bullying. When we consider sexuality, large bodies, especially large bodies of those who identify as women, can be judged undesirable, not sexy, or even asexual.

When I serve young people as a counselor and educator, my primary goal is shoring up their self-concept and self-worth. I hope to inspire them to see themselves through a positive lens. Often, their self-image is distorted by the way they're perceived by others. Cultural bias towards large bodies can color a young person's life and sexuality forever.

I was asked once why my size didn't undermine my confidence. The questioner was a friend who probably didn't realize her words were a microaggression—a hurtful statement said without filtering or thinking. I shelved it away with other comments and actions by adults who thought their intentions were good but had the potential for harm. Over the years, I've been offered sweaters, coats, and whole outfits by people who'd lost weight and said, "I hate to throw this out. It should fit you." One dear friend even told me she knew why I didn't lose weight. "You carry so many teens in your heart. You support them. Your body needs to be solid—a foundation they can lean on."

The truth is, I take these types of comments with the proverbial grain of salt. Do I want to lose weight? Sure. I'm currently focused on eating for nutritional health. I'm a healthy person in her late sixties. I intend to remain healthy and active. In that sense, I try to eat healthy foods and get some exercise (I'll never be a gym rat, but I do walk!). My friend wasn't wrong, though. My size doesn't undermine my confidence. This story will tell you why.

I started gaining weight at puberty. Fifth grade wasn't easy. In our community, our elementary school extended through fourth grade. I was a leader in that small school, president of my second grade and fourth grade classes, and active in student government. I loved school. I've always loved school. Socially, I was at the top of my world. I walked one block to school, and my best friend Stephanie lived another block from me. Life was easy.

For fifth grade, I was bussed to the other side of the city, where all the elementary schools merged to form one school. I only knew a fifth of the students. My best friend and I fell apart the summer before fifth grade, as children may. That summer, the weight slipped on easily. I don't recall eating any differently, but soon I was wearing "chubby" clothes. There was no plus size movement then, and I was relegated to a wardrobe that was more expensive than we could afford and less fashionable than I liked. My mama did her best and began to sew me outfits. Her creations were beautiful, but certainly not "in" or "cool." Until fifth grade, I didn't know I cared.

Being bullied is a fact of life for children who are different in ability, size, skin color, ethnicity, belief system, sexuality, or class. As a certified Olweus Bullying Prevention Program trainer, I know certain types of young people are bullied more than others. The three primary targeted groups are LGBT youth, those with a disability, and those who are overweight. I'd always been an outspoken student, with my hand up to answer questions. In my new school, I found myself holding back. Although I loved learning and wanted to respond, I began to doubt myself.

Riding the bus was a new experience. My ex-best friend was skilled at relational aggression, so I often sat alone and endured her stares and the glares of her new friends. Rachel Simmons' book, *Odd Girls Out*, discusses the type of aggression girls most often use, where friendships are volatile, back-stabbing is common, and popularity is elusive. Think of the movie *Mean Girls*. Like most children, I didn't want to disappoint my parents. Their image of me as a well-spoken, assertive leader would be tarnished if they saw the new persona I was adopting. I told them all I was fine in my new school. I didn't miss Steph. I was okay. I wasn't.

One day, an eighth grade boy on the bus called me "fat" as I walked up the aisle to depart at my stop. My ears reddened as I heard laughter behind me, but I didn't look around or respond. I simply disembarked. I had four blocks to walk from the bus stop to my home, and tears began in my first few steps. By the time I arrived home, I was sobbing.

Papa was working night shift at the glass factory then. It was late spring, and he was busy in his garden as I approached. Papa's garden was as big as our house; he cultivated vegetables with care and love. He was bent over the small tomato plants he'd just transplanted from his makeshift greenhouse (a large rectangle dug in the Earth and covered with an old window). He straightened as I came into view. By then, I was gasping for breathing, which often accompanies a good cry. My chest heaved. My eyes were red. My heart was broken.

When I studied for my master's degree in counseling, I was introduced to reflective listening. I learned to seek to understand a person's idea, hearing with empathy, and offer back the speaker's words to confirm I'd gotten it right. I was taught techniques for drawing out a person's pain, I was supervised in the art of hearing. Papa had no such classes. His formal education was limited to what he learned in Italy. Education wasn't his strong suit, but wisdom - ah, the man owned wisdom.

Papa took one look at my face and motioned me to his side. He sat down, right there in the dirt, and told me to do the same. He didn't ask me what was wrong. He simply was there with me, silent, offering his presence. He held space, although the term would have been unfamiliar to Papa. In time, my staggered breathing eased, and I looked up at his face. He was beaming at me. "*La mia bellissima figlia* (my beautiful daughter)," he said. "You were sad."

I nodded. Finding words was tough. He sighed. "The world is hard at times," he said, his tone a cloak of comfort. Then, he waited. Patient and accepting, he gave me time to find those words. Finally, I told him the tale. He listened intently, as he always listened. Nothing was in his hands, nothing distracted him. Today, when my grandchildren need to share something, I remind myself to put down my phone or turn off my computer. The gift of listening to a child is huge. Papa knew this.

When I was finished, he gave me his biggest smile, the memory of which will always feed my heart. Then he spoke. My body, he explained, was the container God gave me for my spirit to walk around in. *Would God give me the wrong container?*

I remember contemplating his words with skepticism. *How did he know this? How was he so sure my body was right for me?* I didn't know then how much he endured bias when he first came to America. Much later, I would learn of the epithets hurled at his teenage self: *dago, Black Italian, wop*. I only saw a strong man who never backed down, who protected others, and who stood for his beliefs.

He sensed my doubt in his gentle advice and his smile softened. "Some people don't understand," he said. He ran a chaste hand over my hair. "You are so incredibly beautiful. All of you. How sad that some cannot see this. You must know it. You must feel it. Then, they will know." He grinned and his eyes grew mischievous, "Who is this *stupido ragazzo* (stupid boy)?" I told him my persecutor's name. "Where does he live?" I shared what I knew. Papa grew solemn and asked, "Do you want me to kill him?"

A visual. My Papa was built like Tony Soprano. Unlike Tony, he had no ties to organized crime and never hurt a soul. I knew this. I also considered his request with the solemnity with which it was offered. *Should this boy suffer for his words?* I had, after all, just turned eleven. *No,* I realized. Death is too harsh a punishment for ignorance.

The next day, I walked to the bus stop early. The boy was there alone when I arrived, as I hoped. I walked up to him, channeling my papa's courage. I looked him in the eye and said, "You can't hurt me by calling me fat. This is my body and it's okay." Then I turned away from him and ignored him for the rest of the school year. I don't recall if he responded. I do know he stopped calling me names.

Self-Concept

In our educational mentoring program, we measure self-concept with a valid, reliable instrument called the Piers Harris Self-Concept Assessment. It assesses children and adolescent's conscious self-perceptions. The instrument helps us measure the nebulous concepts of self-worth and self-awareness.

School districts often ask me to teach self-esteem to children. I'm saddened by their requests. On one hand, I'm honored they respect me and ask for my expertise. On the other hand, it gives me pause to realize most people don't get it. We can't teach a child self-esteem; we can only guide them to realize and own their own worth. Self-esteem is dripped into a child moment by moment, not given in a bolus. Offer it daily.

When I became a parent, both my parents affirmed their philosophy of raising children. One of my little ones was strong-willed and independent. Mama smiled when I shared. "Just like you!" she crowed. She assured me each baby was their own person. All adults could do, she reassured, is guide. We shouldn't try to change a little one's core personality—nothing but resentment comes from drawing a line between your child and you.

Both Papa and Mama agreed. One thing a parent can do, they said, was tell their child they possessed good characteristics. If you tell children they are strong, they will become strong. If you tell them they are kind and compassionate, they will become kind and compassionate. If you tell them they can do something, they will become capable. If you tell them they are responsible, they will become responsible.

I noticed how often the young parents I served said, "He's so bad," or, "She's out of control" to describe their toddlers. I created a *Tell your kids they're great* jar and told parents to deposit a quarter in the jar every time they announced something negative about their littles ones within the child's hearing. It's a start.

We parent as we were raised. Flipping parenting scripts takes a conscious effort and commitment to change. I've observed young people take extreme steps to parent well. I admire their courage. I don't believe age determines positive parenting; I've seen adults make poor parenting choices. Teens can be the ones to break the cycle.

Young People and Pressure

Accepting one's own body isn't always easy. We come in all shapes and sizes, but society posits the "best body" in the media, and this impression seeps into tween and teen peer groups. Once, I primarily saw eating disorders in young women, but those days are gone. Six packs are coveted, and young people are intimidated by "perfect" bodies, regardless of gender or gender identity.

One of the toughest adolescent body image scripts is that of being "thick" or heavy. We discuss body image in class and at our teen center. The connection to sexuality is real. The key to healthy sexual decision making is self-concept and self-worth. If young people feel unattractive and undesirable, it's easier for them to be less selective in relationships. Vulnerability can lead to a drive to be accepted.

Perhaps the most important choice we make in our lives is a partner, if we choose to have one. Marriage was part of my culture; I expected to marry. I selected my partner with care, and he did the same. In days of VCRs, I brought a VHS tape to school to show the end of one of the *Indiana Jones* movies. Rewinding it to the correct segment ten times a day for each class was arduous, but I loved the message. Harrison Ford is in a chamber with a wizened old knight. He and the villain, a Nazi officer, are asked to select which cup was the chalice. The Nazi selects a gem-studded goblet and drinks from it. He immediately melts.

The knight turns to Indiana Jones and says, "He did not choose wisely."

Consequences of poor choices are not immediate but can set the tone for life. I know the connection between low self-worth, body image, and unhealthy partner choices. Teaching young people the beauty and worth of their own bodies is a major step to connecting for health.

*Inspire young people to see who they are
and acknowledge their own beauty and worth, inside and out.*

Step #7: Remember, Sexuality Includes Positive Body Images

Be open and affirming about body parts and bodies.

Avoid diet culture with children.

Affirm each child's worth daily.

Positive body image leads to confidence, and confidence leads to healthy relationships.

Healthy relationships bring joy to life.

CHAPTER NINE

Consent

As I write this, sexual harassment is in the news.

As the Sex Lady in our community, I've fielded many questions about consent. *Who is right? Who should be believed? Why is this happening now? What do I think?*

What DO I think? Here we go. Pretend I'm wearing my Opinion Hat! Too often, the adults who query me miss the point. The word "consent" is seldom used—the connection to healthy sexuality is often missed.

When Do We Teach Consent?

As with sexuality, our consent messages begin at birth. Start teaching consent early. Children listen. Children watch. Children remember. In 2018, I wrote *Nonnie Talks About Consent* with my wise friend Dr. Lexx James to help trusted adults and parents explore this topic with third–eighth graders.

- Healthy relationships model consent, so the easiest way to teach consent is to show it.

- Begin consent education without connecting it to sex.

- Use tickling (stop when a child says *no*) as a first teaching tool.

- Give children the power of their *no*. A child doesn't need to kiss grandma or grandpa. Adults need to respect children's personal space.

- As children grow, use life to teach. There are plenty of news articles, movies, and books where rape is discussed. Talk about it.

- Honor children's bodies as their own.

Yes, there are times when children must listen. School happens. Dentist visits are needed. Sleep must be obtained. Sometimes a child's *no* must be overruled. Please think, though. There's a wide difference between a *no* involving body ownership and personal space and a *no* that protects a child from running into the street or touching a hot stove.

Consent is Foundational to All Sex Ed

Why do we live in a rape culture, where survivors are not believed, are often emotionally and physically battered, and where rape may be treated as an insignificant crime? How is it that predators often do not face consequences?

Here are my thoughts:

1. **We handle sexuality education poorly.** In truth, we handle sexuality itself poorly. Mandated sexuality education is painfully rare. As of this writing, nineteen states require that sex ed defines sex as okay only if it happens after marriage. Only California mandates comprehensive sex ed that includes the concept of consent. We teach to prevent danger – unplanned pregnancies, infections – but not to model sexual health. Our young people turn to the media and online sources, some of which are porn, all of which are narrow perceptions of sexuality, instead of a caring interaction with an informed adult who can provide medically accurate facts.

2. **We handle sexual pleasure, especially female pleasure, badly.** I've already shared my dismay at the way female anatomy is dehumanized and mocked. At best, it's described in reproductive terms. Pleasure, and the mutual expression of sexual pleasure, is seldom mentioned.

Too many young women think sexual contact is owed – *He was so nice, he wanted it so bad* – and don't even think sexual pleasure is something they deserve. Years ago, I asked a group of ninth grade girls why young people they knew gave oral sex. Their response? It makes guys happy. *It makes them stop nagging.* What about their needs?

Consider this: To get my child abuse prevention education program into schools, I had to remove the diagram of the clitoris. The penis could stay. What does that tell you?

3. **We don't teach consent.** Too often, sex is all about conquest. Too often, power rules, not attraction. Too often, body language and words signaling a lack of interest are ignored. Too often, people, especially women, are sexual objects.

Until young women are validated and taught their bodies are amazingly made and pleasure is their right, consent will be a problem. Until young men are taught consent is the first thing to address with any sexual encounter, harassment will exist. We need to transform our culture. The concept is basic: sex is for individuals who communicate, respect, and value one another. Adults need to model respect in relationships, in sexual encounters, and in our culture.

What do we do first?

Detoxify Sexuality. Sexuality is part of what makes us human. It is far more than sexual acts. In my book *Nonnie Talks about Sex... & More,* I received permission from Dr. Dennis Dailey to use his Circles of Sexuality concept. In it, he looks at holistic sexuality through five lenses: intimacy, sensuality, sexual health and reproduction, sexual identity, and sexualization. I teach the children in the book about all five components of sexuality. Intimacy includes the concepts of love and vulnerability. Sensuality teaches us about skin hunger—the need for touch, so vital for babies and the elderly. Pleasure and body image fall under the category of sensuality. Sexual health and reproduction are the only topics typically taught in our schools if sex ed is presented at all. Sexual identity includes our gender, gender identity, and sexual orientation. Sexualization opens discussion on challenging topics like sexual harassment and rape and sexual abuse. Children in my focus groups were ready for these concepts. They hear them on news channels and read them online. They exist in the real world, not in a bubble. They're ready for sexuality education. Are we?

Teach life-affirming topics with medical accuracy. Teach mutual consent. Teach healthy and unhealthy relationships. Teach the importance of pleasure. Teach inclusive education, where everyone is taught their worthiness, regardless of ability, age, belief system, class, ethnicity, gender or gender identity, race, or sexual identity.

Hire diverse educators. If we don't offer role models who are people of color, members of the LGBT community, disabled people, or of different ethnicities and backgrounds, we offer a slanted view of sexuality.

Handling Critics with Respect

We have work to do. Years ago, I supported a teen mother whose church shunned her. The congregation physically stood and turned their backs on her because she sinned. A few years later, I went before a school board to fight for the right of a young parent to remain in National Honor Society. Her physical manifestation of her sexuality was deemed an honor code violation. No wonder we lose connection! Mentoring with respect works. The data in our young parent program shows a consistent graduation rate above 85%. National graduation averages for young parents hover around 30%. In 2016, twenty-eight of our young parents were eligible to graduate. Twenty-eight did.

When I first started the Outreach, a community leader asked to meet with me. He was kind but condescending. "You are a good woman," he said, "but have you considered what you are doing?"

I assured him I had.

He proceeded to draw an analogy for me. "Sex," he said, "is like fire. Both wonderful and dangerous, fire can warm the home or burn it down. Any sex outside of marriage is the dangerous kind. Any sexual act that happened between two men or two women is an abomination. Any person who plays God and pretends to be the wrong gender is disgusting." As he spoke, his tone became angrier.

I listened, then I asked if he would admit the fire analogy could be taken in another direction. I'd listened to him. *Would he hear me?*

He agreed.

"What if," I asked respectfully, "the desire to start a fire was internal? Genetic. What if as individuals mature, this desire became more intense?"

"I can go there," he said.

I continued, "If adults know this compulsion to start fires is inevitable, shouldn't adults teach *fire education?*"

He looked smug. He agreed about *fire education.* I sensed he was preparing to win this argument by telling me how we must teach our children to avoid fire.

"Forever?" I asked. "Do we teach our children to avoid fire forever?"

"Well, no," he smiled. "Only until they're mature enough to handle it."

"Suppose," I countered, "this intense desire to start a fire can happen any time. Any place. With anyone."

"No matter," he said confidently. "We teach them to avoid fire."

"What if they catch on fire? Not planned, it just happens. We already teach little ones to 'stop, drop, and roll.' Would we continue teaching how to help a child on fire?"

He agreed. "Yes," he said, "of course."

"What if," I explained, "someone invented a raincoat that would protect children from being burned. Perhaps the raincoat was not 100% effective. Perhaps it failed at times, but most of the time, this raincoat worked. Would we teach young people how to put on the raincoat correctly? Would we provide lockers at schools where the fireproof raincoats were easily accessible? Would we encourage communication about raincoat use? What if the drive to start a fire involved more than one young person starting fires together? Would we teach them how to obtain consent? What if a young person's desire to jump through fire differed by individual? What if some people were driven to jump with someone? What if that person was different than them in sexuality or in gender? Would we teach how to talk about exactly what type of fire was desired, and where it would be started, and why?"

I ask you as well:

Would we judge young people based on how they want to start the fire?

What if we could respect all young people?

What if we listened to all our young people, heard them, respected them?

What if?

A Consent Question

I received this question for my *Ask Mary Jo* column. My response is included:

Question: What if I have sex with a girl and she doesn't like it and later accuses me of rape? I haven't had sex, but this worries me. I asked my parents and my mom said not to worry about something like that because very few women lie about rape. My dad said you can't trust women, which made my mom very mad at him. They both said I should ask you!

-fourteen-year-old

Mary Jo's Response: Thank your parents for listening to you and sending you to me. I wish your mom and dad luck sorting this out! Your question is a common one now. It was seldom asked in our classes before a few years ago. One of the results of the #MeToo movement is conversations about sexual assault and harassment. I think talking about these tough subjects is healthy, especially if young people discuss them with parents or trusted adults.

Your mom's correct. A 2010 study showed only 2-10% of rape accusations over the last twenty years were proven false. The FBI says the number of "unfounded rapes" is 8%. Since I regularly teach the idea of consent in relationships, I'd like to give you food for thought:

1. Respect is important in encounters between people, especially sexual ones. If you prioritize respect for the people you meet, you'll be careful to enter into an encounter while thinking of a partner's needs and wants. Respecting others is a major life skill.

2. Consent means both partners want the encounter to take place and both partners agree to what happens. Consent is mandatory. A few important concepts about consent:

   - If a person is drunk, high, sleeping, or unable to communicate, they cannot give consent. This rule is not flexible and it's legal: no consent, no sex.

   - If you respect each person and yourself, you shouldn't want to be sexually involved without consent. This is a moral and ethical choice I believe each person must make before getting involved sexually.

   - Consent can be taken away. A person may agree to something and then decide it's not okay. This is an important responsibility. If someone says stop, stop.

   - No person has the right to touch or use another person's body. Even hugs and kisses should be given with consent.

   - Rape is never the fault of a victim. It's not about how a person dresses, or what time they're out of their home, or where they are, or how they act, or if they drink, or if they flirt with another person. Rape is rape.

   - Rape is about power. Most survivors of sexual assault know their rapists. Some people call that date rape. It means a person trusts another person yet is assaulted. Remember to honor and respect others. Set a high standard right now and keep to it all your life.

3. Choose a partner wisely. Be able to communicate easily.

4. I tell my students a conversation about consent, sexual limits (how far two people want to go), and responsibility for protection from unwanted pregnancy (if the sex will be penis-vagina sex and could cause conception) or STIs (sexually transmitted infections) needs to happen while two people are clothed, before sex. Talking about limits and consent when naked is too late! I even recommend this conversation occur in a public place where there's no possibility of becoming sexually involved. Here's an analogy – an example of what I mean. I'm not supposed to eat ice cream, even though I love it. It's easier for me to abstain from ice cream if I stay away from an ice cream parlor. If you're not ready for sex, don't put yourself in a situation with someone you're attracted to where sex can easily happen. If I do end up at a place where ice cream is sold, it's smart if I have a plan to set my own limits before I arrive.

5. As a young person reaching for adulthood, you own your own body and mind. Make choices with maturity and respect.

If you conduct yourself as a person of character and worth, respecting and honoring the worth of any partner in your life, if you are careful to talk about sexual limits before you get sexually involved, and if you continue communication with a partner, there should be no reason for anyone to accuse you of something you didn't do.

Sex is a grown-up activity that involves adult-type decisions and possible consequences. Give yourself time to mature, and please continue talking with your parents or with me as you grow.

The first steps to transforming rape culture to one of respect
are education on consent, respect for all people, and communication.

Step #8: Communicate, Teach Young People to Own Their No

Even small children have the right to body autonomy.

Model respectful relationships.

Use the news to discuss teachable moments about relationships.

Which celebrity enjoys a healthy one? Which appear unhealthy?

Use your adult power and mentoring to transform rape culture.

CHAPTER TEN

Privilege

I had a budding awareness of my own privilege as a child. I lived in a unique type of cultural bubble. Papa exposed me to complex insights about humanity. Mama taught me different cultures using books. However, one cannot know what one does not know. I was surrounded by my culture. I came up with privilege, but didn't name it or really understand it. It's been a growth process, and my learning curve was long. I'm still learning.

As a child, when my mama taught me about the Holocaust, slavery in America, and the truth behind the Westerns Papa was so fond of watching (he thought John Wayne was Italian, calling him Giovanni Wayna), I was shocked. The reality of the near destruction of an entire culture, the sordid history of slavery in our nation, and the pillaging of a people's homeland overwhelmed me.

I never heard Mama use the word genocide to describe the destruction of America's native peoples, but the inference was there. She cajoled Papa into turning off his beloved Westerns—he watched them when she was absent. Even as a preschooler, I played cowboys with him. One memorable day, when I was around three years old, I allegedly nagged him to play, but he was weary. As the story was told to me, he agreed to play, then stretched out on the sofa and promptly closed his eyes. Evidently, I demanded he get involved, and he opened one eye. "I'm playing with you, honey," he said. "I'm the dead sheriff."

I was a sensitive child. I felt guilty when I learned of racism and bigotry. I told Papa we were horrible people. Mama muttered about a common topic of hers: *man's inhumanity to man*. Papa said, "No, stop crying. Our people did none of this. Our people were hungry in Italy and came to America to escape." His message was clear. We were good white people.

I learned perspectives my classmates weren't exposed to from my story-teller mother's tales. As a young couple of limited means, my parents rented rooms from a Jewish family. It was the thirties. They witnessed refugees from Hitler's Germany in their landlord's kitchen. From her, I understood the Holocaust was no secret while it happened, yet apathy or politics or finances worked together to keep our strong country from interceding (Mama's words).

Nonetheless, as I've described before, Papa treated people with genuine respect. His house and his heart were open. Was he in denial about racism? To some extent, yes, as is our nation.

My Papa told me how he was treated as a fourteen-year-old immigrant in 1927. He was called *wop* and *Black Italian* and *dago*. He faced prejudice from people in the mines who didn't like his immigrant status and his accent. When he shared, he was also careful to explain to me - and I was a child, so adults should GET this - that this country was horrible to people of color (I think he said "colored people" - it was a long time ago). He told me about men he selected for his work team and how some white team leaders wouldn't pick men of color, but he picked men he trusted, and he trusted men of color and they made a great team. He said everyone on his team had each other's backs. He also reminded me of my responsibility. I was white, which made me part of some very bad things. I was supposed to stand up for what was right. Papa took the phrase "I am my brother's keeper" literally.

Desegregation

I don't remember Papa ever telling me to take a stand for civil rights, but I do remember his example. In the early sixties, our local swimming pool integrated. I was too young to know if there were protests, but I vividly recall the day things changed. I went to the pool daily that summer, weather permitting. Papa went with me this day, which seldom happened, since he was always working. I didn't know then he'd taken a vacation day to be with me, to teach me.

I didn't question my good fortune. I was just pleased he was with me. My friends and I were playing in the water when suddenly, without warning, everyone began to exit the pool. Confused, I followed my friends to our blanket. In a flash, Papa was standing beside me. "Come with me," he said, his tone firm, brooking no discussion. I rose and followed him back into the water. This shocked me since he disliked any body of water. A near drowning as a teen frightened him. He often quipped he'd return to visit Italy when someone built a bridge (flying was not even a consideration).

I remember looking around as I re-entered the pool. Papa and I were nearly alone on one side of the water. There were a few children and one or two adults in the water, but the pool was practically empty. My Papa nodded to the other end of the pool, where three families had entered the water. They were people of color. I realized in a rush that the white people had left the pool because these people entered. Papa said again, "Come with me." We splashed our way to the other end of the pool, making sure to keep to the shallow end of the water. Papa introduced himself and me to the newcomers. I learned their children's names.

Papa was embarrassed for those who left the pool. "I'm sorry," he said sincerely to the father.

"Change takes time," I remember the Black children's papa said. I went off to see who could hold their breath longer with the children while Papa wrestled back his fear of water and stood his ground. On the way home, he said, succinctly, "We need to stand for what is right, even if it's hard."

Race and Ethnicity

Race and ethnicity were complicated topics. Like many European immigrants, Papa divided his native land into groups. He was Napolitano and came from people who were fun-loving, according to his bias, but didn't make much money. Calabrese were good cooks, but you shouldn't invest with them. Sicilians were involved in the Black Hand and you needed to be careful or you'd end up dead. He made these statements without malice; his culture imbued him with prejudices within his own country of birth.

When I brought my future husband home, he took me aside to worry aloud. *Didn't he "have any Italian?"*

"No, Papa," I said, with defiance in my voice.

"Well, what is he?"

"American." I received a glare for my comment, and hastened to add, "His dad's family is Polish, and his mom's is English and German."

"Aiii," he sighed.

When his grandchildren were born, Papa would proclaim loudly to anyone around that our unique ethnic combination "made the best babies." Nonetheless, as I've described before, Papa treated people with genuine respect. His house and his heart were open. Was he in denial about racism? Certainly, again, as is our nation.

Learning

As an adult, I attended many workshops on diversity, racial justice, and social justice. The young people I served taught me as well. Young men of color told stories of women clutching their purses to them tightly when they passed them or exiting an elevator when they entered. I watched as clerks followed them when we went on field trips, but not the white teens. I learned, as I said, to slowly understand my white privilege had nothing to do with income (we were not of means) and everything to do with judgement thrust on a person solely based on skin color. My white skin opened doors. I was accepted in ways a peer of color could not be—not in the sixties, not now.

At one of these trainings, the group was separated by race. I felt awkward. *Why would we be segregated? What couldn't my colleagues and I share together?* The facilitator, a young person of color, patiently explained I had my own work to do. It wasn't my friends of color's job to teach me. They didn't represent all Latino or Black or biracial or Asian people any more than I could speak for all white people. By the end of the two hours of separation, unpacking privilege and learning about racism, microaggressions, and denial, I was near tears. I wasn't a good white person at all. I was part of systemic racism and part of the problem.

Mama introduced me to people unlike myself. I was small when she took me to a synagogue to talk with the rabbi there, a little older when she brought me to a mosque to meet the imam. The world was her classroom. If I expressed curiosity about how doughnuts were made, she'd march into a bakery and ask for a tour. Teaching me about diversity was part of her lesson plan. She was teaching. I was used to it. At both the synagogue and the mosque, she explained patiently that all people have the capacity for goodness, and that all can be cruel. Human decency was not relegated to one country, one race, or one belief system.

My First Job

I loved my work at Children's Hospital of Pittsburgh. It was my first job. I worked on the Metabolic Unit—the name was changed to Clinical Studies after my first year. We were responsible for the care of children with endocrine challenges like diabetes, ambiguous genitalia, and short stature. I learned to do nocturnal blood studies for growth hormone and administer epinephrine challenges. It was good work with good colleagues. I was in love with it.

I discovered my love for teaching when I was handed a shoebox and told to teach the parents of a newly diagnosed diabetic child. I had twenty minutes to prepare, and the box contained only alcohol wipes, syringes, and a vial of sterile water, but I finished the session beyond excited. I wanted to teach! In no time, I was creating learning activities that I could use to teach with heart. I doubt I ever would have left Children's if we hadn't moved to New York City. Indeed, I returned for a brief stint of night shifts before our second child was born.

At Children's, as a newbie GN (a graduate nurse who has not yet passed state boards), I was the only nurse on the night shift when I rotated onto 11-7. I knew so little, I didn't know how much I didn't know. A nurse's aide from Alabama named Ruth, a woman whose skin was so dark you could only see her sclera and her uniform in a darkened room, taught me how to keep sick little ones alive. She also taught me to make the best grits ever. She was a great friend once we connected with heart.

I came to her for help one night when a six-month-old didn't look right to me. His vital signs weren't alarming, but he seemed different when I did my hourly check. I sought her help because the child was Black. I'd trained with all white student nurses, and all my instructors were white. No one, to my knowledge, ever taught me how to look for signs of shock by checking the skin color of a person who was non-white.

I was hesitant. Ruth had a reputation for snapping at people, especially young, annoying, green nurses who got paid more than her but knew less. I looked again at this precious baby. I remember his name. I'll call him David, but, in my heart, I remember his real name. I can still see him. I recall how much I loved rocking him and feeding him. He was on our unit a long time. When he was discharged, I traveled two hours to visit him at his home. That night, something was wrong with this baby. I knew it, *but what?*

I pictured my Papa's courage and found Ruth in the treatment room, on break. I sat down, saying nothing. "What you need me to do?" she said. "I'm on break."

"I know," I said. "I don't need to you do any work, but I do need you to teach me. I'm worried about David. He doesn't look right to me."

"What's his beep (blood pressure)?"

"No different, but something's off."

"You went to college," she said disdainfully. "Why you asking me?"

I spoke the truth. "Because you know more than I do. Because it's wrong that people don't treat you like you do know more, but I know it's the truth. Because…" I was rambling and almost stopped, but I could see my words had mellowed her. She was listening. I finished in a rush of words, "because he's a Black baby and I don't know how to tell if his skin color isn't okay, and I was taught to look for ashen or pale skin in a white child, but I'm lost, and I don't want him to be…"

She was up and running down the hall before I finished and had the light on. "This child is sick. His color's dusky. Grey. Not good. Take his signs again."

I did. His blood pressure was lower, his heart rate faster.

"Call the resident," Ruth said.

I'd never done that. I blinked, and she softened, "You were right to get me. Your instincts are good. I can't call him. You can do it."

I did. I'm sure my inexperience made my voice shake, because the first-year resident on-call told me to call him back in the morning. (There were exactly two female residents in the hospital at that time. It was 1971.)

I returned to Ruth, crestfallen, "He said…"

"Go above his head, honey. Everyone has a boss. Call the chief pediatric resident." David looked worse to me—his respirations shallower than before. I nodded. She squeezed my arm, "Go on, now."

When my children needed a pediatrician, that chief pediatric resident was the doctor I chose. Not only did he respond to my call and come to our unit, where it was discovered David was bleeding from an internal stent, but he chastised the hapless first-year in front of me. CPR in the movies and in real life are leagues apart in reality. I am grateful to this day that this small person recovered well and a cardiac arrest wasn't called. I was told he was close due to blood loss.

Ruth continued teaching me. When she had surgery a year later, I was the RN she asked to stay at her home and offer her post-op care. She cooked so much – I was only staying three days – that I could've been there a month without putting a dent in her mac 'n' cheese, green beans and ham, and collard greens. At a Christmas visit once, she insisted I taste chitlings, crowing with delight when I gamely shoveled in a spoonful and pronounced it good. Everything Ruth cooked was good. In turn, I brought her eggplant lasagna like my Papa made it, my famous three meat meatballs, and homemade gnocchi. She taught me more by respectfully sharing our heritage and recipes and guiding me through the early days of my profession. Ruth gave me insight into racism in America. Her honest conversations opened my mind and my heart.

Learning from Teens

As part of a YWCA seventies initiative to bring races together called *Project Y's Link*, I volunteered with three girls of color as mentors. A friend who trained for the program with me quit after two months, so I took on her three girls. For the next two years, I spent a lot of time with these middle schoolers (when we began, the girls were sixth to eighth-graders). Between giggling, making a mess in my tiny efficiency apartment while we made homemade pizza, and talking - a lot - about boys, they taught me basic truths I use today to reach young people.

- Culture affects teens as much as adults.

- Racism is carefully taught, mostly by example.

- Those Black teens faced different fears than white teens at the time. Being ignored in a classroom was a real fear. Failure to secure work was a real fear. Not getting accepted into college was a real fear. Driving while Black was a very real fear.

- Interracial dating has grown to be more accepted as I've aged. Loving vs Virginia, the landmark Supreme Court case that stuck down bans on interracial dating, only happened in 1967, when I was seventeen. Still, these young women of color taught me conclusively that they found white boys attractive—along with Black boys, sometimes Asian boys, and sometimes girls.

• It wasn't their race that helped me understand young sexuality. It was their age and the trust we developed together. I am grateful to them to this day. When I started teaching sex ed, I had a foundation many adults never find. I knew to listen to young people.

When Teens are Advocates

To honor my papa's strong beliefs, we sent our children to a Catholic school until eighth grade, then they transferred to the city public school. Our district is the only truly diverse district in the county, and all three of ours received a great education there. When our second daughter started high school, I was actively teaching in the district. One night, a few days after she started, she received a prank call that was sexually harassing. The mother lion in me rose, roaring. I fumed, called the police, and wanted to wrap her in bubble wrap. Our daughter was calm and confident. I was not.

The next morning, I went to teach eighth grade in the district. I remember the lesson: we were playing a game I call Relationship Hang-Ups, where each student creates a t-shirt out of construction paper using a few easy tears to the paper. (My thirteen years as a Girl Scout leader left me not only creative but frugal with supplies; no scissors needed!)

My students divide into dyads and work on the shirts together. On one side, they write the things that can make a relationship unhealthy. We then discuss as a group. They then turn over the paper and write a quality that will counter those negative traits. For example, if control is an issue in a relationship, they will typically write compromise. We hang the paper shirts on a clothesline with clothes pins I bring with me.

We were in the middle of the unhealthy discussion when a boy interrupted, "Did someone prank your daughter last night?"

Shocked, I almost reacted, but another boy stood before I could speak. He strode purposefully to my desk. "I need to speak out of turn. I mean you no disrespect. May I?"

I nodded, still surprised.

He walked to the first boy's desk and hit his fist on it hard, "You know who did this? I know you do."

The first boy stared, mouth open. The second boy hit the desk again, harder. "I know," was sputtered out.

"Then you stop it. No one disrespects this woman or her family, you hear me?"

No one ever pranked my daughter again. The first boy was white, the second boy was Black. His older sister was a teen mother I mentored; her newborn needed cardiac surgery and I'd accompanied her to and from Pittsburgh hospitals for months. He didn't forget.

I told my family I almost initiated a racial incident, but they all laughed at me, rightly reminding me it wasn't race that figured in the confrontation but loyalty. To this day, I don't know. I do know there was tension in that class before this happened. The tension fled.

Giving Thanks

Privilege colors our reaction to life. Consider traditional Thanksgiving. I'm happy for the opportunity to be grateful those Thursdays. I eat good food, love and treasure family, kin and friends, but I finally understand that we should not perpetuate a lie.

I was taught the happy "Pilgrims and Indians" story, just like most people.

Please take a moment to consider the reality of colonization. Please visualize the genocide. Please think about the Native Peoples who lived here - whose land was taken, whose children were subjugated and forbidden their own language, who were denied the right to vote in this nation until 1924.

In my typical teen-driven Thanksgiving *Ask Mary Jo* column this year, where teens write about their gratitude, one of our brave peer educators shared his Native heritage. He wrote: "I'd like to share the other side of the Thanksgiving story. At the time, Native Peoples were in mourning over a massacre caused by the settlers. Traditionally, Natives would begin a fast on Monday and end it by celebrating with a big feast to celebrate the fall harvest. This is the real reason for Thanksgiving - not to sit around and give thanks. A traditional Native Thanksgiving would include corn, squash, fry bread, and buffalo, deer, rabbit, or duck would be the meat source. There would be no turkey or potatoes. No pies, because sugar wasn't yet used. One of my parent's heritage is Native from the Seneca tribe. I wanted to tell the story that isn't taught in schools. Not only did the settlers massacre Native people, they also dug up Native graves and stole jewelry buried with the Natives."

I am grateful for those who can face the horrors of the past with the conviction that we must not repeat them.

Using Privilege for Good

At our Common Ground Teen Center, we discuss everything our teens wish, but we maintain our guideline of respect. It's okay to agree to disagree, it's fine to debate without hate, but we do not tolerate any of the isms – no racism, no ableism, no heterosexism, no ageism, no classism. All religious beliefs are honored. We leave our anger for one another at the door.

This year, I've engaged an amazing colleague to Skype into our center once a week and present a series called Teens Dreaming Solutions. Our speaker is a young professional who is gender queer, uses they/their pronouns, is disabled, is a person of color, and is in grad school. Our teens are learning Privilege 101. Their discussions after the thirty-minute Skype sessions are rich and deep and insightful. I'm grateful, Aaminah.

Teaching a sensitive subject like sexuality means opening oneself to human needs. Once we decide to look at our humanity - and our sexuality as a huge part of our humanity - we are committed, in my opinion, to supporting all people.

As a white person, it is my responsibility to learn. It is my responsibility to dismantle white supremacy and white fragility. It is my responsibility to step back. It is my responsibility to ensure people of color and other minorities are given equal pay for their work. It is my responsibility to protect their work and not take it for my own purposes. It is my responsibility to seek and model equity.

I am determined to use my privilege – in all areas – to speak out and support. I've been honored to be recognized with many honors during my life, all of which matter to me. When I received the NAACP Humanitarian Award in 2008, I felt many emotions. Humility, first, since receiving an award for doing the right thing made no sense to me. One does the right thing because it is the right thing, even if it is hard. Along with gratitude, I also experienced frustration. There's so much to be done.

Social changes must be made if our grandchildren are to live in a culture of respect. It starts with us.

Step #9: Recognize Privilege

Use privilege – which we all have in one way or another – to create a better world.

Step back as an ally or accomplice.

Do not take the microphone.

People do not need a savior.

Teens teach one another best. Give them resources and they'll do a great job.

CHAPTER ELEVEN

Change

❋

"Change takes time." When I heard those words at the desegregated swimming pool by my father's side, I was too young to know their full import.

I've seen many changes in my life. One of the biggest surrounds informed choices for women during birth. I became a birth advocate for many reasons—chief among them was the inequity I saw during my first birth experiences as a student nurse.

How Birth Changed in My Lifetime

The very first birth I attended in my first week of my obstetric service, I was instructed on how to catch the newborn. I was nineteen. I was given a white, sterile apron with a long, wide front. All birth attendants were garbed in surgical gear, as if for an operation, even though the baby was moving down the vagina, a non-sterile environment.

We now know so much more about natural birth. I tell my students the book of what we know is small compared to the book of what we don't know. The term "human microbiome" was coined by Joshua Lederberg in 2001, and it refers to the totality of micro-organisms and their genetic codes on and in the human body. Scientists now believe babies acquire their mother's microbiomes during birth, breastfeeding, and first touch. These microbes assist babies' digestion as their own gut microbiomes develop. In 1969, without this knowledge, the standard protocol for birth was sterile technique.

My job at that first birth was to stand by the obstetrician, who was perched between the mother's legs. Her legs were carefully covered with sterile foot-to-thigh booties, her perineum (bottom or vulva) was draped with sterile sheets, and the doctor was gloved and dressed for surgery, complete with a mask and head covering.

I wasn't scrubbed in. My job was to pull that apron tight in front of me, extending both arms under the apron, palms up. When the baby was born, the obstetrician would cut the cord, lift the newborn by the feet, slap it on its bottom, and toss the baby to me.

My heart was thundering so loud in my ears I worried I wouldn't hear the doctor's instructions. *What if I dropped the baby?* Older student nurses terrified us with tales of students who did just that. I planted my feet on the floor and waited, staring at the doctor, barely breathing. The forceps on the surgical table were formidable. *Don't faint,* I chanted to myself. *Don't you dare faint!*

The baby cried. Suddenly, she was in my arms. As taught, I pulled her close to my chest and made my way, quickly but carefully, to the warming bed. I helped the RN do an initial assessment on the baby. My peripheral vision observed another nurse waking the groggy mother to tell her she had a daughter.

I'd excitedly anticipated seeing my first birth, but I felt no joy. It was impersonal and cold. I knew the mother was given a drug cocktail during labor that included scopolamine, an amnesic, and nitrous oxide to inhale immediately prior to the birth. I was overwhelmed. Birth should be better. We could do better than this.

We did, but it took time, effort, education, and an army of committed childbirth educators, doulas, midwives, and parents to make change. I will be forever proud of my time as president of Lamaze International. I am a Lamaze certified childbirth educator to this day.

How does one make change reality?

Educate for Change

Education is my tool and my path, but change can be so slow it can appear glacial. In fourth grade, I wrote an essay about who I would be when I grew up. In it, I stated with conviction I would be a nurse. I am. In many ways, I have not changed. When people first meet me and ask what I do, I reply I'm a nurse, even though my journey has taken me in many directions. I'm not a frustrated physician. I'm proud to be a nurse.

I'm also an entrepreneur, although my childhood self wouldn't have known the word. I approach life as a series of possibilities, learning from failure. My dreams are huge. I'm not afraid to strike out alone. I created ECHO (Educate Children for Healthy Outcomes), a one-on-one educational mentoring program, a year before I had funding. I love shooting for what looks impossible and making it reality. My godson, LeBron, recently told me he plans to be an entrepreneur, speaking with confidence, as an eighth grader, about something elusive. I'm proud of him. To strike out on one's own takes courage. In my generation, as a woman, it took uncommon courage. In this, I have experienced radical change.

I obtained my doctorate in my fifties because I loved education, because I promised myself I would achieve a terminal degree, and because I was hungry to learn. I embrace education because it inspires change and internal growth. My students' paths are their own. I'm their ally and their advocate, but their choices are theirs. Nelson Mendela's quote gives me courage: "Education is the most powerful weapon which you can use to change the world." I believe it's truth.

What are educators trying to achieve? Can we teach without finding common ground? How united should adults be in their core values? Do we teach to test or to encourage the best impulses of our students? Are we striving to raise humans of good character? Do we teach kindness and empathy—more importantly, do we model both characteristics? When we write curricula, how much do we rely on teen wisdom? Do we invite young people to the table? A popular Broadway show *Into the Woods* tells us children will listen. Do adults listen?

In high school, our son was in a play based on Deitrich Bonhoeffer's *Letters and Papers from Prison*. Since then, I've studied Bonhoeffer's words. He throws down a challenge: "Silence in the face of evil is evil itself. God will not hold us guiltless. Not to speak is to speak. Not to act is to act." I think of the Nazi doctrine of Untermensch, where people who were considered inferior were made to be subhuman. To hurt a group of people, propaganda first labels them as less than, and, in time, people deny that group's humanity. History reveals this, over and over. The Armenian genocide. The Khmer Rouge in Cambodia. Stalin's Gulag. Rwanda. Jim Crow laws and continued systemic racism in America. Hate crimes against transgender individuals and people with different abilities. This is why I believe so deeply in education. Maya Angelou famously said, "Do the best you can until you know better. Then, when you know better, do better."

I am convinced each time we educate young people to think critically, we set the future in motion. I know adults who fear young people's voices, and I am confused by their anxiety. One school refused to allow peer education. They respected me but were concerned. "How will we know what these teenagers will say?" they asked. Ah. How does one know what anyone will say? Training and trust.

I often use a quote attributed to Socrates when I present to adults: "The children now love luxury. They have bad manners, contempt for authority; they show disrespect for elders and love chatter in place of exercise." I explain these words demonstrate an ongoing fear of young people that accompanies generational criticism. It seems adults have always been suspicious of youth.

One Kid at a Time

Our original mantra was "one kid at a time," because we seek to tailor education to each individual young person's needs. If we listen to hear, will we provide young people with the education **we want them to need**, or the education **they truly need**?

Perhaps the most important change of all is internal. How do we challenge ourselves? Do we select apathy and indifference, or do we stand for our convictions? It is easier to remain silent. What message do we convey when we do not speak?

Our peer educators go on to serve in the military, are peer advisors or resident assistants in college, and become peer mediators at work. They are leaders. Malala Yousafzai's words, "One child, one teacher, one book, and one pen can change the world," guides these fine young adults. My pride in them runneth over.

I don't lose faith in humanity because I spend my days interacting with young people. Are they perfect? No more than me. They overreact and they are often emotional. They can be selfish and arrogant. Me, too. In other words, we're human. These teens are also good-hearted and empathic and eager to learn. They embrace change in a way few adults can.

Ralph Ellison wrote, "I am an invisible man... I am a man of substance, of flesh and bone, fiber and liquids—and I might even be said to possess a mind. I am invisible, understand, simply because people refuse to see me." I began this book by stating too many of our young people are invisible. I see them. Open your hearts to see them, too. All of them. You will be made better for it.

A new day is coming. Young humans will lead the way.

Step #10: Have Faith in Young People

Teach critical thinking skills and step back, watching them think.

Set high standards for behavior and step back as they fulfill them.

Teach them the tools to communicate, and step back as they discover facilitation and compromise.

Help them register to vote, and step back as they take on adult responsibilities.

Model empathy and compassion, and step back as they connect with others.

CHAPTER TWELVE

Please Don't Make Me Say What My Daddy Did...

"I washed my mouth out with peroxide

the first time I kissed a girl. Sloshed it around and then spit it out. Tasted shitty. I was ten. In my family, there was nothing worse than being a dyke. I figured I'd wash away the kiss and everything that came with it. Just a piece of advice. Peroxide's not the way to go. Liquor would have done the same thing and tasted a whole lot better. But I wasn't all that when I was ten, and I grabbed the first thing I found."

My dissertation looked at the lived experience of young parents. I knew many of my subjects; I was a doula for the mom who began her taped interview with the words above.

I cannot imagine what goes through a ten-year-old's mind when she feels this alone. To prove she was straight, she found an older man, "smoked herself silly" before having sex, and got pregnant. She gave birth as a thirteen-year-old. I held her baby right after birth. Her sexuality wasn't altered, but her life was forever changed.

Izzy was part of my dissertation, but I knew her story long before I interviewed her for my research. She came out to me when her little one was less than two. Telling me and her therapist in the same week and receiving acceptance from us both, she felt comfortable telling her foster mom. She disclosed on a Monday and was removed from the home the next day, described as an incorrigible teenager. I tried to advocate for her. *How could she turn into an out of control teen on Tuesday when she had been fine on Monday?*

She was moved to a foster home over an hour away. My staff and I maintained contact. Her history was difficult, her family of origin barely functioning. The new foster home was run by people who read her the same Bible passage daily and told her she was an abomination. I'm not sure how she endured those years. I visited her on Christmas Eve in juvie once.

Sexual abuse is a hard topic. Most people turn away from stories about abuse, and a few people shout out hatred towards those who abuse, without considering their own trauma. I've never worked closely with perpetrators, but I have wonderful friends and colleagues who do. Acknowledged trauma doesn't excuse behavior, but therapy isn't possible until a counselor is able to see each person as worthy and go from there.

What does it say that it was easier for Izzy to disclose her sexual identity as lesbian than it was to disclose the sexual abuse she'd endured in her preschool years? Her little one was a preschooler when an intense need to protect her overcame Izzy. Terrified, she connected with me to help fight a shared custody battle against the father of her baby. Even though she planned the sexual encounter with the intention of changing her identity, she knew she was a child when her little one was conceived.

Time, in Izzy's case, was healing. The father of her baby married and became stable. She found a woman she loved and who had empathy for her past and helped raise her child. Izzy made it. Her courage continues to impress me twenty-nine years later.

LGBTQIA Isolation

Since then, I've learned Izzy wasn't alone. Young bisexual, lesbian, or gay youth are two to seven times more likely to experience early childbearing than teens who identify as straight. Too often, LGBT youth are ignored in sex ed. Too often, they are invisible. They are not invisible to me.

When a young person comes out to an adult, it is a sign of trust. It is an honor. It is an opportunity to mentor and learn. The first teen who told me he was gay did so in the first months of my teaching, back in 1988. He lingered after class, often showing up at the end of the day to help me carry my supplies to the car, talking of football and tests and food. (I remember the food for some reason – he liked Italian!) I began delaying my departure to spend time with him. Finally, one day, as we walked down the now empty school hall, he said, "You talk about respect. Does that mean respect for everyone?"

His affect was off. Normally jovial and outgoing, his words were whispers and he didn't make eye contact.

I assured him I respected all young people. Silence. I paused in the corridor. I said his name.

He took a shaking breath, glanced at me, and said, "Even gay people? Do you respect gay people?"

I found an open room with two chairs and sat down, and listened, my heart weeping. This amazing young person, this young man of great worth, thought he would be diminished in my eyes because of his sexual identity.

I vowed to do all I could to avoid heteronormative teaching. Inclusivity became my norm. This young man taught me. He was the first of many who trusted me with coming out. In 2005, with two amazing, dedicated women, I co-founded the first GSA (gay straight alliance) in our county. I will stand strong with all young people, and I am a committed advocate for LGBTQIA youth.

Abuse

The concept of postponing sexual involvement is important at this age. Unlike Izzy, who tried to change her sexual identity by giving birth, most eleven-year-olds are not sexually involved, although their online contact opens a world of sexuality that would shock most parents. Contrary to popular belief, though, fifth and sixth graders are exploring their sexuality, even if only mentally. Many young LGBT adults have shared that they knew who they were at ten or eleven or earlier, but words to explain their questioning or their identities were lacking. Growing up in a home where homophobia is the norm is a torture I cannot conceptualize. What does it feel like to know you are a person like the ones your family members mock and even hate? To me, that environment is one of emotional abuse.

Again, I learned from young people. I didn't consider abuse when I began teaching. When I began in the eighties, I thought just teaching about delaying sexual acts would make young people react positively and avoid risk. How naïve I was! Like many adults, I didn't consider the *why* of teen sex. No behavior happens in a vacuum. Some young people are sexually involved due to curiosity or peer pressure. Some are simply physically and emotionally ready. Some don't understand they own their own bodies and can decide their own boundaries. Some are conditioned to do whatever necessary to please a partner. Some are sexual abuse survivors. In time, I learned the links between childhood trauma and behavior.

When I first began working with young survivors of sexual abuse, it was overwhelming. I was young. I had no frame of reference for this pain. Even now, many years later, I cannot conceptualize the trauma, but I've learned how to ease the hurt and move the child towards healing.

A six-year-old boy taught me my best lesson. Sent to me by CYS (Children and Youth Services), I began to take an assessment at his first visit. I'd already set the stage for a safe place: I had toys and Koosh balls and dolls. Music he selected was playing softly in the background. We started with a game, he seemed relaxed, then suddenly looked at me with eyes so large they tugged at my soul and said, "Please don't make me say what my daddy did to me."

The more I counseled young survivors, the more I realized adults needed to step up to lower the trauma of post-abuse testimony. Our community developed a child advocacy center to allow for children's videotaped testimony. I played a very small part in its creation by connecting CYS and our hospital. Prior to the center, we ascertained a child needed to repeat the story to at least twelve people when they report abuse. If the abuse is disclosed at school to a trusted teacher, they need to then tell a guidance counselor, the principal, a CYS caseworker. Eventually, parents are told. There may be a pediatrician, a caseworker, a social worker. Then, an attorney, a magistrate or judge... the list is long.

That six-year-old's wisdom inspired me to approach young survivors differently. Now, when we first meet, I say, "I won't ask you what happened to you. You may share anytime you like, but I won't ask." We then play games. In all these years, I've never gone longer than four sessions without disclosure. On their terms. In their own time. With their own voices.

I schedule young survivors to see me again when they're in puberty. Sexuality is complicated. Processing abuse through the lens of body-positivity is rare. Healing takes time.

I wrote my child abuse prevention program, *Inside Out: Your Body Is Amazing Inside and Out and Belongs Only to You*, because due diligence made me cringe at what often passes for child abuse prevention education. The Red Flag Green Flag program coined the term "stranger danger" even though a full 90% of sexual abuse survivors were abused by an adult they knew. Other programs pressure children to stop an abuser; children have no power. In my opinion, such an approach is cruel.

Teaching children the lessons in *Inside Out* can help them sort out adults who groom them for sexual abuse by teaching about secrets, trusted adults, and their own bodies. Children are more likely to disclose sexual abuse if they know real names for body parts and if they're taught about their bodies without shame and fear. *Inside Out* clearly tells children they're worthy and demonstrates worthiness through interactive lessons where they are free to participate or be silent.

"It's not your fault" is a drumbeat throughout the book. The book teaches medical names for body parts. It's taught in third and fourth grades by school faculty I train.

Kids Teaching Parents!

Every summer, I try to bring *Inside Out* to summer camps without cost; I often volunteer to present the program myself. One year, as I distributed the coloring books at a local camp called Camp Challenge, a young person cried out, "I already have this book!" She was a fourth grader who received the class at school the year before. I told her she didn't need to attend, but she wanted to stay. She assumed the role of elder, encouraging the other children. "This book is important," she said.

Before we began, I asked her what she learned in school when she took the program. She moved both of her hands over her torso. "All this is mine," she said. I was pleased.

"Anything else?" I asked.

"No one touches my body unless I say yes," she added.

"Wonderful," I said.

Then she grinned. "I learned something else," she said, her expression mischievous as only a ten-year old's can be. "I learned I gots a vulva. My mama didn't know she had one, so I taught her."

Before I could speak, one of the other children in the class asked, "What's a vulva?"

Said my young student, with a matter-of-fact shrug, "It's a koochie."

Language matters. We teach our children the proper names for other body parts. Ears are ears, eyes are eyes, feet are feet, yet we avoid naming our genitals correctly, as if they're insignificant or, even worse, shameful.

Unwanted Sexual Touch

My work with young sexual abuse survivors also guides me to convey the body's autonomic response. Programs that teach about different kinds of touches or good touch and bad touch often forget our bodies have a hot-wired response to sexual touch. A skilled abuser can cause sexual pleasure, and a child who is orgasmic as a result of abusive sexual touch is often confused. When I work with a young child survivor, I arrange a meeting when puberty hits. It's important to affirm a survivor's worth as they discover their sexual identity. Giving birth and breastfeeding as a survivor is another area where a caring counselor or educator can ease trauma and pain. Trauma lasts a lifetime.

Sexual excitement is normal as young people's bodies mature. *How do I convey this concept to young people?* I never know if a survivor is in my sex ed classes, but one in ten American children experience abuse prior to their eighteenth birthday, so the odds are strong survivors are in attendance.

I use chocolate as a teaching analogy. I love chocolate. It doesn't love me. I need to avoid it for health reasons. Our community is home to a delightful chocolate factory, where my two favorite vices are sold: chocolate and ice cream. I share my enthusiasm for chocolate and ice cream with my young students. Their expressions mirror mine. Sometimes, they lick their lips.

We talk about how just thinking about the treats can make our mouths water. We're hot-wired for pleasure, I explain. Our bodies react to pleasure in ways we cannot control. The easiest way to avoid eating chocolate and ice cream? Stay away from the chocolate factory!

Our sex drive is stronger than our desire for chocolate, at least physiologically. Unless a person is asexual, and is not interested in physical sexual experiences, the body reacts powerfully to sexual stimuli. Pornography is meant to excite—few view porn for the plot.

When young people experience sexual abuse, their bodies may respond physically. Sorting through feelings of sexual pleasure that may accompany abuse is one of the biggest challenges faced by survivors. I use my chocolate analogy to reinforce this reality. One more time: abuse is never children's fault, even if their bodies react. Our culture's reticence surrounding sexuality adds to a survivor's confusion. Just naming body parts can be intimidating to many adults.

Protecting Children

When a child knows facts beyond those figured out by playing doctor (think of the small actor's line from *Kindergarten Cop*, "Girls have vaginas, boys have a penis"), a red flag should immediately arise. While teaching a growing up class for parents and nine to twelve-year-olds, a nine-year-old girl once said, "I hate that men make so much noise when they stick it in."

I knew this child was either exposed to pornography or experienced sexual abuse. I consulted with the parent after class and talked gently with the child. She disclosed a two-month ordeal of sexual abuse by an uncle. As a mandated reporter, I called Childline and law enforcement. The uncle was charged, and the child protected.

I am proud to be a Darkness to Light Stewards of Children authorized facilitator. I've taught hundreds of adults the signs of abuse. My audience includes teachers, counselors, youth ministers, coaches, and parents. Adults abuse children. Adults need to dismantle a culture that excuses and covers up that abuse.

The signs below are adapted from Darkness to Light:

- Physical signs of abuse aren't common. In my personal practice, I find most abusers of small children use oral sex instead of penetrative sex. There are few physical signs of oral rape.

- If there are physical signs, redness, rashes, and swelling in the genital area, urinary tract infections, or other genital discomfort are red flags.

- Children often show anxiety and depression with stomach aches and headaches. Even if abuse is not suspected, adults should be alert to chronic complaints of these physical issues.

- Emotional or behavioral changes are more common. Consider "too perfect" and pleasing behavior, withdrawal, depression, and unexplained anger or rebellion as signs a child needs support and possibly therapy.

- Sexual behavior or sexualized dress or language that is not age appropriate may be a red flag.

- In some children, there are no signs at all.

The connection between child abuse and teen pregnancy is well established. It may take years for a young parent to disclose. One of our young parents only revealed her own child sexual abuse when her toddler developed genital sores. Panicked, she contacted me. I held space with her in the ER as she paced back and forth, desperate for a cigarette, terrified of what her gut told her was true. When the pediatrician on-call told her the baby's diagnosis of genital warts (a STI – sexually transmitted infection from a strain of HPV – human papillomavirus), she was stone cold and silent. Hours later, she melted down. Her immediate reaction, despite her emotional withdrawal, was to call Childline herself while holding my hand tight, initiating a process she knew might place her baby in foster care. Her passion to protect her daughter was so intense, she was willing to be separated from her. They were assigned to the same foster home, her mother's boyfriend was arrested, she disclosed her own abuse, and voluntarily entered rehab for the alcohol she used to self-medicate her pain. Her well-adjusted daughter is nearing twenty-one and I smile when I think of her. The resiliency of the survivors I've been honored to serve humbles me.

If an adult suspects abuse, be an advocate. Contact your local Child Protective Services. Use Childline. The National Children's Alliance offers support at www.nca-online.org or by calling 1-800-239-9950.

Talk honestly with the young person prior to reporting. It may be hurtful to hear this from you, but, in my opinion, they need to know. Otherwise, you violate trust. I've been told to keep your report anonymous—in many agencies, it is against policy to talk with a young person before making a report. I believe the opposite. I stand on my conviction. I will not lie to a young person.

In my ideal culture, the crime of child sexual abuse would be universally maligned, abusers who cover up their abuse would be persecuted, there would be no statute of limitations on abuse reporting, and children would be protected.

Only adults can stop child sexual abuse.
Be an adult who protects children.

Step 11: Be Alert for Signs of Abuse Child Sexual Abuse is Not a Child's Fault

If you're talking about sex, abuse will eventually be disclosed to you if you're connecting with young people.

Consider disclosure a great gift, because it is.

Always report. That is your legal duty as a mandated reporter and your ethical responsibility.

Be there, no matter what happens.

If young people are placed in foster care, follow them.

Do not abandon.

CHAPTER THIRTEEN

Nude Pics, Phones, & Social Media

Nude Pics

When I was a child, young people at the age of ten were typically child-like. Social media altered childhood. Most of the court-ordered referrals I receive deal with ten to fourteen-year-olds. I recently consulted with distraught parents whose eleven-year-old daughter sent a nude picture of her breasts to an eleven-year-old boy who asked her to "lemme see sum" via text.

I've listened to one young person after another explain their actions when they send nude pictures as "I don't know why I sent it," or, "I didn't know how to say no," or, "I wanted to be liked." In this eleven-year old's case, she took off her t-shirt in the bathroom and looked critically at her chest. Nope. Not enough breasts there at all. Resourceful, she found a voluptuous, topless woman online, downloaded a picture of her without a top, and Photoshopped her face on this stranger's body. Then, she texted the picture.

The young man was also eleven. He wasn't mature enough to realize this wasn't the girl's breasts, but the body of a grown woman. He distributed the picture to one friend, who sent it to two. In short order, the picture was spread throughout the school.

Both children were terrified to speak with their own parents. Once again, trust eases pain, encourages communication, and opens doors. Trust is the key to connection, even between parents and their own children. As my papa sat me down in the earth of his garden to hear my tale of woe about bullying, parents need to put aside everything else and listen to their kids without judging them.

Trust and Social Media

Children today are inundated with sexual images and content. It's no longer 1905 or even 1950. Our children need our guidance in the real world of today. A common question I receive from adults deals with social media. A very real fear is associated with it. To deal with that fear, I trained our peer educators – teens who teach with me – to teach adults about social media. They've presented with me at professional conferences, taught middle schoolers, and have conducted webinars on *Making Sense out of Social Media.*

Currently, our peer educators are presenting a four-part series called *Respect Online* to seventh graders. The course covers empathy, compassion, moral decision making, cyberbullying, and consequences. I selected teens to teach it because they are closer to middle school student culture. Their role modeling makes a real difference.

If less is more, how do we guide our young people when they see so much MORE online? Do we remove phones, or do we teach them how to handle images and information today's adults never faced as children? Education matters. I say we teach.

How to begin?

Remember the foundation of sexuality education we initiate when we present bodies as body-positive? Think of the way we teach by example and the openness we offer when our children seek answers to their questions. I've personally held focus groups with hundreds of teens; my staff with hundreds more. As soon as an adult scrutinizes a teen's phone for content, the teen feels violated. It's a little like laying the first brick upon the wall of connection between adult and teen.

As one young person said, "It's like they're reading my diary." Teens are clever—they're way ahead of adults! If one app is closed, they find another. Our best bet is to involve them in a relationship where online use is discussed from the start. I like to create contracts for behavior for teens and parents. I do the same at our teen center. I don't gather all phones and put them in a basket during peer educator meetings. We establish guidelines for phone use and adhere to them. We create trust.

I believe each new phone should be accompanied by gentle, kind, but firm messages. Be clear. Define respect online. Use your own values to augment this list, but please be aware of a common thread. Young people are worthy. Set high standards and hear their voices.

- There is power in this device. Use it wisely.

- Images sent online through apps will last forever, especially when screenshot.

- Your phone is personal, I don't want to invade your space. You need to earn my trust, however. Once violated, trust is hard to regain.

- Use your phone or tablet wisely, with self-respect and respect for others.

- Avoid online drama. It only intensifies and objectifies problems.

- If you wouldn't say something to a person's face, don't post it.

- If you wouldn't post an image or words on a huge billboard on a busy highway near your home, don't post it.

- Face relationship problems in person.

- Talk with a trusted adult if you see confusing images or videos online.

If you want to connect, be that trusted adult. Most children are simply curious. Establish yourself as a safe adult, an adult who can be trusted, who can protect and empower children. If no one talks about bodies with little ones, they may be ashamed to disclose unwanted touch.

Sexualization

Bodies in American culture are sexualized. Consider breasts. I breastfed all three of our children, and my daughters and daughter-in-love nursed my grandchildren. Our family sees breastfeeding as a positive parenting choice. In some parts of our country, women are chastised or even arrested for nursing their babies in public. A woman posted this online comment following an article discussing the legality of breastfeeding in public: "No one's ready to see THAT!" "That" is a body part perfect for nurturing human babies.

In Italy, I toured Venice with two of our children. In the Piazza San Marco, surrounded by people and pigeons, I witnessed a twenty-something Venetian woman nurse her baby. The child appeared about four months old. Unremarkable, unless I note her state of dress. She wore no top. It was a hot fall day, and both breasts were exposed. No Italian men seemed to notice. They went about their business. My twelve-year-old American son? His eyeballs nearly fell out of his head!

Sexuality Can Be Complicated

Sexuality education in America can be complicated. Sex ed is often controversial in a nation that is too often schizoid regarding sexuality. We fear sex, but we exploit others using it. Sex sells everything from cars to clothing, yet we seldom mandate education for sexual health. How often do sexual scandals bring down those in power, not just in our nation, but in many others? I believe these scandals come from an attitude of denial. We deny our inherent human right to our sexuality. We deny sexual expression. We pretend sexuality is only about sexual acts, when, in truth, sexuality includes intimacy and identity and reproduction and sensuality and human connection and body awareness and body image and self-worth.

Sexuality also encompasses negatives like sexualization, rape, incest, and sexual harassment. Ignoring these realities leads to rape culture. Denying the need to facilitate open discussions about this huge and vital topic denies our children the skills they need to be fully human.

Teaching young children about consent, healthy relationships, their bodies, and their sexuality takes commitment and a caring heart. Too often, parents do not trust anyone else to teach their children about sex, saying they will "cover it at home" and then saying little beyond "Do not." I use permission forms in all our classes because I honor and value parents. Few sign their children out of our programs. When they do, I respect their choice, but it often saddens me. Schools are responsible for monitoring who is permitted attendance—our staff doesn't know the children we teach prior to meeting them, so sorting out those without permission isn't possible. It's the school's responsibility.

When I first started hiring other "Sex People" to teach in the early nineties, a mother approached me after graduation. She'd recently joined my church. She apologized to me. "I had no idea you were such a good person," she gushed. "I wish I'd given permission for you to teach my daughter when she was in middle school. I didn't know you, so I didn't trust you. Would you meet with her before she goes to college? She's saving herself for marriage, but it wouldn't hurt if you talked with her and gave her some hints on remaining abstinent." Of course, I agreed to the meeting, but my heart was in my throat as she spoke.

I knew her daughter well. She'd snuck into my classes since sixth grade. She'd spoken with me in confidence. She'd had many sexual partners, at least three pregnancy scares, and often entered relationships bordering on abusive. How she managed to get into class escapes me. I smiled and nodded and set a date to meet, thinking all the while how I'd personally feel if my own children were so afraid to be honest with me that they put a wall between me and them and lied for most of their adolescence. *Do parents really want to encourage such a wall?*

Adults need to be aware of sexualization. Children are curious about their bodies and that curiosity is healthy. Teaching limits is important, as well as regulating your tone to one of calmness. The music behind an adult's words – their tone of voice – can shame or offer validation for a child's humanity. The music behind our words matters. If I wouldn't scream to a co-worker, "Look at the mess in your office! I don't pay you to live like a slob!" I shouldn't use such a tone with a young person. Talk about concerns, but be proactive and open and respectful. Give and take.

Young people need support in the era in which they live. Longing for the past won't help. Teach them to deal with the technology they face.

Step #12: Listen to Young People

When adults listen, they need to sit or stand at the young person's level. Do not tower above, as if all-knowing.

I prefer sitting beside one another, so eye contact is not forced.

Grounding a teen for phone use can be harsh. Use such a consequence as a last resort.

Hear a young person's side.

Teach empathy and compassion and moral decision-making and respect.

CHAPTER FOURTEEN

Hockey

✺

I could fill a book with the questions I've received from young people alone. Their curiosity inspired me to create a game I call *Myth or Fact*. Small cards contain one word or a phrase connected in some way to sexuality. Students each take a card, then the group decides if the concept is true or false. Students are, as always, given permission to pass or not play the game. Cards are placed in piles labeled *Myth* or *Fact*. The *Myth* pile is always much higher than the *Fact* one. The game consists of over 130 cards now and is always growing.

Some myths are universal, even in an age when online searches are easy. Here are a few I've picked up from listing to young people:

Some Common Myths:

1. **Eating green M&Ms will not make a person horny.** No explanation needed. I'm unsure where this myth originated, but it's common.

2. **Drinking Mt. Dew doesn't lower sperm count or make genitals shrink.** Nope. This myth was very common in the early 2000s, but is less prevalent now.

3. **Two men engaging in sex can't make a baby, neither can two women.** Conception requires two body cells: an egg or ova from an ovary and a sperm from the testicles. Babies can be created in-vitro – out of the body – but the same ingredients are needed!

4. **Sex before athletic events will take away strength.** I've been told coaches often tell young men to be "hands off," referring to masturbation, before a big game. Untrue.

5. **Vaginal sex during a menstrual period is when babies are most likely to be made.** The opposite is true. Most adults think a person with a uterus ovulates twelve to fourteen days after a period. The truth is ovulation occurs twelve to fourteen days BEFORE the next period.

6. **Sex in hot tubs prevents pregnancy.** It's possible to make a baby if one type of sex happens in a hot tub, even though the water is hot, provided the sex involves a penis and a vagina and a sperm and an ovum. The show *Glee* caused a temporary spike in myths surrounding hot tubs after a main character coerced her boyfriend into believing she'd gotten pregnant, even though they never did it (engaged in penile-vaginal intercourse or PVI), because he ejaculated in a hot tub while he was with her and his sperm swam inside. Nope. Water kills sperm. Bath water, hot tub water, swimming pool water, lake water, ocean water.

A Few Facts:

- STIs (sexually transmitted infections) can be spread orally. Not all young people understand or believe this fact.

- Sperm can live inside a fallopian tube for three to five days, which means conception can occur after penis-vagina sex, even if the two people don't touch one another during those days.

- Pregnancy can happen if two people engage in PVI in water—the sexual contact needs to happen.

- An ova (egg) only lives for twenty-four to forty-eight hours.

- A person with a uterus and ovaries can get pregnant before the first period if PVI occurs.

- HIV (human immunodeficiency virus) is only spread through infected blood, semen, vaginal fluid, or breast milk. It is NOT spread by casual contact, breathing the same air, using the same exercise equipment, hugging, kissing, shaking hands, drinking from the same water fountain, or using the same eating utensils.

An Unexpected Teachable Moment

While playing *Myth or Fact*, one teen's spontaneous question gave me an unexpected teachable moment. A young man blurted out, "I ain't never gonna make no babies!"

The grammar person inside me cringed. *How many negatives!* I simply responded with, "Good," and moved on.

Another young man said, "Yeah, that's because you don't get any," to which my first student growled defensively, "Yeah, I do!"

I stepped in, firmly stopping mockery on all sides, then tried to teach. "If you have vaginal sex without protection, you might…"

I was interrupted, "No, man. I'm always careful."

I wondered if he really used condoms, or if he used withdrawal (commonly known as "pulling out").

The *careful* young man said, "I don't use no condoms."

I remember taking a deep breath, then trying again, "If you don't use protection and you have vaginal sex, you're going to…" when once more, he cut me off, "I'm always careful because I think about something else when I do it."

Wow! This young man genuinely thought mind over matter, or, in this case, mind over sperm, worked. I strive to refrain from laughing at a young person. I laugh in class – and in life – loud, often, and with enthusiasm, but laughing AT a person isn't okay. I struggled to keep a straight face. I mentally imagined the mortgage on our outreach office. I thought of my checkbook. I stayed calm.

Another boy asked, "What do you think about?"

"Hockey!"

Laughter bubbled in my throat. I closed my mouth, lest it escape. I stood strong. Until…

"He shoots and scores," cried out a young hockey lover in the back of the room, his bright Pittsburgh Penguins jersey advertising his fandom. I laughed. I'm human. Luckily, the "careful" young man was grinning widely, eating up the attention.

I calmed everyone down and started a discussion. I asked, "Are there things you fear? In life, not just sexually." Critics who think I only teach sexuality would be shocked to see how often my focus is on life and living with respect for others. I knew this group of young people needed to look away from sex for a moment.

I think my students were confused by my abrupt change in topic, but they responded quickly. "Dying like Tommy," someone mumbled. A high school friend was killed in a car accident a few days before—we'd begun the class processing of his loss and it was fresh on their minds. "Not graduating," said another. "My mom finding out about my boyfriend," was met with hoots and a, "She already knows," comment that caused general merriment. Finally, someone said, "Flying. I've never been on a plane and I'm afraid to fly." *Bingo!* The words I wanted. I knew these young people and they're shared concerns about my air travel before, so I wasn't far off in thinking the topic would arise.

I nodded, "Good answers. I fly a great deal. When I get on a plane, do you think I'm saying to myself, *I bet this plane will crash?*" The consensus was *no* or I wouldn't board.

"May I tell you a story?" I asked. No matter a group's age, people listen to stories. You may call them parables or anecdotes or analogies, but they inspire attention. Teens are no different. It's like they're preschoolers again, sitting on a red, blue, and green library story rug. They're all ears.

"I flew into Mexico with my daughter once. I was presenting at a conference in Mexico City. The plane was small, only eight seats. The pilot was separated from the passengers by a tiny curtain. As we took off, the pilot said, 'Get ready to rock n roll. We've got some great winds ahead.'"

My daughter was quickly asleep. I was not. I spent the flight staring out the window at the changing horizon as the plane bucked up and down. When we landed safely, I took a huge breath. My daughter opened her eyes, peered at my relieved face, and asked, "Heavy plane, Mom?" My students laughed.

"I knew I wasn't really keeping the plane aloft," I added. "I think it's human nature to think we have control over things. We think bad things will happen to someone else." I gestured around the room at each of them in turn, and they nodded. Tommy's death sobered them. "We don't have control, not always. No matter how much we want our minds to control what happens, we cannot do so."

Mocking the young man who used thinking about hockey as a contraceptive would've been easy. It took effort to re-direct my students and find ways to help them assimilate their current life experiences with an almost universal desire to control our circumstances. I needed to help them own the message. Some things are out of our mental control, so we must act. Proactive prevention is the best way to prevent an unplanned pregnancy if sexually involved. Denial is not a contraceptive.

Right before the class bell rang, another student asked, "Where can you get condoms?" This was a common concern in our community, where access is challenging if young people don't drive or have their own transportation because no schools in our community allow condom distribution. City teens can walk to a store, but rural young people are stuck. As one teen told me, "I live with my grandma. I go shopping with her. Am I supposed to say, 'Hey, Grandma? I'd like this box of Captain Crunch, and this box of Trojans?' No way!"

Be an Adult Who Opens Doors to Communication

These young people were all sexually involved. Few of their parents knew they were. Almost all of them were taking risks with unplanned pregnancies and the spread of STIs. *How many of them used consent in their encounters. How many were in healthy relationships?*

When adults ask me how to connect with young people, I share simple truths:

- Articulate the obvious.

- Share what you think everyone should know, gently and without judgement.

- Teach what your students need, not what you think they need or want them to need.

- Be matter of fact.

- Don't assume.

- Respect each young person.

- Look for the *why* for behavior.

- Be sensitive to trauma.

- Don't judge. Each young person is unique. You are not living their lives, nor do you know what they face daily.

Remember, we never know what young people don't know, or what they need to know. Often, neither do they.

Step #13: Don't Assume Young People Understand

Repetition is key to connection and retention of your message.

Key points must be repeated in different ways, using different types of learning.

Education shouldn't be boring. People daydream when bored.

Keep young people engaged. Use interactive games to teach.

Young people are their own best teachers. They learn when they teach; their students gain from a shared culture and perspective.

CHAPTER FIFTEEN

Fear

One of my joys in the last few years has been writing my *Nonnie* series. I'm a nonnie—a grandma! My first grandchild turned the nonna of my family tradition into "Nonnie" and it stuck. It's my very best title. Being a nonnie is my best job.

I've taken on challenging subjects and written *Nonnie Talks About* books for young people (typically in grades three through eight) and their trusted adults. I want to enhance communication in areas adults may find difficult to address, but children need to know. Children listen. They sense when something is troubling, even if no one tells them.

Learning from a nonnie is safe. It also bridges the wisdom of older adults to young ones. Naming my series after me as a nonnie will, hopefully, encourage young people to connect with their own grandparents or trusted older adults in their families. Families matter.

Before we go to print on each book, I conduct focus groups consisting of children from the ages targeted in the books. Their honest feedback, and the wisdom of great friends and colleagues who serve as reviewers, make the books culturally relevant. During each focus group, I ask the young participants about the current book. I then ask them what topics they'd like me to address. This year, several groups asked me to write *Nonnie Talks About Fear*.

I was surprised to hear so many children of varying ages request support about fear. I quickly ascertained they didn't mean the fun kind of fear one gets from watching a scary movie or telling a ghost story. No, these young people's fears were real.

The first focus group I facilitated as preparation for the *Nonnie Talks About Trauma* book was sobering. The reality of violent death visiting their schools was the elephant in the room until I called it out, then they all began to talk at once. One seven-year-old said, "If the monsters with guns come to my school, I'm not afraid. I can run fast!" Then, she paused, pensive and troubled. This child has a twin brother who is autistic. "Should I go back for my brother?" she asked. "If they tell him to run, he may not know where to go."

Since I'm an itinerant teacher, going from school to school, I'm seldom aware of lockdown drills. When the warnings sound, I don't know if the threat is real or not. Neither do my students. I was teaching sixth graders once during an unexpected lockdown. We closed the doors and barricaded them as prepared. We stood away from windows. We heard heavy running feet in the hall outside. *An adult? Adults?*

I looked at these wonderful children and said, "If this is real, I want you to exit outside if those feet in the hall get closer and you hear what sounds like shots. I'll tell you what to do. Go into the woods. Everyone pick a buddy."

These kids – who moments ago were excitedly playing a game called *Liar, Liar*, were deathly quiet. One said softly, "What about you, Ms. Mary Jo?"

"I'll be fine," I reassured.

Several young people looked determined, their body language shouting their stubbornness, their shoulders high, many of their hands in tight fists. "We'll stay with you," "We won't leave you," and, "You go with us." It wasn't long after a school shooting; this was real to them.

Life in schools was different before school shootings. Spring and fall in Pennsylvania can be hot. My own children were playing soccer then, so I carried many blankets in the back of my van to use as impromptu seats at games and practices. When a school wasn't airconditioned and the heat was oppressive, I'd take my class outside under a tree, spread the blankets and teach in the fresh air. The week after Columbine in 1999, it was incredibly hot for April. I was teaching under an impressive oak tree with many shade branches, when the vice principal came towards me in huge studies, oozing authority. "You can't teach out here anymore," he said. "A shooter might come."

I didn't argue. I've never hesitated to discuss my thoughts with school administrators, but I do so in private and with respect, not in front of young people.

As I motioned my students to rise and gather my visual aids, a young person picked up one of my plastic vulvas, waved it like a flag and said, "But Mr. Jones, we have all we need to learn out here."

I'm troubled we don't know the long-term effects of lockdowns. We do know how emotional stress affects young brains. I'd love to see research connecting the two.

Facing Fear

Were you fearful as a child? I was, but not of typical child-like anxieties. I didn't stay awake thinking of spiders or snakes, and although I've never enjoyed horror movies, they didn't haunt me.

No, my childhood fears dealt with death. When my mother was depressed, she would often send me to school with these parting words: "If I'm not dead before you come home, I'll see you tonight." No wonder I threw myself so wholeheartedly into school. The distraction was healthy. She didn't fall so low often, and she was always there at the end of the school day, but her words affected me.

Papa was a rock of support, a blanket of stability around my shoulders.

Now that I'm a mental health professional, however, I finally admit his role in Mama's depression. His own fear of doctors and the power of hospitals kept him from seeking help. Mama needed therapy. His lack of awareness and intense desire to protect her denied her treatment.

I'm aware these childhood moments were traumatic. I know they influenced my life in both positive and negative ways. Acknowledging trauma was a first step for me.

I was also afraid of nuclear attack. In this fear, I was not alone. We ran drills at school where we were instructed to get under our desks, put our hands on our heads, and pray. Whispering Hail Marys under my wooden desk, even in elementary school, I was smart enough to know this fragile cover wouldn't protect me from a bomb.

For some reason, I decided Pittsburgh would be one of the first cities attacked. The steel mills would make it a primary target. In fourth grade, our class planned a field trip to the Heinz pickle factory. I was terrified. We lived only forty minutes from downtown, but I wasn't wise enough to realize we'd be within ground zero even while sitting at home. I was sure the Soviets would attack while I was at that pickle factory! I begged and pleaded to be kept home when my class made the trip. I reasoned with my parents to the best of my ten-year-old ability. *"Don't you want to protect me?"* I whined.

My parents were firm. I was going on the field trip. The night before, I lay awake, staring at the white ceiling and the ceiling lamp I'd pretended was a cat face as a child. Finally, Papa took pity on me. He brought me to the kitchen and made me chamomile tea. "Why are you so frightened?" he asked as the tea brewed.

I explained, again, my obsession with bombs. "It will be the end of the world, Papa," I wailed.

"Ah," he said. "That's it. That's what you're afraid of. The end of the world." I realized he was correct. I'd read Revelation on my own—a poor developmental selection for a child. He smiled and placed two cups of tea on the table, rose, and cut a hunk of fresh bread, topped it with tomato and parmesan cheese, and eased into a chair. I know now he was tired—his day started at 6 a.m. and he left the house at 4 a.m. I was keeping him from sleep, but he didn't complain. He smiled again.

"The end of the world happens when each of us dies," he said confidently. "Each person dies alone, even if loved ones are with them. Each person then accounts for what was done with the gift of life."

"That sounds scary," I said, shivering.

"Oh no, honey. Not at all. Just live well. Do the right thing, then there's nothing to fear."

I went to the pickle factory. I received a small green pickle pin, which I treasured for years. When I looked at it, I remembered my papa's words. There's no fear if you live well.

Fear and Sexuality

Fear and sexuality education are often companions. I've mentioned the fear and shame used to teach abstinence until marriage education. Fear-based sex ed is emotionally damaging. When teaching sex ed, I play a game where I use candy as an analogy for sex. I divide the class into small groups of "families." Each "family" must contain a pretend thirteen-year-old, and the other students are adults. I give the young people time to create this "family"—it's fun to watch. I then give out their assignment. The pretend thirteen-year-old will be given a piece of candy—they pick their favorite from my candy bag (I use chewy candy for reasons I'll explain later). They may not eat the candy until I ring my bell, but when the bell sounds, they may eat.

The adults in the "family" are responsible for using their words to convince their pretend thirteen-year-old to delay eating the candy. I establish rules: The candy remains with the pretend thirteen-year-old—the adults may not remove it. The adults may not physically touch the pretend thirteen-year-old. They may bribe the pretend thirteen-year-old but are obligated to deliver on all promises. If they offer a dollar for delaying the gratification of eating the candy, they need to pay up when the game ends. I clearly clarify one thing before I ring my bell. I ask, "What does the candy represent?'

Inevitably, someone shouts out, "Sex," and I laugh.

"No," I say. "Don't get freaky on me. It represents candy! Just candy."

After a few minutes, I ask each '"family" to report back to the whole group. Did the pretend thirteen-year-old eat the candy? If yes, why? If no, why? Either way, what did the pretend adults do to teach?

When we process the activity, I ask a young person to write on the board. We list the techniques the "families" used to teach. Fear is at the top of the list at least 80% of the time, followed closely by bribery, threats, guilt, and shame. They're often quite original. I've heard, "You'll get diabetes," "There's rat poison in the candy factory," and, "You'll get an STI," despite my admonition that the candy was not sexually linked. A few pretend adults will reason with their charges. I hold my breath each time, hoping someone will speak to my message—typically they do when a young person reports, "We talked about cavities, tooth decay. This is sticky candy. Unless my kid can brush and floss after eating, they're at risk."

They're at risk! Eureka! I'm looking for those words.

I facilitate the conversation to the usefulness of tooth brushing and flossing in lowering cavity risk. They agree. I then switch the discussion to sex. What if your "family" is hoping to teach a pretend thirteen-year-old about delaying sexual involvement? The conversation turns somber immediately.

"You can't," some say. "If a teen decides to get busy, they will." Others immediately disagree, "My parents have me under lock and key. Their threats scare me."

Fear jumps to #1 again. I let the class bounce around ideas, still imagining themselves as parents or adults. Ultimately, someone will say, "You can't keep a teen under lock and key forever. Eventually, most people do it."

To which I calmly ask, "Why is teaching about condoms so much more difficult and frightening than teaching oral hygiene?"

I love the discussions that results then.

Fear and Shame

In the nineties, I waived my honorarium to travel to a Pennsylvania town and teach a day-long training I called *First, Do No Harm: The Art of Teaching Abstinence Without Emotional Trauma.* I'd observed a presenter at a state-wide conference as she presented an exercise on abstinence. She provided each student with a bag of chips, then instructed the chip bag be opened and a handful of chips be chewed up and then spit back into the bag. Then, students were told to exchange bags and eat someone else's chewed up chips. If a person had sex before marriage, she announced with authority, they were those chewed up chips. They were damaged goods.

I invited her to lunch. Breaking bread with people helps with connection. I gently asked her if she'd considered the reality that some of her students were sexual abuse survivors. To her credit, she was shocked. No, she hadn't. I shared that one in ten children are sexually assaulted prior to their eighteenth birthday. I told her young people should never leave a sex ed classroom on their emotional bellies. She invited me to her community. I taught my approach to sex ed. She heard me.

I ache with sorrow and frustration when I consider how many young people in our nation receive messages of shame as part of sex ed.

A Cascade of Questions

Fear and sexuality can mix again when young people consider becoming physical with a partner. Digital culture has changed radically since I first taught, but some fears remain unchanged. Unless a child is very bold, first questions are basic. Over a few weeks, their questions cascade into more personal and serious topics. So many fears are instilled in them regarding sexuality that nearly every class series I teach, young people ask:

"Does it hurt the first time?"

"How do you keep from being raped?"

"How do I know I won't be accused of rape afterwards?"

"What if I make a fool of myself?"

"What if I can't get it up?"

"What if my parents find out?"

"I'm gay. In our small town, how can I find someone like me?"

"How can I talk about the sexual assault that happened to me when I was twelve?"

"What if my partner leaves me?"

"How do I know if love is real?"

Fear is part of living, but for some young people, it grows into a persistent anxiety and morphs into a pervasive shadow on their lives. The first step to connecting with young people about their anxiety deals with trust. Teens will say, "I'm fine," or, "I'm good," rather than admit angst until an adult is trusted.

How do you affirm and support an anxious young person?

- Listen to the question behind the question. The questions above can be summarized in a short one: "Am I okay?" Knowing that can make connection smoother. Honor worthiness.

- Say, "I'm here." Repeat with confidence. Be there.

- Teach mindful breathing. In a crisis, ask young people to match their breath to yours.

- Say, "Tell me about your fear. Is it big? Does it center in your body or in your mind?"

- What's something I can do to make you feel better?

- Do you want to journal about it or draw a picture of your fear?

- Imagine a time when your fear is gone or more manageable. What happened to get to that time?

Back when I volunteered with young parents, I created personalized casette tapes for each of them to use in labor. I recorded myself guiding them through relaxation. I repeated their names frequently. The tapes seemed to help.

Today, I use Skype or FaceTime to talk young people through panic attacks or to help them ease anxiety. My goal is to convey these skills to them, not to become a part of their routine. I also teach the common technique of grounding for anxiety. Young people can learn these steps:

1. Look around you.
2. Find five things you can see, four things you can touch, three things you can hear, two things you can smell, and one thing you can taste in your environment.

Panic can make young people feel lost and without control over their surroundings. This process can help them focus.

Considering fear as it relates to sexuality helps with connection.
Be observant, be aware, and be present.

Step #14: Seek Courage

Adults may need to face their own fears before supporting young people.

Stand for what is right.

Sexual health is a human right.

You're not alone. Seek like-minded people to reinforce your messages.

Check out resources and use them to enhance your teaching.

Just because some teens are smoking weed or using drugs or doing sexual things doesn't mean they all are.

Be kind.

CHAPTER SIXTEEN

Silence and Truth

Some teachers are afraid of silence.

Have you ever attended a class where educators ask a question and then quickly respond to themselves? Even if you had an answer, there was no time to formulate it or respond. This is especially true when the question seeks an opinion, not a fact. Yet, most teachers seek class participation. We want to hear from our students— we want to know their thoughts. We often assess, and grade, based on a student's contribution in class.

I learned to value silence. I practice what I call *Breathe and Wait* when I ask a question in my class. Breathe. Wait. If necessary, mentally count off seconds. Pause at least fifteen seconds with your query in the air. Remember the teacher in *Ferris Bueller's Day Off*? "Anyone? Anyone?" only elicited boredom.

I also recommend asking open-ended questions—the kind that elicit a full response, not just a "yes" or a "no." Certain questions can spur discussion and help facilitate a rich conversation on any topic.

To encourage facilitation, questions need to be simple. One thought per question. Clear, concise, and to the point.

Parents may find these types of questions helpful as well. Each developmental age requires different listening skills. Younger children often chirp about their days. Listening when you feel you have no more energy to listen is part of parenting most five to eight-year-olds. A child's "You know what?" leads to a play-by-play of he said, she said. This is the age of storytelling. How do we communicate and listen to children?

The listening comes first. The children in my *Nonnie* series focus groups are hungry to be heard. Listen as my Papa did. Put down devices. Turn off the TV. Sit with the child. Hear them. Ask questions that show your interest. "What did you feel at lunch when your friends weren't talking with you?" can lead nowhere or can open a door to an empathic awareness of a child's needs. No matter the topic, let the child lead you. Repeat names, make intermittent eye contact (too much is, well, too much), and lean in. Children are worthy of a good listening, too. Convey that with both your words and your actions.

Adolescence is different. Every encounter with an adolescent is a cross-cultural experience. Many teens are monosyllabic at home. "I'm good," "I'm fine," "Nothing," "Everybody," and "I don't know," are standard thirteen to fifteen-year-old responses to "Are you hungry?" "How was your day?" "What happened today at school?" "Who did poorly on the test?" and, "Why did you do that?"

Getting Past Barriers

Try enhancing communication by asking questions to encourage and respect a young person's opinions and thoughts.

1. *What do you think?* This type of question is based in respect. The adult genuinely solicits a young person's opinions and thoughts. Body language is important. Lean forward, look interested, react without judgement.

2. *What makes you think this way?* Following up with this question empowers the teen and leads to deeper thought. Critical thinking encourages young people to connect cause and effect. Looking at the foundation

behind their thoughts can help them examine their sources and be open for your next question.

3. *How do you know this?* The key here is to accept a young person's rationale for their thoughts without judging them.

4. *What more can you share?* Keep the conversation going. Involve other students by asking them to react. *What do the rest of you think?*

5. End the discussion with, *What other questions do you have about this topic?* or, *Are you curious about anything else?*

An astute young person can still block your questions if they feel invasive. *The Zits* cartoon is written by someone who is culturally connected to fifteen-year olds! In one comic, the main character, Jeremy, reacts to his parent's question, "How was your day?" with a mental image of a woodpecker pulling back his skull to pick at Jeremy's brain! Just being there and offering your presence in comfortable silence while articulating the obvious - *I'm interested in you. I'm here if you want to talk* - can help.

A common technique called *Newsprint* encourages class participation in a safe, almost anonymous way. It works best in a classroom where all students can write and go to the board, so I tailor this activity to my class composition. If a young person lives with a physical disability and cannot go to a whiteboard or flip chart, I adapt the activity by passing blank sheets of paper around the class. I write simple, open-ended questions or prompts on the board or the paper and encourage students to complete the sentences.

Each open-ended prompt leads into the topic for the day. For example, I teach a class at Washington and Jefferson College on sexuality. EDU208 is entitled *Teaching and Dealing with Sexuality in Schools*, but my class roster extends beyond education majors. The class fills up quickly, with a long waiting list. Our first class, my prompt is "Sexuality is…" Each class, a different newsprint greets my students, who automatically go to the board to complete the sentence. We then discuss the prompts. After the first class, one of my students facilitates the discussion, not me.

Teens Teaching Teens

Our teen peer educators are skilled facilitators. They select their topics and conduct discussions at our Teen Center. Training peer educators is an art and an investment of time. I love when they present at a conference with me. I'm proud of them. I began using peer educators in my young parent program when I discovered how powerful messages could be when an experienced teen parent spent time with a pregnant one.

County fairs are a big deal in my community. One early September class at a school, I had three young parents whose babies were under a year old, and five pregnant teens. Right after guidelines, a parent of a nine-month-old turned to another teen and said, "Your baby is, what, four months?"

The second parent said, "Just turned four months."

The first parent glared, "Then why'd I see you holding her on the Tilt-a-Whirl at the fair? You can't hold onto her on those rides. It's not safe."

I gently repeated our guidelines of respect and no judging. The second young mother looked pale, "I never thought..."

The first teen locked eyes with me and nodded, "I know. That sounded mean and judgey. I just did some stupid things with my baby, and I don't want you to make my mistakes."

I began training young parents to teach the next week. The message coming from a peer meant more than my words.

Peer Educators and Sexuality

My first sex ed peer educator experience wasn't as smooth. It was 1995. I personally taught in ten school districts then, having just hired my first educator. I arrived at school one day to be met by an excited eighth grader. "I'm going to prom," she declared, practically vibrating.

I did my *Breathe and Wait*, then asked, "With whom?"

A senior.

In those days, even after teaching sex ed for fourteen years, I still hadn't shed my adult perspective—still didn't realize adolescent culture is not mine. I assumed that prom night equaled sex, and that a fourteen-year-old with an eighteen-year-old equaled coercion. I now know sex can happen on a Tuesday, no prom needed.

I sought support from the high school principal, a man of integrity I still call a friend. We discussed the policy of permitting eighth graders access to a junior-senior prom. He agreed, it needed revision, but the prom was the next day. *What to do?*

I asked the principal for an assembly with all the eighth graders. He arranged it that afternoon on two hours notice! Then, with no time to spare, I connected with four of my senior students. These young people were very outspoken about waiting to have sex until marriage.

I've shared I believe virginity and hymens are about ownership and women as property. In 1995, I was still caught up in the conventional virgin concept that assumes a definition involving sex between a man and a woman on their wedding night. Defining virginity in a heterosexual manner (sex that counts is penis-vagina sex) and placing a double standard on sexual experience, where girls are labeled as "sluts" and boys are considered "the man" after sex, is not only sexist, it damages all young people. Young people with sexual abuse histories bemoan the loss of virginity, when, in my opinion, what matters is consent. We add shame to their trauma.

As I prepared to walk out on the stage to face the entire eighth-grade student body, flanked by my four self-proclaimed virgins, I felt I was ready to take this on. I asked the students if they would be comfortable teaching eighth graders. *Would they be willing to convey the idea that prom night didn't mean they were obligated to have sex?* I had no time to really prepare them. I shared the essence of good body language while presenting: make intermittent eye contact, look confident, lean forward, keep your tone warm, be truthful. Ten minutes later, we walked into a packed auditorium filled with buzzing and laughing thirteen and fourteen-year-olds.

It went well to start. My senior wannabe peer educators shared the need to obtain consent (I was on target with that one). One of the eighth graders raised a hand, "Are any of you going to prom?"

I was feeling pretty good about myself. I'd checked this out. The four seniors assured their audience that yes, they were all going. They all had dresses and dates.

Life often shuts us down when we become cocky. The same eighth grader's hand flew up again, "Do the boys you're going with know they're not gonna get any prom night?"

One of my seniors leaned forward, looked confident, made excellent eye contact, smiled warmly, and modulated her tone to be accepting and welcoming. She said, "No, not at all, but, you know, I give the best head in school."

I am seldom speechless. I sat there, dumbfounded, listening to the gasps of shock and the rumble of laughter that followed. If I'd really been a talk show host, I would have cut to commercial. The bell rang and the eighth graders left.

It never occurred to me that a young person would proclaim her intent to remain abstinent until marriage and then, in the next breath, proclaim her proficiency with oral sex.

Truth

Learn from mistakes. Here is some wisdom for training young people to be peer educators: Training is key, and learning the art of facilitation takes time. Some self-evaluation to ponder before you begin peer education or a youth advisory board:

- Are you comfortable surrendering power?
- Do you trust your peer educators' wisdom?
- Can you respect adolescent culture?
- Can you accept all young people, no matter their sexual identity, their

gender, their gender identity, their race, their ability, their class, their academic prowess, or their social skills?

- Are you prepared to support these young people?

My most recent book is a training manual for peer education. Its title is *Peer Educator Manual for Real Teens.* Teen voices are incorporated in the book. Here are a few of their comments:

"Being a peer educator is less a responsibility and more of an honor. I get educated on very many subjects and topics and I get to put in all of my input. I get to educate so many of my friends. If I wasn't introduced to being a peer educator, I can't tell you where I'd be, to be honest. I'm just incredibly thankful I was born in this day and age and to have this beautiful opportunity."

–LaShauna Carruthers

"To me, being a peer educator shaped me into who I am today and continues to teach me everyday. It has become a tremendous part of me. Many friends, lessons, and adventures in my life happened because of the time I got to spend as a peer educator with the teen outreach. I can honestly say I don't know where I would be without the abundance of memories, people, and morals. I have learned that I have a voice to be heard, even as a teen, how to reach out, to speak up, and how to come out of my shell and show my true self to others. Also, I have seen and heard countless different perspectives, giving me a greater understanding of empathy and kindness towards others. 'Each person is a person of worth,' is a great quote by Dr. Mary Jo Podgurski, but furthermore a concept everyone needs to grasp and understand. I am ever so grateful for the time I got to spend as a peer educator and would do it all over again in a heartbeat."

–Maggie Thompson

"Being a peer educator means being a friend to those who need one—to see others who may be shy or afraid and try to make them as comfortable as possible. It means going the extra mile for those in need and stopping the spread of misinformation."

-Landan Weakland

"A thought is literally a construct, which, in many cases, may be biased or misleading. Having the opportunity to share thoughts in an open forum allowed me to learn more about HOW 'each person is a person of worth.' Thank you for all that you have done, are doing, and will continue to do for young people."

-Zhiere Patman

When an adult teaches, it's heard as a whisper.
When a teen teaches, it's heard as a shout.

Step #15: Silence is Golden

Use it to listen and learn.

Try not to fill in the silence with words.

Pause and wait for young people to share their wisdom.

Surrender power and teach teens how to connect and teach and facilitate.

It's not about us.

CHAPTER SEVENTEEN

Snow and Ice

Early Lessons

In my culture, feeding people ranks high in the social hierarchy. I love feeding people – at my home, at our teen outreach office, at the Common Ground Teen Center I run. Breaking bread with someone sparks connection, connection inspires empathy, and empathy leads to compassion and social change. It's also fun.

I grew up in Western Pennsylvania, long before PennDOT became a factor in snow removal in my small community. We lived in a tiny house with a large garden, perched on top of a steep hill. Inevitably, snow and ice would cause fender benders; out of control drivers often drifted into our yard or became stuck on the periphery of our home.

Papa loved people. He was my mentor in feeding people as well. My mama cooked with passion, but she was an introvert at heart and the sight of strangers conjured up danger to her. Papa felt no such anxiety. When it began to snow in earnest, he was watchful. A large bin of cinders was placed on our corner by the city. Papa kept a shovel near the door. When a car slid into the curb by our house, he'd put on his black galoshes and tattered red knitted hat and brown workman's gloves (all of which embarrassed me as a teen) and saunter out into the elements. He'd shovel cinders and help the hapless driver get out of the ditch.

When he failed, he brought these strangers into our home to use our phone. My current students are incredulous when I describe the black rotary phone I knew as a child. I don't know what surprises them more: the reality that phones were tethered to the wall and cell service did not exist, or the concept of a party line, where one shared phone time with a neighbor.

We host an annual youth conference at Washington and Jefferson College, where I'm an adjunct professor in the Education Department. In 2014, our theme was Respect for Older Adults, and the conference focused on culture. We looked at the changes in culture from 1964 to 2014, and projected possible changes for 2064. Our Adolescent Advisory Board examined six areas: business, education, gender, healthcare, race, and technology. Two adults over the age of sixty-five facilitated small group discussions with our students. My favorite young person's comment dealt with the idea of a party line. The young man was fourteen. His brow was furrowed, his expression confused. He asked sincerely, "But... who selected the ring tone?"

Open Door, Open Heart

Sharing a home phone in the fifties might have been an act of courage. I was around ten when I began to realize my papa's behavior was unconventional. Not only did he welcome strangers into our home, he fed them. We had a rounded white refrigerator. It was always stocked. Weekly excursions to the local Italian butcher were part of my Saturday mornings for as long as I could remember. A long stick of pepperoni was a weekly purchase. While his guests used our phone to call for help (AAA didn't exist in those days), Papa would throw open the fridge door and stare into its belly, like a gleeful hunter examining potential prey. He'd emerge with that stick of pepperoni, a hunk of provolone cheese, some green onions, cured red peppers, and a plastic butter container full of green and black Italian olives. While coffee brewed, he would cut these treasures, arranging them on a dish as if he were plating the items on a modern day cooking show. Pride oozed from him. He'd carve thick Italian bread, the grain as dense as cake, and drizzle olive oil and herbs over each piece. Finally, he'd slice whole tomatoes, baptizing them with freshly grated parmesan cheese. Invited to our large oak kitchen table in our four-room house, these strangers were admonished to *mangia*, eat.

My family used food to cope with emotional pain as well. This is both positive and negative. I've been on a program for food intake most of my life. A memory: when a beloved family member died, our immediate family gathered at the hospital. There were so many of us, the frazzled nurses relegated us to a waiting area and closed the door. I was in high school, planning to be a nurse. After a few minutes, the head nurse entered, carrying a tray of small medicine cups. Each cup contained one small round pill. My nonna was near the door. I heard her ask the nurse to explain the pills. I moved quickly to stand beside her. I doubt I knew much about medicine, but, in my family, I was already an expert in healthcare by my intended career. I heard the nurse tell my nonna the pills would calm everyone down. I think I remember her saying they were phenobarbital, but my memory may be poor. Would a healthcare professional really provide barbiturates to a room full of grieving people? No matter the clarity of my memory, I am certain of my grandmother's response. She firmly dismissed the hapless nurse. "We'll be fine," my assertive nonna said. "We'll go home and eat."

My papa's winter weather company made real his belief that all people were worthy of respect. I don't think he thought he was teaching his only child to respect the culture of others, although I may be wrong. I knew, even then, that he taught me by example. *Esempio.* I also know what I learned sitting at my kitchen table and listening to Papa converse with people he didn't know. I watched him listen with intention. I watched his food, offered with such joy, ease people's tension and make them feel safe. Long before I was taught as a young teacher to create a safe place for learning, my Papa showed me the way. He didn't care about our temporary guests' skin color or gender, age or ability, class or belief system. I witnessed him firmly refuse money when the travelers left. I observed their gratitude and the graceful way he simply said, "My pleasure." I'd go to the bedroom where my mama was hiding - "These people will rob us blind," she'd say - and coax her into the warm kitchen. Mama could be the life of the party, and her emergence would make my papa's face glow. He'd defer to her ability to facilitate a good conversation, content to watch her and his guests eat.

A young person of color once asked me why I didn't see color. I corrected him gently. Of course, I see color. If I didn't see color, I didn't see all of a person. I had a gentle, persistent teacher, however. I learned early that all people are worthy of respect.

Social Justice and Sex Ed

The connection between social justice and sexuality education is huge. My primary message in education remains the same, regardless if I'm teaching birth education or sex ed or presenting to adults on how to reach young people. People are worthy. Establishing that mantra as my educational foundation opened my eyes to the differences between equality and equity.

Equality is more common. In *Nonnie Talks About Race*, I quote a man named Dr. Naheed Dosani who wrote this tweet: "#Equality is giving everyone a shoe. #Equity is giving everyone a shoe that fits."

I link sexuality education with an awareness of equity when I provide the same message to all young people yet tailor my messages to the needs of individuals. Connecting means hearing a young person's needs and adjusting. Gender and gender identity should not limit or alter a lesson. Unlike the 1905 sex ed books, I don't water down my message for girls.

Let's talk about gender identity. My first *Nonnie* book was *Nonnie Talks About Gender*. I wrote it for the children who came to me with gender non-conforming feelings. It astounds and confuses me when I hear people attack parents who support their children when they are gender fluid (not conforming to societal norms for gender) or gender non-binary (not fitting into a binary or male/female definition of gender). Parents guide children to become people of character and to find their own path. Accepting a child unconditionally means honoring their identity.

Trans Youth and Suicide

Letting the child lead means parents hear their child's needs and support them. The suicide rate for young people who identify as transgender (not identifying with body parts but with gender) is harsh. A recent American Academy of Pediatrics study showed high levels of attempted suicide among transgender youth. Trans boys and non-binary youth had the highest rates—more than half of transgender male teens attempted suicide in their lifetime. Transgender female rates are lower, but still alarming, revealing suicide attempts at 29.9%. Non-binary youth report a 41.8% rate of attempted suicide.

In contrast to all these groups of transgender teens, just 18% of females and 10% percent of males who are cisgender - meaning their gender identity matches what it says on their birth certificate - have attempted suicide.

Many trans or non-binary young people experience family rejection, bullying, and harassment. They often feel unsafe at school or social events simply for being who they are. My experiences with trans youth reveal depression and self-doubt, but also phenomenal perseverance and resiliency.

Young people are strong, but adult support
is vital to their survival and mental health.

Step #16: Sexuality Education is a Companion to Social Justice

Model empathy.

If an adult doesn't understand a young person's identity, seek information.

Even if an adult disagrees with a young person's identity, respect means a teen must be honored as a person of worth.

Adults need to protect young people, not add to their angst.

Remember, we only see the first layer of a person's "onion."

CHAPTER EIGHTEEN

Sex on the Road

I've had the great honor of teaching in thirteen countries. I learned quickly to acknowledge and honor each nation's culture. I was a visitor, a traveler, a stranger in their homes.

My favorite trips were to China, where I taught with my dear friend Teri Shilling in 2008 and 2009. Teri and I co-presented our workshop *Games Educators Play* for over a decade. She is the founder of Passion for Birth and a strong advocate for birthing women. Teri also followed me as president of the board of directors for Lamaze International.

A young Chinese woman was my guide. She took the English name Mabel as a second name—most of the people I met on that trip assumed English names to use with their Asian ones. She asked me once if Mabel was a popular name in America. I gently responded that it depended on a person's generation. I'm not sure my words clicked with her. She just beamed and said, "I knew I picked a good one."

I'm not sure what I taught in China. For that matter, I'm not sure what I taught in Russia or any other nation. Like many Americans, I'm not fluent in another language. Consequently, my words when I teach are translated. One learns to make frequent pauses when teaching in another country, to allow the translator time to convey the message. In China, I would sometimes speak a while, perhaps two or three minutes, while the translator patiently waited. Then, she would say two or three words to the class! Other times, I would say very little and my translator would talk in Mandarin for a long time! I know some topics were intimidating. My students were parents, educators, nurses, and childcare workers. One of the areas my Chinese students were most interested in was communicating about sexuality to children and young people. Yet, I could sense tension by my translator's hesitation as she paused, as if considering ways to respect her culture while faithfully conveying my information. I was proud of these brave women (they were all women) for their courage.

I taught in Russia with Magee Womencare International, led by another dear friend and childbirth educator, Michele Ondeck. We taught childbirth education to professionals. It was 1995, only a few years after perestroika made huge changes in the Communist Party. We taught nurses and obstetricians and perinatologists. Many of these good people had not received paychecks for months. They existed as best they could.

We started in Moscow, where my husband and our two youngest children accompanied me, then traveled to Suzdal, where the training was held. My family left after five days while I remained to teach. In Moscow, we were provided with an old Volkswagen van and a jovial driver. In an attempt to connect with him, I engaged him in conversation. We hit upon a funny routine. I would ask him to share the sounds animals made in Russian. For example, if a rooster said "cock-a-doodle-do" in English, what would a rooster say in his language? He loved this game. The rooster, he told me, would say "cookero-cookero!" This always made my children laugh.

On the last day, our driver shared his real job. He was a professional business man, but business was poor. He was barely breaking even. I asked if he was driving because his normal work had fallen off. He said *no* and that he was driving vans for tourists to avoid the Russian mafia. His family made vodka to sell on the black market, and they were late in paying their roof. Spellbound, I inquired the meaning of "roof." Their payment to the mob, he explained. I looked around the van, suddenly feeling less secure. "What would happen," I asked, "if the mob finds you?"

"Oh," he said, matter-of-factly, "they'll kill me." I was glad this was our last day in his van, and appalled that this was how he survived.

Traveling as an educator left me with two intense impressions. First, it was an honor to see a country as a consultant. I've traveled as a tourist, and my experiences as a trainer were more intimate, more face-to-face, and real.

Advocacy and Humility

My second impression isn't as positive. I've been an advocate for change for most of my life, striving to make a difference in my own small way. For example, I try to boycott Nestle. I've done so since the seventies when I discovered they were sending lab-coated, non-medical personnel to countries to sell formula. Mothers successfully breastfeeding would be coerced to buy their product. When money was tight, the formula would be watered down and thriving babies went hungry. As a strong breastfeeding advocate, this angered me. I say I *try* to boycott because my mother's guilt overwhelmed my activism when our son was small. One day, in the checkout line at the supermarket, Nate said, with great sorrow, "I know we don't eat Nestle, but I wish I knew what a Crunch Bar tasted like. Everyone at school eats them."

I capitulated.

I share my advocacy story to explain the sadness I felt when people in other nations assumed my colleagues and I were always correct, and our standards of care better than theirs, simply because we were American. In Russia, for example, birth happened in a culture of normalcy. One of the challenges faced in American birthing deals with medicalization. We often lose sight of the reality that birth is a normal part of life.

I once observed a native midwife assist at a birth in Mexico. My Spanish is poor, but a colleague asked the midwife, "What will you do if the baby doesn't fit?" I wondered the same question. We were far from a hospital or clinic. The midwife spoke in rapid fire Spanish, and we were dismissed from the room. Later, she explained that women are strong, they can labor and birth their babies. Doubting their ability to do so was not acceptable. In Russia, this acceptance of the normalcy of birth was also obvious. Birth was not seen as pathology, but as a condition of health. American hospitals in 1995 were so medicalized it was tough for women to have a normal birth experience.

There were glaring areas where our tutelage helped in Russia, however. I witnessed poor sterilization techniques; an obstetrician helped one woman give birth using thick surgical gloves (at the time, they didn't have disposable ones). He washed his hands, kept on the same gloves, and moved to another birth. Women in one of the hospitals we visited brought a basket and a length of rope with them to give birth. Since there were no cafeterias or food supplies in the hospital, and no visiting, they would lower the baskets to their families, who filled them with bread, milk, cheese, and vegetables. Yes, there were areas ripe for change.

The concept that birth is normal may sound like a no-brainer, but women's right to informed choice and a voice in their own births is often a battle, even today. When I first became a birth advocate, Suzanne Arms had just written *Immaculate Deception* (1977), Ina Mae Gaskin was promoting midwife birth at The Farm, and the woman who would become my dear friend and mentor, Elizabeth Bing, had written the first guide to women's independence and autonomy in birth, *Six Practical Lessons for an Easier Childbirth* (1969).

My colleagues and I did offer knowledge, but the culture of women birthing normally in Russia was superior, in my opinion, to ours in America.

My strongest impression of traveling as an educator is simple: people are human the world over.

Lessons Learned

Openness to learning is a prerequisite for empathic understanding. I've been a student all my life. I'm a student now.

I was honored to attend one of the Advocates for Youth's European Study Tours in the early 2000s. Led by my friend Barbara Huberman, this three-country experience brought American sexuality educators to Europe. We were exposed to curricula and cultural attitudes different from our nation. We shared our expertise with one another and with our hosts. Barbara was not only a friend, we had common roots in Lamaze education. She was the force behind these international events. Her passion for young people and for education is her legacy. I miss her.

The trip was teeming with lessons. I saw the inclusive, factual way sexuality was addressed in the Netherlands, met with students in Germany from both university and trade-focused secondary schools, and had an audience with the French leaders from their Department of Health. It was eye-opening. It was inspiring. It was also depressing.

While meeting with French health administrators, we asked if the French required parental permission forms for their sex ed classes. "Non, non." Our host appeared confused. When pressed, he added, "This is a condition of health. We do not require permission forms to teach proper handwashing. Why would we need them to teach children about their bodies?"

Someone said, "Isn't this a Catholic country?"

I remember this doctor's expression. "Perhaps," he said, smiling, "religion is separate from education. Families may teach their children any religious belief they wish, but the public school system teaches facts." He paused a moment, as if contemplating us, then added, "We use American research to support our curriculum with facts. Don't you?"

Youth Culture

Generalizing young people will give you incorrect perspectives. Teens, like adults, are not the same. Too many adults judge teens as a group, as if they shared the same beliefs, used drugs, smoked weed, were irresponsible, and had sex with many partners. Untrue.

An exchange on Facebook brought this to my attention. Someone posted the question, "Should the voting age be lowered to sixteen?" I was interested in the responses. Our peer educators created an original game called *Debate Without Hate* in 2016. They selected and researched the topics, designed the play of the game, and made it work. *Debate Without Hate* is purely teen driven. In 2017-2018, we created an interactive website (debatewithouthate.com) with generous help from the Three Rivers Community Foundation. One topic addresses lowering the voting age to sixteen. Our teens were evenly split, some feeling sixteen-year-olds are mature enough to vote, others arguing to keep the age at eighteen.

The Facebook posts showed an extreme lack of awareness of young people's culture, needs, and assets. If was as if these adults were from another country. Every single one of the seventy-plus comments said "no" in various ways, but some elaborated:

"Hell no! They're still eating Tide pods! Raise it to twenty-one and hope they mature enough by then to make a decision based on facts."

"Hell no. That's the age that our sixteen-year-olds are being brainwashed at our schools."

"According to Obamacare, a person is a child until twenty-six. Therefore, some people want to lower the voting age and include people that will not be an adult until ten years later. The dems don't care about anything other than keeping power by any means they can think of."

I typically avoid confrontations on social media, although I do use Facebook as a platform to teach. With nearly 5,000 friends, I think it's a forum where my messages of respect can be spread. The sheer volume of hateful responses attacking the young people I love motivated me. The primary guideline in our

Debate Without Hate game is respect—civil discourse. These adults hiding behind their computer screens were disrespectful. I responded:

"Interesting comments. Our peer educators created a *Debate Without Hate* game and this is one of the questions they selected for debate. Teens debate the question honestly - some in favor of lowering the age and some against it. It's sad to me that so many adults in these comments appear to not even consider the other side of this debate. I know sixteen-year-olds who are better informed than adults, who read all types of news from different sources, and who never watch TV news because it's automatically slanted one way or the other. I know teens who can discuss history like scholars and tell you how we repeat the mistakes of the past. I've facilitated discussions with teens about government and they can tell you the differences between a democracy, a republic, an oligarchy, a monarchy, and a dictatorship. I know teens who carry intense school schedules with AP classes, hold down jobs, help in their families, and work at our teen center. Teens are not all the same. So, sure, some sixteen-year-olds aren't mature enough to vote. From what I see, neither are some twenty-year-olds and some thirty-year-olds and some forty-year-olds and some fifty-year-olds and people my age."

Denying Sexual Information

Negative attitudes about young people can add to denying sex ed. If teens are seen as immature, stupid, out of control, useless, or any of the other many hurtful adjectives I've heard adults use to describe them, they are not respected. If they're not respected, they're not seen as able to learn about their own bodies and their own relationships.

Our own country is a mosaic of states, each with their own culture. The CDC (Center for Disease Control) 2014 School Health Profiles show fewer than half of our high schools and only a fifth of middle schools teach all sixteen topics recommended by the CDC as essential parts of sex education. Basic information on HIV and STI transmission is missing as well as vital communication and decision-making skills.

A recent study published by the Guttmacher Institute found that fewer teens are receiving timely information in sex ed. In 2011-2013, 43% of teen females and 57% of adolescent males did not receive information about birth control before their first sexual experience. The study also showed these teens were not increasing sex education conversations with their parents.

Voting

I was fourteen when Julie Andrews and Dick Van Dyke introduced us to supercalifragilisticexpialidocious in the *Mary Poppins* movie. I was at the age when I was supposed to be above such childish fare. I was not. I sang the songs for weeks.

I don't know if I truly understood the ramifications of the song *Sister Suffragettes*. I mostly recall the tune. Researching the lyrics today made me pause:

> *We're clearly soldiers in petty coats*
> *Dauntless crusaders for women's votes*
> *Though we adore men individually*
> *We agree that as a group they're rather stupid*
> *Off the shackles of yesterday*
> *Shoulder to shoulder into the fray*
> *Our daughter's daughters will adore us*
> *And they'll sing in grateful chorus*
> *Well done sister suffragettes*

I sang those words when I was young, but I doubt I believed men were rather stupid. The men in my life were wise and respectful. Young people now sing songs without really hearing lyrics, shocking the adults around them. Music connects, it also instructs. Instead of horror, perhaps adults could react with education. Life is a teachable moment!

I do remember being appalled when I learned the Nineteenth Amendment granted women the right to vote in 1920. *Why,* I pondered, *didn't women receive this right from the start of our republic?* I was in college before I learned how the American suffrage movement marginalized women of color. Instead of uniting as women, the racism of white suffragists excluded Black women. Poll taxes, the concept of an "educated suffragist," and twelve-hour waits to vote in some states made it impossible for many Black women to vote until the sixties.

My mama's brother was a United States congressman. I grew up distributing emery boards and keychains embossed with his name, standing with Mama at polling booths, and listening to spirited political debates in our kitchen. I recall the way my relatives agreed to disagree with respect, although the process of finding common ground was often loud. Very loud. And emotional.

Voting was part of our family's culture. I registered as soon as I was able, and I've not missed an election since I reached legal age. Voting rights for eighteen-year-olds missed me by a few years. I was already twenty-one in 1971 when the age was lowered. Cultural currency is what matters in a culture—each family creates its own culture and has its own currency. In mine, being informed mattered.

I was thirteen when John F. Kennedy was assassinated, and not quite fifteen when Malcolm X was killed. In my family, both deaths were met with deep sorrow. My papa had few words of wisdom. He was in shock. Rich and I graduated high school in 1968. On April fourth of that year, Martin Luther King, Jr. was brutally killed. Within a week of our June graduation, Jack's brother Bobby Kennedy was assassinated, and one of our classmates was tragically killed in a head-on collision. My girlfriends and I returned to school, wearing our white graduation dresses, at the request of the dead girl's family. I think they wanted to help us hold onto innocence—once a member of your peer group dies tragically, mortality feels fragile. I'd been an officer in NHS, and we went to the home to prepare food after the funeral. We were reeling. Death was too real for new graduates. My papa remained stunned. His beloved America was changing. Mama's response to the deaths and political turmoil was clear. Vote. Vote. Vote. Vote.

Adults need to advocate for young people.
No vote equals no voice – adults must speak!

Step #17: Be an Advocate for Young People.

It isn't enough to respect young people; one must strive to see life through their lens.

An awareness of sexuality as it is approached in different nations brings insight into our own cultural expectations and rules.

Sixteen-year olds voting isn't the issue, although it is a debatable topic. What matters is that voting adults consider the human rights of young people and support them.

Vote!

CHAPTER NINETEEN

Lessons Learned

As much as I enjoyed teaching in other countries, most of my lessons have been homegrown. The young people I've served and the patients I've cared for are my best educators. It is when I've been least prepared that I've learned the most.

More Life Lessons

A memory: I did a short period of casual nursing when my babies were small. Instead of my chosen fields of pediatrics and oncology, I joined a pool of nurses who could select which days they wanted to work in a month, but then were sent to any unit in need.

One 7 a.m.–3 p.m. shift, I was sent to obstetrics. I was a childbirth educator but had little experience as a clinical OB nurse at that time. The hospital in which I worked was not progressive. I traveled over an hour to reach it, and it wasn't my first choice for employment, but it was the only hospital with flexible scheduling, and I needed flexibility more than anything. I rotated units. My primary choices were obstetrics, pediatrics, oncology, and the psych floor. Once I was assigned as supervisor in the cardiac step down unit and my hands shook when I drew up meds. I'd never given cardiac drugs in adult doses!

Women in this hospital, at that time, labored alone. No labor coaches accompanied them. This situation changed perhaps six months after I left. Pressure from women and their partners altered policy. At this moment, please visualize windowless single labor rooms, lining a long hallway, with windows on the other side of the hall. As I started my first patient rounds, I heard a woman screaming, "Help! Help! The baby's coming!"

I looked around. It was a busy unit, and there were many people in the hall. IV nurses with their baskets, nutritional services with their carts of food, maintenance workers, doctors with their heads together. No one paused. No one seemed to notice. I glanced at my day's assignments. The woman in 314 was not my patient. She continued screaming.

I entered her room and approached her bed. Long fingers shot out and she grasped my arm hard enough to bruise. "The baby's coming," she yelled.

"I'll get someone," I soothed. I was a newly trained doula, but not a midwife. I needed help from a more seasoned professional.

At the nurses' station, the charge nurse barely glanced at me when I shared the laboring mother's distress. "Dr. Jones just checked her. She's only four centimeters dilated." She shot me a look I was accustomed to as a casual nurse who didn't know the staff on a unit and wasn't yet trusted. "You do know what that means, don't you?"

I grunted that I did. As a childbirth educator, I was very familiar with labor and birth. The cervix of the uterus must open to ten centimeters before pushing begins, and four centimeters is a long way from the baby coming.

I set off to see my patients. The screaming was unabated, as was the steady indifference from professionals walking up and down the hall. I went into the room. I removed a cervical dilatation chart from the wall and tried to teach. "You're only at four," I said. "You need to dilate to ten."

She persisted, "The baby's coming!"

I thought, I'll look at her bottom and reassure her. The charge nurse had also firmly admonished me to avoid doing an internal exam, where a healthcare provider inserts gloved fingers into the vagina to feel the cervix or the baby's head. The risk of infection from too many internals was real, and, allegedly, Dr. Jones had just performed one. My intent was to reassure only.

When I lifted the sheets, the baby was crowning, which means the head could be seen coming through the vagina with the vaginal opening forming a type of crown.

Shocked, I started to tell the woman not to push, when she did. With enthusiasm. In her defense, the baby WAS coming. She didn't know I was inexperienced and had never caught a baby. My scrub suit looked official and my name tag did not say, *No experience. Don't trust her.*

I got out one foolish word, "Wait!" when she pushed again – two pushes – and her son was out! I instinctively grabbed him, without gloves. He howled lustily, thank goodness. I've been at births where babies need help with their first respirations. This little guy seemed to know whose unskilled hands held him. He cried on his own!

I remember my own tears sliding down my cheeks. The mother fell back on the bed, exhausted. Then, she looked at her baby, pinking up nicely in my arms, covered in birth fluids and vernix (a whitish coating that protects the fetus' skin in utero before birth). She checked out my expression, which I'm sure was frozen in shock. I was young, I suppose, from her point of view, and it was now obvious I was ill prepared for the birth. She patted my arm gently. "You're doing good, honey," she said.

I had a dilemma. *How to get help?* The mom was stable now, but I had no desire to deal with the placenta (afterbirth). I knew yelling would do nothing. So, I cried out, "Code Blue, Room 314." Code Blue in that hospital meant someone's heart had stopped. Instantly, people ran into the room, pushing crash carts, ready to resuscitate. I stood there, holding the crying newborn, and said, "Hey!"

Later, I learned it was her ninth birth. I suppose, after nine pregnancies, the uterus just goes, "Hey," and the baby is born. Since then, I've caught six other babies who came quickly. I've served as a doula to more teen mothers than I can count. I'll never forget this mother, though. She taught me a lesson I've carried into education ever since that birth: People know their own bodies. They know what they feel, they need to be heard.

Advocating for Teens in Labor

Young people are often misheard, ignored, or invisible. I've witnessed young people in labor as they were treated poorly. One of my doula roles with teens is advocating for decency and respect.

I served as doula to a wonderful sixteen-year-old teen of color many years ago. This young person managed to smile during a difficult pregnancy, in the face of her mother's abandonment, as she moved into her boyfriend's home with her mom's permission, when he broke off their relationship and she ended up with a grandmother she barely knew, as she held down two minimum wage jobs, refusing to take welfare, and as she struggled to study and graduate. She triumphantly walked with her graduating class, telling me in tears that she pushed herself to graduate for the eighteen-month-old she clutched in her arms as soon as she stepped off the stage with her diploma. She disliked whining, often spoke of her ability to face anything, and was the first pregnant person to whom I gave the title "warrior."

Her labor wasn't easy, but it wasn't abnormal. We did a lot of walking and rocking and rhythmic breathing. It was a long night. The obstetrician came in to check her near morning and pronounced her fully dilated. He told me she could push.

I gestured to the young mother, "She's right here, doctor. Why not talk with her?"

I received a glare for my words, and he did an internal exam without warning. She squeezed my hand.

"Um," he said, as if discovering something, "this baby is breech."

Residents were in and out throughout her labor, but no one mentioned the baby's position as breech. A breech baby is presenting butt first. Nature meant for the head to exit first, since it is the biggest part of the infant. The vaginal mucosa will stretch, but pelvic bones, although they do give a bit, are more rigid. No ultrasound had been done during the pregnancy, but that wasn't unusual this many years ago.

The mom and I exchanged looks. Before I could protest, the doctor was giving me instructions, again, as if I were giving birth. "We seldom do vaginal births with a breech, but I think she can do it."

With more force this time, I said, "I'd like you to talk about it with her."

He glared again. I glared back. He shrugged. I interpreted his body language as dismissive, but he peered at me, mumbled something about me being persistent, and addressed the teen for the first time since he entered the room. "So, sweetie, here we are. This baby is upside down. I have a choice. I can cut this baby out of your belly, and you'll be very sore and have a scar here," he gestured to her abdomen, "or we can get this baby out the regular way, but you'll need to help me."

I knew the minute he said "cut this baby out of your belly" that she would opt for a vaginal birth. As a birth advocate, I had no problem with avoiding a cesarean birth unless it was medically necessary, but I remained troubled by the way he seemed to consider her needs superficial. The words "this baby" had my guard up. I wrestled back emotion; this was her birth. *Was I overreacting?* I asked her what she'd like to ask the doctor. Her eyes were wide, "Will my baby be okay?"

He assured her, yes, but they had to hurry. In moments, she was being rushed down the hall to the delivery room. This was years before birthing rooms became popular. The room was grim, but I'd prepared her for reality, and she didn't flinch. "Come with me," she cried. I knew better than to ask the doctor, who was striding purposefully away from us, but I knew my nurse colleagues would let me stay.

I was supporting her at her head, making eye contact, talking softly, when I heard a commotion. Looking up, I saw twelve residents crowding into the room. Stunned, I spoke again. "No one asked her if she could be used for an educational lesson," I sputtered. Many residents looked away, a few looked at the doctor. I received yet another of his glares.

He said, "Sweetie, this kind of birth is rare. You don't mind if these future doctors get to watch, do you?"

Her contractions were intense, she locked eyes with me and said to him, "It's okay."

I lifted one shoulder and a delivery room nurse took her other shoulder. Our eyes met over her in solidarity. We puffed with her to help her slow down the urge to push. We positioned our upper bodies to cushion her from so many eyes.

The doctor said to his audience, "See, not too many OBs know this anymore. Breech births are tricky. Here's what you need to remember. She screwed to get the baby in, you need to screw the baby to get it out." He demonstrated by turning the emerging fetus to manipulate the head through the pelvic opening.

The birth was smooth. After three pushes, her son was born. The delivery nurse, who had more power than I, whisked the newborn to the warming bed, did a perfunctory check, wrapped him in a blanket, and returned him to his mom. The nurse whispered, "You're a very brave young woman. I'm very impressed by you."

My own eyes teared as I saw tears run down the new mother's cheeks. "I did it! I did it!" her cries of joy filled the room. "He's healthy and beautiful and I did it!" She kissed his perfect forehead, called him by name, and beamed.

To their credit, at least half of the residents spoke to her, in turn, respectfully, thanking her for allowing them to be part of the birth. She glowed. After directing the chief OB resident to assist with the placenta and "clean things up," the obstetrician left the room without a word.

I remained with the new mother until she fell into an exhausted sleep and left to get her food. On the way, I stopped at the Director of Nursing's office. The hospital was new to me, I was unsure how I would be received. The director heard my tale with respect. She explained that this doctor was very close to retirement, was abrupt with a poor bedside manner, but was very skilled. After all, she reminded me, the baby was born healthy.

True. The baby was healthy. *How often do new parents excuse behavior during labor or decisions made without their permission because the baby is healthy?*

I asked the Director one thing: if this mother were a twenty-seven-year-old white woman, would her experience have been the same?

Empty Cups

When I first began teaching, I imagined my students as empty cups. How excited I was to fill those cups with knowledge! I envisioned my role as one who would give young people wisdom.

I'd been trained to teach. I'd student taught. I knew how to create lesson plans and use different teaching modalities to reach my students. Direction was supplied by my teachers and professors. I was ready. I was cockier than I'd been as a brand new nurse. No one would die if I messed up. I could do this.

In time, I learned my students already possessed wisdom. I discovered how often the word "empower" is ill-used. It does not mean to give another human power. Empower means to guide young people, with empathy, to find their own power. Young people already have power. Teachers are not their saviors; that reeks of privilege. We are guides, mentors, and an adult connection in their often chaotic lives.

I did my first childbirth education training at Penn State in 1987. The night before, I met with my two co-presenters, faculty from Lamaze. One of them asked what we wanted from our trainees. She said, "Knowledge." She wanted our new childbirth educators to know the material. The other said, "Organization." She wanted our new trainees to be organized and present a six-week series with fidelity. I said I wanted passion. Passion means anything else can be taught, but without passion, educators fail.

I haven't lost passion for serving young people yet. If I do, I'll retire.

Young people respond to sincerity, to genuineness, and to real people. They can sense fake in no time. In response to an adult's commitment, they are open, responsive, and often hilarious.

Teaching topics where young people cannot envision themselves facing consequences for their actions stretches a teacher's creativity. An example of such a subject is sexually transmitted infections (STIs). A bright young person told me in the early nineties, when AIDS was inspiring fear, cruelty and misinformation, that he wasn't afraid of an HIV infection. He said, "I only have sex with people I've know since kindergarten. They can't be infected." Denial is strong.

Avoiding lectures is wise. Lecturing is passive education and is often not retained. I want my students to experience education. I create interactive games to teach – how else could I make learning real?

In 1996, while my papa was dying, as I sat beside him and watched the rise and fall of his chest, I wrote my first educational drama to enhance learning. Entitled *Till Human Voices Wake Us*, it tackled teen pregnancy. We created a teen educational drama troupe called the Real Talk Performers. Since then, we've released an original play annually, covering a wide array of topics from relationships to the meaning of love to cyberbullying to social justice. Our play *Fifty Shades of Social Justice* premiered the same year as the book *Fifty Shades of Grey!*

One of my favorite lines from *Fifty Shades of Social Justice* is: "Allies are like sports fans. You cheer at games. You support your team. When it comes time for the press conference, though, you don't take the microphone. You step back."

Our peer educators now write, cast, direct, and perform the plays they present at conferences, for students, and at community events. I am hands off. These are their works of art. We often do pre and post-tests in the audience. One of our most successful plays, with a 67% increase in knowledge about STI transmission and symptoms, was called *Gonorrhea Monologues*. Each player was cast as a different STI. Their dialogue and songs demonstrated the difference between bacterial STIs, like gonorrhea, syphilis, and chlamydia, and viral STIs, like herpes and HPV.

Everyone coveted the role of chlamydia, whose costume was a full camo outfit to represent how asymptomatic the bacterial infection could be. The day after we cast *Gonorrhea Monologues*, I was walking down the hall of a high school when I heard a young person cry out, "Hey, Mary Jo, is it true you gave chlamydia to that girl from Wash High?" Only the Sex Lady!

Advocacy requires introspection and humility.
Are we reacting for our own needs or for those of the young person?

Step #18: Know When to Step Back

Give young people the power to make their own life choices.

Guide, but do not direct.

Surrender your concept of curricula to expand it and include their thoughts.

Teach the skills of facilitation and small group work to young people. They get it.

Let your students lead you.

CHAPTER TWENTY

Trauma

Which of us matters? *Do we all? Do we matter in different ways, with different equity?* Our bodies react to threat or stress with fight (defend yourself) or flight (get away). A third, less healthy reaction is to freeze, paralyzed by fear. Traumatized children may become frozen in the body's normal fight, flight, or freeze cycle.

Imagine yourself in the middle of a busy city – maybe New York's Times Square – alone, in the middle of the day. What do you see? Who is around you? What do you hear? Do you notice any odors? Are you frightened? Imagine yourself in the same spot in the same city, but the time is now 3 a.m. Would your anxiety rise? Now, imagine how a traumatized child feels without treatment. They may be frozen in a fear cycle with no way out.

Trauma may be categorized as big 'T' and little 't.' Big 'T' traumas include serious injury, sexual violence, or life-threatening experiences, where serious physical injury, death, or violence causes intense trauma. This type of trauma can occur even if the person is not physically harmed. Big 'T' trauma commonly makes a survivor vulnerable to PTSD (post-traumatic stress disorder).

Little 't' traumas are very distressing events affecting an induvial personally that don't fall into big 'T' areas. The death of a pet, bullying, non-life-threatening injuries, emotional abuse, or harassment are some of the experiences that can cause little 't' trauma.

Trauma, like grief, isn't about a disappointment or a failure. We can learn from failure and grow from disappointment. Trauma can change our lives. In children, trauma actually can change the brain. As a counselor, I've spent innumerable hours with young people. They know when bad things are happening. We don't preserve innocence by avoiding these topics or sheltering young people, we deny them the best coping mechanism of all: contact with a caring, trusted adult. Studies tell us how important a long-term relationship with a significant adult can be to a growing youth. It is particularly important after trauma. Many researchers believe this prolonged, positive contact can heal brains damaged by childhood trauma. Think of your own childhood. Did an adult support or guide you through difficult times? If not, can you think back to a traumatic event or death of a loved one and imagine how guidance from a loving adult could have eased the trauma?

Don't Assume a Child Doesn't Need Information

I remember two brothers, Eric and Matt, and their families' approach to one boy's cancer. They were eight and ten years old. The parents decided the boys were too young to understand the reality of the younger boy's diagnosis, to spare them both emotional pain. I found the ten-year-old crying in a corner of the playroom one evening while his brother was having a lumbar puncture (commonly known as a spinal tap). I joined him, handing him a slice of pizza. He nodded, trying to hide his tears, and ate. We sat together in comfortable silence

"He's gonna die, isn't he? Eric. He's gonna die, right?"

I asked, "Do you think so?"

"Yeah," the tears returned. He wiped his runny nose. "Mom and Dad think we don't know. We both do."

"Would it help you if your parents knew the truth?"

He shook his head, "Maybe, but I don't want to hurt them. They like to pretend Eric's okay."

Our conversation humbled me. He continued talking, sharing the many ways he and his brother deceived their parents about their awareness of reality. "It's like Santa Claus," he added. "We haven't believed in Santa since I was six and he was four. My fault. I heard at school and told Eric. We pretend because it makes Mom and Dad happy."

The elephant in the living room is almost always felt. The parable of the elephant and the blind men was a play our Real Talk Performers presented a few years ago. Blind men approach an elephant, having never encountered one. One touches the ear and declares the elephant to be like a fan. Another touches a leg and says the being is like a tree trunk. A third touches the trunk and says, "This being is like a snake." Yet another encounters the elephant's side and is sure it is like a wall. One man touches the tusk and says it is like a spear. The last man touches the tail and says, "This being is like a rope." Yet, the elephant is still an elephant. If we don't talk with our children about challenging topics, who will? Parenting by Google allows no discussion or connection.

Racism

I was raised to believe all people had worth. Over the decades, I've woken to the reality that many groups of people are *less than* in our nation. This awakening is a condition of privilege, one definition of which is *privilege means you don't need to think about it.* I raised a son, but never felt the need to teach him how to react if stopped by police. I did tell him to show respect, but never felt I had to caution him to keep his hands visible and not reach for something abruptly. My son's skin, like my skin, did not mark him as a threat.

Immigration is a hot political topic these days. It's been a challenge for our nation for decades, under many presidents. April of 2018, a zero tolerance policy mandated that children be separated from their parents at our southern border. A year later, these children remain traumatized.

As the news filled with images and stories of migrant children in distress, I wrote *Nonnie Talks About Trauma*. I was surrounded by thoughts and images of pain and violence and sorrow. It was a tough book to write. Traumatized children break my heart. I pushed through with the book, because adults and young people need support communicating about this challenging subject. Children are affected by other children's trauma—by the images they see and the words adults hurl at one another when they disagree.

My staff and I are reading *The Deepest Well* by Dr. Nadine Burke Harris. In it, she discusses ACEs or adverse childhood experiences. Research tells us childhood trauma can cause neurological changes in a child's brain that leave lifelong physical and mental problems. Many children deal with the trauma of abuse, domestic violence, or a national disaster. Why are we inflicting trauma on children as a deterrent to immigration? There must be a better way.

What if these children were our children? How silent would we be? Where are these children now? How are their parents coping with the not knowing? I lost our first child for about five minutes in a store once. She slipped under a clothing display and was playing hide and seek. There's no comparison to the intense fear these parents must feel as their children are taken from their arms and taken to places where the parent cannot reach or touch them. No comparison, yet I clearly recall my thundering heart, my instantly chilled skin, my rapid breaths. *Where was she?*

I've cared for children like this before in the seventies, when Vietnam fell. I recognize the behavior. I vividly recall seeing a five-year-old Vietnamese child over a period of months—a little girl so traumatized she exhibited none of the behavior a typical child would. Blank stares, withdrawn, clinging to me because I was a person who didn't hurt her, even though I was a stranger. Those children in the seventies suffered the horrors of war. *Why are we politicizing and traumatizing children now?* Frankly, I believe anyone who seeks to debate the purposeful traumatizing of children doesn't get it. This isn't about politics, this is about human decency, lifelong trauma, and neurological changes in innocent children.

Our border staff are ill prepared for this. They are not trained in support-ing little ones. I hire staff for our outreach with such care, making sure they can serve young people with kindness, with empathy, without judgment, seeking to empower—making sure they can teach with heart. Who trained the people in-teracting with these children? Are our agents at the border treating people with humanity and respect? Regardless of politics, can we really condone treatment where children are called donkeys, where they are so traumatized by prolonged separations that last so long the little ones no longer recognize their parents, where teens are bound naked with bags over their heads in solitary? My skin crawls with the very real possibility that these unprotected children are also enduring sexual abuse.

Are We Born Kind?

I'd like to believe we come into the world ready to be kind. Studies with babies show we are certainly born with the capacity to be kind. Our brains contain neurons that are called mirror neurons. These neurons respond in the same way when we experience pain in ourselves as when we see someone else experience the same thing. The term "empathic distress" refers to the human tendency to react to another's pain. Babies are more likely to cry when they hear another baby crying than to cry from any other noise. However, anyone whose raised a child will tell you we're born selfish. We must be taught to share, and it's hard.

More ominous are the results of a University of Toronto study where infants as young as six months showed a preference for members of their own race versus members of a different race. I shudder to think this is the start of racism. Parents and teachers need to model kindness in words and actions. "Look, honey, that little girl fell and has a boo-boo on her leg. You know that hurts! How can we help her?" Children benefit from parents like mine, where the differences in people were not only respected but also celebrated.

Illegal = the "Other" = Subhuman?

I witnessed hatred for others in my early years as a sexuality educator and hospice nurse. I remember my nurse colleagues looking around at one another when we received our first patient with GRID (Gay Related Immune Deficiency) —the syndrome that would later be called AIDS (Acquired Immune Deficiency Syndrome). One of my co-workers quipped about drawing straws for this assignment; there was a definite sense of *please don't pick me.* I said I'd take him. He wasn't all that much older than the teens I typically cared for and he died at twenty-two. I remember people telling me I shouldn't go to his home to offer care because I had young children and I would "*bring it home.*" After that young man, I was the go-to AIDS nurse.

When I started our outreach in 1988, I stopped clinical nursing but never stopped advocating for respect and education. "It's a virus," I'd say. "Not a judgment. And it doesn't spread casually. Let's talk." I sponsored our first county-wide AIDS Awareness Day program on December 1, 1993. Over three-hundred young people sang and performed spoken word on the courthouse steps. Right after that first AIDS Day program, a teen in one of my sex ed classes told me to stop eating at salad bars just in case someone who was gay selected food. *I'd get infected*, he said. *We should tattoo gay people across their hands*, he said, *so we would know.*

I don't give up on young people. I gave this young man a copy of Elie Wiesel's intense first-person account of the Holocaust, *Night.* I asked him to read it and discuss it with me. He read *Night* and brought the book back. "You think I'm like those people, like the Nazis in Auschwitz?" I asked him if he saw similarities in his thinking. He was only fifteen at the time. I didn't have a peer education program until 1995, but he started hanging out with me when I taught at his school. He listened. I listened to him. One day, another student said something hateful about those living with HIV. This young man looked at me, took a deep breath, and said, "It's a virus. It's not a judgment. And it doesn't spread casually. Let's talk."

Teen Decision-Making

The first of two times I took a busload of teens to D.C. to view the AIDS quilt was in the early nineties. My son was ten and accompanied me. Act Up was demonstrating at the quilt. Two men, dressed all in leather, were kissing with enthusiasm. My boy paused to look, then asked me, "Mom, do those men love each other like you and Dad?"

I said, "Maybe. At least, they seem to be attracted to one another."

My son shrugged, dismissing any adult kissing as incomprehensible, then said, "Okay."

I said, "Many people would be hateful if they saw those men kissing."

My boy asked, "Why? Kissing is weird, but they're just people."

This trip taught me another lesson. Research on adolescent brain development is real. The pre-frontal cortex, the part of the brain responsible for decision making, is maturing as teens reach for adulthood. It's a work in progress. I witnessed an example of the brain's immaturity in D.C.

As my students and I walked around the quilt patches, each one the size of a grave, one of my teens named Alexa approached me. Her face was swollen, her breathing shallow. Alarmed, I asked her what was wrong.

"I'm having an allergic reaction," she said calmly.

"To what?" I looked around for an allergen that could cause these types of symptoms.

She shrugged, non-pulsed. "I'm allergic to chocolate," she said.

I looked at the chocolate ice cream pop dangling from her rapidly swelling fingers.

She shrugged again. "My mom's not here to stop me," she said matter-of-factly.

I sent one of my staff with her to the hospital. Thank goodness, it was close. An entire busload of forty teens and chaperones drove to the hospital on the way home to pick them up. She grinned as she entered the bus, laughing. "I love chocolate," she said. "It was worth it!"

Teachable moments are everywhere!

Was this eighteen-year-old unable to make a good decision because her brain's pre-frontal lobe was still developing? Maybe. Or was she human and rationalized her behavior with the hope her mom was wrong and she'd be fine? Maybe. I only know educators need to teach for all possibilities.

We processed many things on the four-hour bus ride home. We processed the quilt and discussed living with HIV or AIDS. How it must feel to be shunned by family while dying. Why our culture judges people based on their sexuality. How easy it is to hate. How to be an ally, an accomplice, an advocate. And I discussed with Alexa why testing our bodies for known allergens on a field trip wasn't wise!

I will rejoice when no child or adult is treated as if their lives are disposable.

Step #18: Reach Out Without Judging

Hatred is carefully taught.

Children do not hate unless adults coach them to do so.

Stress kindness.

Encourage children supporting others.

Model respect.

CHAPTER TWENTY-ONE

Words Matter

The first time I used the term "words matter," I was in graduate school. A member of my cohort appeared to be a compassionate counselor, but consistently told the kind of jokes that put people down. She was an equal opportunity person when it came to put-downs. Racist jokes, jokes about disabled people, gay jokes—she knew them all. Laughing hilariously after the joke, she said, every single time, "Just kidding."

I invited her to lunch—there's a pattern here about me feeding people to connect, right? To be fair, when I share lunch with someone, I seldom have an agenda. This time, I did. We spoke of her dream of counseling teens. She shared her feeling that this was a calling, a vocation. Hesitant, unsure, I finally brought up the jokes. Shocked, she stared at me. "I don't mean any of that," she argued.

I told her I believed her. "Words matter," I said. Everyone, especially if a person is in power, needs to weigh their words with care. Teachers are in power. Counselors are in power. Parents are in power.

I don't know how she fared, since she left before graduation. I often ponder her cognitive dissonance. Cognitive dissonance refers to a situation where someone's behavior conflicts with their beliefs and attitudes. An example is smoking. In today's world, few people are unaware of smoking's health dangers, yet some people continue to smoke. My grad student colleague allegedly wanted to respect teens and counsel them, but her words contradicted her expressed belief.

The R-Word

Culture changes over time, albeit slowly and sporadically. As a child, saying the R-word was common. It was hurled at friends in a joking way - *You're such a retard* - and became an oft-used adjective - *Look at those retarded shoes!* I don't remember thinking twice about using this word. In my naivete and privilege in ability, the idea of hurting others by slinging this uniquely strange word around never hit me. It sounded weird. We all did it. It was fun.

I was nine or ten the first time my papa heard me say "retarded." It was spring; I know the temperature was pleasant, not too hot. I was jumping rope with friends. Before Title IX, there were few sports experiences available for girls. We jumped rope nightly after school, weather permitting. I don't recall the context—no doubt I told one of my friends they were a retard for some reason that now escapes me.

Papa said nothing. He was consistent about not correcting me in front of peers. His sensitivity to my emotional wellbeing extended even to discipline. When my friends left, he asked if I'd like to go to work with him.

I loved going to work with my father. At the time, he worked as a pressor in a glass factory. The factory was alien to a child—it was hot, with large fires looming from kilns. There were many men, all of them sweaty, all of them acknowledging my papa with respect. As a child, I took this respect for granted. Now, I know it was earned.

My mama and I were studying the book of Revelation. I was too young for its contents and it terrified me at first. I was sure my papa's factory was a sign of things to come. The heat, the fires, the perspiring and solemn men—in my child's mind, this was what hell was like. Still, I loved going to work with Papa. We were alone and could talk or sit in peaceful silence as he drove. Being quiet with my father was one of his best gifts to me. He taught me the goodness of amicable silence in relationships. He was comfortable saying nothing—there was no need for me to fill time with conversation. Plus, we always got ice cream on the way home. Papa was not supposed to eat sweets due to diabetes, but he would wink at me and say, "Don't tell your mother." Inevitably, he'd confess to her – or the dollop of chocolate on his shirt would tell the tale.

The day I called my friend a retard was no different than my other trips to work with Papa. I expected him to pick up his paycheck, introduce me to a few of his co-workers, and leave. I was anticipating ice cream. This day was different, but I didn't know so at first. He brought me deeper into the factory than ever before. I was distracted by the heat until we were standing in front of a large man—a man taller than my papa. Even as young as I was, I knew immediately something was off about this man. His head was large. He limped. One arm was curved toward his chest, as if frozen. His dark eyes peered at me, and I looked away. I felt Papa's hand on my arm and looked up at him.

Papa introduced me to this strange man with great respect, as if I were meeting the pope or the president. His words resonate in my memory. "Mr. Smith," Papa said, "I'd like to introduce you to my daughter, Mary Jo. Mary Jo, this is my co-worker and friend, Mr. Smith. Because of his work, I can do my job. His work is very necessary and good." Papa smiled at us both. "My daughter," he said to the man, "is a kind soul. As are you. I thought you should meet."

Mr. Smith responded, but I don't remember what he said. I remember his speech was slurred and he stuttered. I also remember his smile, and the way he beamed at my papa.

We went for ice cream. On the way home, my father said one thing to me, "Do you understand?"

"Yes, Papa," I said. "I won't say that word again." I have not, and it was painful to me to even write it in this story.

When Papa died, so many older folks came to the viewing that my aunt quipped, "It's like an old age home came on a field trip." One of the mourners stood by the casket, tears streaming down his cheeks. I approached him quickly, seeking to comfort. It was Mr. Smith. It was only then that I heard the story Papa didn't share. Mr. Smith was not part of the union at the factory. As such, he had few rights. His job was to gather the glass that fell or was broken and sweep it up. Papa noticed how he was treated. Men mocked him. Hot glass was put down his trousers. A bully regularly took his lunch, and one day urinated on it, ruining it. Papa saw this. He brought his lunch to where Mr. Smith was seated, sharing his salami sandwich. He rose and went to his boss. Papa requested Mr. Smith be part of his work team. The supervisor told my father Mr. Smith could not do real work. Papa argued to give him a chance.

Mr. Smith told me, at Papa's casket, how he was made the carrying-in boy in my father's work team – the man responsible for taking the hot glass from my Papa and carefully bringing it to the next step in the process. He told me he became part of the union with my father's mentorship. He made a living wage. No other workers bothered him again. Still crying, Mr. Smith said, "Your father made me a man!"

Papa's example taught me without words. I never forgot this lesson and it influenced me when I introduced sexuality education for people of all abilities with our local Arc (The Arc is an organization for people with developmental disabilities). I imagined Mr. Smith and the dignity with which Papa graced his life. I instinctively knew all people deserved information on their sexuality.

Years later, when I overheard teens say, "That's so gay!" I was able to model my papa's wisdom to teach them acceptance and kindness. The bias and microaggressions hurled at LGBTQIA plus teens diminishes their humanity and creates them as "the other." My commitment is to all teens, and Papa's example gave me my foundation for respect.

Empowerment

The word "empowerment" is bantered about in social service and educational circles with impunity. I've read grant proposals, of which few narratives fail to state they will empower youth. As a popular character once said in *The Princess Bride,* "You keep using that word, but I do not think it means what you think it means."

Mentors need to step back after providing young people with guidance and the skills they need to go forward independently. The word "empower" assumes people have no power. Young people are powerful. I cannot give them power they already have, but I can listen to them, support them, and help them use their power. As I write this, the teen survivors of the Parkland school massacre are leading adults. Skeptics claim they are coached, but these people seek to drain their power. We need to listen to hear these young people. They are the future.

Adults enter the helping professions for many reasons. Some seek adulation—they want teens to like them. That's not me. It's not about us. I started the teen outreach with two primary goals: to serve young people with equity, no matter their background or identity or needs, and to nurture the staff of professionals I selected to serve on this mission. When a person becomes part of our staff, I gift them with a book written by one of my heroines, Marion Wright Edelman. *Guide My Feet: Prayers and Meditations for Working with Children* is motivational and inspiring. I don't expect people to pray. We are a secular agency, and each person's belief system is respected. I do find her words support our work. Ms. Edelman is the founder of Children's Defense Fund. I inscribe the book with the date and the words, "Welcome to my mission."

One of my favorite passages from *Guide My Feet* is:

"An African proverb reminds us that the rain falls on all the village huts and not just on some. So it is with violence and drugs and family and cultural decay today. All of us are affected by other people's children, in the fears we harbor, the taxes we pay, the prisons we build, the welfare we love to hate, and in the nagging sense that we're not living up to our professed values of fair opportunity to all."

Her words are as relevant today as they were nearly twenty-five years ago.

Another of my heroes, Dr. Michael Carrera, describes those who serve young people as lifeguards in his book, *Lessons for Lifeguards*. Dr. Carrera's analogy is apt. Lifeguards teach individuals to swim and safeguard them in the water, but their students ultimately swim alone. They're there in a crisis. New staff at the outreach may be surprised when I explain they need to be available for their young clients 24/7, 365 days a year. I don't expect them to forget about their lives, obviously. In fact, I am clear that their families – and children, if they're parents – matter most. If we fail our own young people, we are hypocrites. I help them set boundaries and create a positive work-life balance.

Inappropriate

I try to stay away from teacher lounges. My professional team taught in those forty-eight schools, but I introduced our programs to every one of the thirty districts representing those schools. I taught the first series of classes in each school. Translate those numbers to reflect a lot of teacher lounges, break rooms, and teacher cultures.

I've found amazing, dedicated teachers in each of those schools. Some remain friends to this day. Even when I felt among friends, I was careful to avoid groups of teachers, especially when they thought it was important to alert me to the many behaviors their students engaged in—that they somehow thought I could correct.

One principal told me, "If you can take on sex, you can do anything. Can you fix our drug and alcohol problem?"

A combination of those hands-on experiences in schools and my years serving young people in trouble made me dislike the word "inappropriate." What is appropriate, please? I've listened to so many young people "in the system" bemoan being judged as inappropriate from foster home to foster home, with the rules constantly changing.

People in power define normal. The old joke that normal is just a setting on a dryer is applicable here. In the Netherlands, a Dutch teacher drew me aside to ask for advice. His son was an exchange student in America and had just been given detention for saying a word. I knew immediately which word he meant, but he dutifully continued, "He said 'fuck.' I don't understand. 'Fuck' just means sex. He was told it was inappropriate to use the word."

I explained our cultural standards and said the word was considered profanity. He studied me, then nodded, looking sad but no longer puzzled. "I see," he said. "My son said he often hears Black teens called an English word I taught him never to say. It begins with an 'N.' He hears boys in the locker room call one another a second English word I told him not to say in America, 'faggot.' There are special needs children in his high school, and he hears them called names I won't let him say. No adult seems to correct these teens, but saying a word that means sex is inappropriate." He walked away, shaking his head. My papa would've agreed with him.

Rape

Serving young sexual abuse survivors for decades guides my perspective on other words and their messages. For example, I've never understood why so many headlines read of "underage women" in rape cases. Underage women are children. Language pushes us away from the reality of child sexual abuse to make us picture adult women, not children. Children cannot give consent. Children aren't ready to have a conversation about sex with an adult. Children shouldn't even be exposed to these types of sexual environments.

Again, I use permission forms for sexuality education, even after thirty plus years of teaching. I do so because I honor parents, I respect their values, and I acknowledge their young people are not adults. Our classes are uplifting, empowering, medically accurate, and promote worthiness, yet I honor childhood and families and seek permission. We receive returned forms from 95-98% of students, so our community supports our message.

When media outlets use the phrase "sex with a minor," they ignore the truth that minors are children. Minors cannot legally give consent. Sex with a minor is rape. Call it rape. We need to stop minimizing the exploitive nature of these alleged crimes.

I also see the phrase "child prostitute." Again, a child cannot give consent. A child cannot willingly be a sex worker. Those children are victims of rape or are sexual assault survivors. If we use these words, we can distance ourselves from the reality of child trafficking, the exploitation of runaways, and parents who sell their own children for sex or child pornography. We must talk about this with transparency.

Words make a difference. Rape is rape is rape is rape. The term "non-consensual sex" is hurtful and wrong. Rape isn't about sex, it's about power. If a sexual act is non-consensual, it's rape. Stop watering down these crimes against children.

Until we change words, we will not transform our culture into one of respect, where rape is a crime, making it safe for victims to come forward and be believed, and for survivors to seek the help they need to heal. Victims and survivors need validation and protection. I stand with Darkness to Light Stewards of Children as an authorized facilitator committed to making a difference in child sexual abuse. D2L talks about child sexual abuse as a "crime that thrives in secrecy."

Actions Matter, Too

I was a Girl Scout leader for thirteen years, first for our daughter Amy's troop, and then for Lisa's. At one point, I had forty-five Brownies in the troop and needed to close registration! At each first meeting, I scheduled one parent to attend for each five girls the entire year. We did amazing things! Our ceremonies were fun but serious, our color guard respectful of the flag, our outings planned by our scouts. My idea of camping is a Holiday Inn, but I dutifully took my scouts to Camp Henry Kaufmann and Camp Redwing. One night, a few girls came to me screaming. A spider was in their tent! Every time I tell this story, that damn spider gets bigger in my mind. I patiently coaxed it onto a large leaf (it was a big spider, honest), and liberated it into the wild. I wanted my scouts to be respectful of nature.

Over twenty years later, I ran into one of those scouts, now in her thirties. We had a joyful reunion, and I asked her if she remembered the spider. Nope, she did not. I rattled off many things we did as a troop. No reaction. Finally, I asked what she remembered.

"I remember going to the Ice Capades in Pittsburgh. Most of us had to go to the bathroom. The line for the women's room was so long. You went into the men's room and made sure it was empty, then stood guard while we used it."

Frustrated, I thought, *THIS is what she remembers?* Then, she said, "You taught us a good thing that day. We were just as important as the boys. It was okay to ask for what we needed." Okay, I'll take it.

Another way I empower is through our Common Ground Teen Center. I'm incredibly proud of the young people who attend. Each May, I hire five or six seniors to supervise the center. They open and close, facilitate meetings, clean up, take care of leftovers (I feed them a lot), and safeguard our guidelines of respect. One teen is hired as the supervisor and creates monthly schedules without my assistance. I pay them at least ten dollars an hour. Young people are worthy.

Each teen attendee signs a contract, which is witnessed by another young person. If the contract is breached, the Teen Executive Board meets to determine consequences. I sit on the board, but I do not direct their decisions.

I taught a webinar on youth self-advocacy for the PA Department of Education in February of 2018. Seven peer educators presented the webinar with me. One of these exceptional young people, Toni Maurer, said this about the topic: "I think one of the things that helps with the advocacy is your trust in us. It's not just that we run the center, we are the executive board, we write our plays, we create the anthology. It's the fact that you trust us to do so, and that makes every person want to do it more. Your trust in us allows us to be open and free to be ourselves and express ourselves in all we do. Adults inspire the next generation."

People ask me why the center works so well. I explain that I assume the best from these young people, and they rise to that standard. They've earned my trust. They don't need me. I enjoy spending time with them, but they can function alone.

I listen to them teach and facilitate and I'm proud. They live the maxim, "Words matter." I see them weigh words with caution and release them with respect. Children have an amazing way of growing into the type of people we tell them they are.

It's worth repeating:

If we tell children they're strong, they grow to be strong.
If we tell children they're kind, they grow to be kind.
If we tell children they're capable, they grow to be capable.
Words matter.

If teens can treat words with respect, so can adults.

Step #20: Think Before You Speak + Be Aware That Children Listen and Model After Adults

Give feedback with care and respect.

Everyone makes mistakes with words. Apologize sincerely if you do.

Don't make the apology about you. For example, if a young person is misgendered – called by the wrong name or addressed with the wrong pronoun – emotional pain may result. Say you're sorry and let it go.

Don't spend time drawing attention to yourself, seeking forgiveness.

It's not about us.

CHAPTER TWENTY-TWO

Labels

When our peer educators worked on the Smash the Stereotypes theme, one brought me a meme that said, "Label jars, not people." I loved it! People do label others, though, consistently and from a young age. Not only do we need to introduce self-worth, sexual health, consent, and body image from early childhood, we also must present our children with kindness and model empathy.

Seven-Year-Old Bullying

As a Brownie leader, a new girl joined my first troop. She wasn't dressed as well as most of the scouts, and the other girls told me she smelled. At times, she did. They ostracized her. I observed, hoping a child would stand with her, but they kept to their own friend groups. I decided to support the child – I'll call her Carrie – by making sure she had a place at the table, literally, for dining and crafts. I placed her near my daughter, whose kindness to this day is exemplary. Amy is a Girl Scout leader now, which proves her dedication to children.

I didn't want to state the obvious. I wanted to preserve the little girl's dignity. I felt I couldn't say, "Carrie may not have the type of home you are privileged to live in. She may not have a shower or a washer and dryer. Her parents may not be able to provide for her."

Instead, I watched who picked Carrie up after each meeting - an assortment of different people in different cars. Troubled, I called her mom and asked if I could arrange a play date. She agreed enthusiastically. When I went to her home, I wasn't surprised. I'd been in far less hospitable environments on home visits with young clients. Carrie lived in a tiny, run-down basement apartment in an unsavory part of the city. Two rooms filled with five children and a mother, no shower I could see, just a miniscule bathroom with a small sink and a toilet.

We spent a pleasant afternoon at the park, where the girls played on the swings and ate a picnic lunch. Carrie was shy at first but warmed up to playing. It was a beautiful day.

At the next meeting, I was determined to make a change in my troop. I picked Carrie up so the girls coming to the meeting saw her with me. Some of them paused, a few ran to my car to help me carry supplies and welcomed her. My heart cautiously leapt. I knew children's social interactions can't be forced, but adults are guides and set the tone. No one would be bullied in my "house."

As we entered the meeting space, a group of six girls ran up to Carrie, hands raised. "Put on your Carrie shields," they crowed. Carrie's face became blank as she withdrew.

I gathered the girls together to start the meeting, placing Carrie near me in our circle. After each child shared something about her day, I said, "Who can tell me what it means to be kind?"

I steered the conversation without referring to Carrie, but firmly directed my Brownies to think of what it felt like if they weren't treated as if they mattered. *Had they ever felt left out?*

I had a large troop of forty-five Brownies. Hands flew up. Girls with parents in custody battles, girls whose older brothers were mean (from their perspective), girls who didn't like a teacher in school, girls who felt their friends from preschool were leaving them out. *Wow!* My craft for the evening was put on hold. I glanced at Carrie. She didn't look at me, but after about a half hour, her hand went up. I called on her.

Carrie took a deep breath and said, "I feel happy when people treat me nice." Her voice shook, "I'd never put up a shield against any of you."

The girls were immediately quiet. I let them sit in silence.

One of the six said softly, "I'm sorry, Carrie. That wasn't kind."

It seemed as if the tension Carrie was holding dripped away, like rain wiped from a windshield. I did our closing of holding hands in the circle and singing and broke out our treats. The girls started their craft, but we completed it the next week. As we cleaned up, one mother slid beside me. "Thank goodness you're a counselor. Last week I was ready to hit my kid upside the head." Her daughter was one of the six who created the imaginary shield. Before I could acknowledge her, another mother came over and boldly told me I had no right intervening in "normal childhood pecking orders."

I told her bullying was not normal to me. I told her I'd be happy to sit and listen to her. I thought she'd pull her daughter from the troop, but she remained. We spoke privately, and, eventually, she mellowed. I never shook the feeling that she was very comfortable encouraging her child to be in power, though.

Carrie and her family moved away from our school in another month—a pattern, sadly, for her family. We lost her.

I know many Carries. Whether labeled by poverty, race, sexual or gender identity, ability or ranking in a school, these labels stick.

Teaching with Theatre

One of our Real Talk Performers plays from 2010 was called *Labels*. It was creative and innovative, and our peer educators were bold and brave. Each performer wore three shirts in a special order. The bottom shirt was printed with a huge label on the front and represented positive character traits. The second shirt was grey.

During the play's first act, each performer received different colored t-shirts imprinted with common teen labels. The labels included: jock, slut, gay, nerd, player, cheerleader, prep, punk, bully, virgin, stoner, loser, boy?, girl?, and gimp.

During the play, the performers discussed the idea of being labeled and brought the audience to an awareness of unjust labeling. In the final act, each performer removed the label shirt and the grey one to reveal the affirmation shirts, announcing "I know I am…" The affirmations included: accepted, independent, complete, sexual, educated, respected, complicated, understood, strong, intelligent, brave, good friends, wise, not alone, resilient, kind, misunderstood, amazing, and compassionate.

Our pre and post-tests showed an increased knowledge of the word "empathy," and statements came from the audience like, "Labeling and judging someone is wrong," and, "Labels are superficial."

Adults have the power to diminish the pain of labeling young people.

Step #21: Avoid Labeling Any Person

Start with example.

Model kindness.

It's okay to not understand young people's identities. It is not okay to judge them or hate them or limit their human rights.

CHAPTER TWENTY-THREE

Perfect

Before you begin thinking my parents were perfect, they weren't. Neither am I, thank goodness. Being human, making mistakes, the reality of frailty - these are attributes that come together to create counselors and educators who connect with young people. I need my imperfections.

My parents tried their best. Not all people can make such a statement. I know I'm blessed. I was the result of a very desired pregnancy after seventeen years of marriage, and raising me was my parents' primary vocation. I benefited from their commitment to me. The areas in which they made errors also formed me. I blossomed under their guidance and I grew in resiliency when they stumbled.

My mama suffered from depression most of her life. In my family's culture, this wasn't discussed, at least not with me. I think she dealt with postpartum depression at my birth, since I was told stories (as an adult) of my aunt spending time with us "until she was better," and I don't think her healing was only physical. I know she had what was called a "nervous breakdown" - which I understand now was a psychotic break – when I was in first grade, because I have vague memories of another aunt moving in with us. Mental illness is not a fault, but the way my

Papa and my extended family reacted to it was.

When my youngest was born, I witnessed my mama's abrupt change in behavior for the first time as an adult. His birth was an emergency cesarean, and my mother's fear of surgery was nearly overwhelming. Her mother – the grandmother I never knew – was admitted to the hospital for a hysterectomy and never returned. Family lore says she was given blood that was typed and crossed incorrectly. When I was sent to the OR for the birth of our son, something slipped in Mama's mind. Her fear of losing me, as she lost her mother, without closure (in 1923 there were no hospital visiting hours for an eleven-year-old), brought her to a clinical depression. She experienced a psychotic break – the first of my adulthood. My papa recognized the signs he'd seen repeatedly during their marriage, but never discussed with me. I recognized the fitful pacing, verbal hallucinations, blank affect, and paranoia I'd witnessed as a young RN in psych.

I found myself postpartum with a newborn, two small daughters, an abdominal incision, and a mom on the edge. Papa tried to cover for her as he did when I was a child; I saw the way Papa tried to camouflage the worst of it from me. It all echoed within me. I was a professional counselor now, and I knew. When she started talking suicide, I secured therapy for her. She did well. Nearly eighteen months later, she remarked to me casually, "I had no idea doctors and medicine could help so much!"

As an advocate for removing the stigma associated with mental illness, I often encounter negativity. I strive for patience, but it's challenging. I picture my mama and the way treatment brought her back to us. I imagine the many years when a lack of education about mental health condemned her to struggle without professional care.

My mom's psychotic break in 1985 brought with it a tsunami of childhood memories and cracked the wall I'd carefully erected over her "sick times" in my childhood. I remembered her disjointed movements, her periodic near catatonia, her lack of eye contact; I recalled the days when she retired to a darkened bedroom alone. Through it all, Papa was there. I often tell families that a child doesn't require two nurturing adults in their lives to survive and thrive – one solid parent figure is enough. Papa held us both up. When she was well, Mama was 100% present. I never doubted her love. In fact, her love for me was fierce and her fear for my wellbeing made her anxiety intense enough to implode. A vivid memory: I returned from a church youth group meeting when I was a new driver. I was about fifteen minutes late. I found Mama in a fetal position in the hallway, rocking back and forth. I now know dreadful images of how a child's possible pain can haunt a parent. For Mama, those images were real.

I also now know education might have penetrated the cocoon of protection Papa created with the best of intentions. Keeping her "safe at home" felt right to him, but it didn't help her heal.

Mental Health and Teens

Stigma still lingers over mental illness. One never hears a person with a fractured limb advised to "shake it off" and "make yourself better," but individuals dealing with a mental health diagnosis receive such messages with regularity. Is it the invisibility of their illnesses driving this attitude, or is it fear? Are we anxious about what cannot be seen? Does the apparent lack of control over mental illness terrify?

Too many young people in need of therapy deny themselves help. Too often, the adults in their lives think their behavior is "just a phrase" they'll pass through.

Depression is particularly troubling. Studies estimate that 20% of our teens suffer from depression. Just as children may not say they're sad but may complain of stomachaches or headaches, teens with depression may show anger or aggressive behavior instead of the withdrawal most adults expect to see.

Suicide and 13 Reasons Why

In my opinion, it is vital to teach education that alerts young people to ways teens may act when they're at risk for suicide. Knowing that depression, withdrawing from social connection, radical changes in eating habits (overeating or undereating), talking about leaving possessions to others, saying "No one would miss me if I was gone," or, "I'm so useless, I don't matter," or talking about dying should not be ignored. Teens are not counselors, they should not be taught they are responsible for the lives of others. They do need to know how to connect with a trusted adult. I believe raising awareness can help young people help others by reaching out to an adult who can make a difference.

In the nineties, I spearheaded a program called Yellow Ribbon in co-operation with several wonderful community agencies. Among other suicide prevention goals, Yellow Ribbon (yellowribbon.org) teaches teens to be alert for suicidal ideation and comments from their peers. Training was school-wide. I encountered an interesting phenomenon promoting the program: many adults feared discussing suicide would cause suicide! Like the anxiety against sex ed and the belief that talking about sex would make young people have sex, suicide was deemed an unsafe topic.

The controversial Netflix series *13 Reasons Why* brought suicide into discussion. We created a lesson plan using the shows episodes, including topics for discussion. My contention that the show was unhealthy is supported by many mental health professionals. The protagonist, Hannah, leaves thirteen taped cassettes accusing those she felt drove her to her suicide, which was portrayed in graphic detail. The idea of retribution after death – of essentially having the last word by blaming people for why she took her life – was troubling to me. I saw it as a teachable moment. Our peer educators facilitated excellent conversations. we addressed the show's messages clearly and with guidance. Our teens supported each other.

The peer-reviewed Journal of the American Academy of Child and Adolescent Psychiatry released a study in March, 2019, reporting a 29% increase in suicides among American teens ages ten to seventeen in the month after *13 Reasons Why* aired. The link between the show and suicides is correlational; it does not prove cause and effect. Netflix added warning signs and also created 13ReasonsWhy.info resource page and promoted the Crisis Text Line (text REASON to 741741) and the National Suicide Prevention Lifeline (1-800-273-8255). SAVE (Suicide Awareness Voices of Education) created an online 13ReasonsWhy Toolkit to help adults help young people process the show. Two years after the show aired, as the third season is being filmed, producers announced they would remove the scene where Hannah takes her own life in Season 1. Too little, in my opinion, too late.

Teens Who Become Their Diagnoses

As a young counselor, I seldom encountered children diagnosed with bipolar disorder. The consensus seemed to be that young people's emotions were naturally labile—swinging in ups and downs. Over time, psychologists and pediatricians agree that some children fit into a bipolar diagnosis. Symptoms to look for in a child are:

- Atypical, severe mood swings unlike the child's usual moodiness

- Risky, reckless behaviors that are not usual for the young person

- Inflated ideas of their own capabilities beyond typically teen or tween invulnerability

- Depressive episodes nearly every day.

- Insomnia or significantly low need for sleep.

- Aggressive, impulsive, or hyperactive behavior.

- Suicidal thoughts or behaviors

These symptoms may originate from ADHD (attention deficit hyperactive disorder), operational defiant disorder, clinical depression, or anxiety disorder, so diagnosis can be challenging. From my perspective as someone working one-on-one with a young person, it can be disconcerting for a thirteen-year-old to sit across from me in my therapy room and declare, "I'm bipolar," by way of introduction.

I've also been told, "I'm borderline," or "I'm depressed," or "I cut," before anything else is said. I typically respond with, "I'm Mary Jo. What's your name?" At times, young people appear to "own" these mental health diagnoses, using them as an excuse for behavior, "I'm sorry, but you do know I'm bipolar?" or vomiting their symptoms without any apparent emotional stress.

I was observed through a two-way mirror and videotaped as part of my master's work in counseling. One of my first young patients said "Hi" and then launched into a detailed story of past sexual abuse, mental health inpatient stays, and several diagnoses. I thought highly of myself; I'd drawn this complicated history from this young teen on our first encounter. My professor was less complimentary.

"She's a professional victim and patient, Mary Jo," she said. "It's not you or your technique. She'd tell the whole story to the maintenance staff. She no longer feels her past."

ACEs and Adulthood

I know my mama's recurring depression colored my choice of profession. If introspective, I realize I wanted to make her feel better, and sought out a field where I could help others. Having a parent with a mental health issue like clinical depression is considered an ACE (Adverse Childhood Experience). A 2018 study in JAMA Pediatrics confirms ACEs as universal and found that one of every five American adults had at least one adverse experience in childhood, like divorce, a parent's death, physical or emotional abuse, or a family member's incarceration or substance abuse problem. One-fourth of adults have at least three ACEs, which other research shows increases risk for common chronic disease, like heart disease, cancer, and depression.

The JAMA Pediatrics study also revealed differences in some groups. People in low socioeconomic groups, people of color, and people idenitfy as LGBT had significantly higher chances of experiencing adversity in childhood.

Adults serving young people need to be aware of the long-term effects of ACEs on their mental and physical health and plan interactions accordingly.

Mistakes

I was fortunate in that both my parents were open to admitting their mistakes. They told me they were sorry when things didn't go well instead of affecting an all-knowing parental attitude. Growing up with my mama gave me resilience and taught me to admit my mistakes. I hope my mistakes and imperfections made my own children resilient. I admitted my mistakes as they grew, and I admit them to my students.

I believe adults need to:

- openly admit their mistakes.

- apologize to young people when they're wrong.

- not act like you know more than them just because you're older.

- listen to them.

- say *thank you* to them when they've done something helpful.

Each of us can learn from the gift of imperfection.

Step #22: Raise Awareness for Mental Health

Be aware of signs of teen depression.

Be an advocate for suicide prevention.

Pay attention to shows young people watch.

Read YA (young adult) books, like *Perks of Being a Wallflower,* and use them to connect.

Remove stigma from mental health issues every day.

CHAPTER TWENTY-FOUR

Me, Too

As I write this, the #MeToo movement is sweeping the nation. As a woman, I applaud this effort. As a counselor serving young sexual abuse and assault survivors for over forty years, my heart is here. Words matter. Young people who endured abuse are survivors, not victims. Any person courageous enough to speak the truth about sexual harassment, gender inequality, and sexual violence and coercion is a warrior. Visibility matters. Young people tell me they often feel invisible to adults.

"I feel invisible when people think I don't want to do well in school."
-fifteen-year-old
"I feel invisible when teachers don't know what my family is really like."
–thirteen-year-old
"I feel invisible when everyone thinks I'm straight."
-seventeen-year-old
"I feel invisible when my parents fight about me."
-ten-year-old

The #MeToo movement brings sexual assault survivors into visibility.

Another group of individuals who are often invisible are those living with disability. My own personal #MeToo advocacy was created long before the #Me-Too movement and hashtag. It isn't connected to sexual harassment or assault. I'd taught young people living with different abilities inclusively since I founded the teen outreach. My philosophy was simple: Each person is worthy of information. Each person is worthy of respect.

When I first refused access to a student's aide in one of my classes, I met resistance, even though I was respectful. The excuses were well-intentioned. *How will my student cope in your class? What if this information is overwhelming?* I patiently explained the way my classes worked. They were conversations, not lectures. They were interactive, not passive. Every student had the right to pass. Every student was respected. I tried to draw a verbal picture. If an adult attended, all the students would be on edge. My class was a confidential one. Our students knew and trusted me, but the addition of a new person would be awkward. Finally, I played my ace card: *I know you want the best for this young person. You can remain directly outside the classroom and I'll send for you if you're needed. This class can give your student something intangible, that no other experience can give. By attending this class without an aide, your young person will be part of a peer group. The topic of sexuality will be normalized for someone for whom the subject is often ignored. Your actions will teach. What you do will speak louder than words and resonate through this young person's life.*

To date, students with different abilities do well in my class. Like all my students, they inspire me to be a better teacher. My fondest memory of in-school inclusion was a young man of fifteen who communicated using a computer. He verbalized sounds, but not words. On the sixth day of class, the subject of masturbation was brought up by another student. As our discussion centered upon how normal touching was, this young man brightened. He cried out, "Uh huh," loudly, and using his own voice. There was a moment of silence, then the other students laughed. He laughed with them, then typed, "Thank you!"

Dating

Another story that resonates with me involved a ninth grader I'd known since sixth grade. Todd is autistic. One day, he approached me and matter-of-factly said he wanted to ask out a fellow student. He asked how to do so. We role played the conversation at least six times. I asked questions to give him a chance to practice, posing as his intended date. *Where would we go on this date?* The movies, he said. *Who would drive us?* His mom, he said. *Would we go out to eat after the movies.* Yes, he said. Finally, he felt ready. The day he asked out his crush, he came to me at lunch and said, "It didn't work."

It's impossible to describe Todd's affect. It's not exactly flat, but his tone of voice is devoid of emotion. He speaks his mind and is articulate, but Spock would rival him in his lack of inflection. Concerned about his emotional wellbeing, I engaged him in conversation, hoping to discover what "It didn't work" meant. When I understood his overtures for a date were rejected, I began to plan a way to guide him through the experience. I asked, "Would you like to share what happened?"

He shrugged. "I asked her to have sex with me. She said *no.*"

Surprised, I stared at him. In the many times we role-played this conversation, sex was never discussed. I shared my confusion, and he shook his head.

"I don't want to go to the movies," he declared with confidence. "I want to have sex."

I asked him how he felt.

"Fine," he said. "I wouldn't want to have sex with someone who didn't want to do it."

Teaching young people communication and respect for consent is a huge part of my mission. If only adults were taught the same, #MeToo wouldn't be needed.

Do You Believe Me?

I'm typically called in consultation when a disabled person's sexual behavior is considered a problem by caregivers. Commonly, that translates into self-touch. Using behavior modification to make masturbation private isn't the problem. Too often, staff don't believe a person who is differently able has sexual needs.

A true paradox exists. One myth about individuals with ID (intellectual disability) is that they are childlike and not interested in sex. The opposite is also a common myth. Some people judge those living with ID as predators who are prone to rape. Neither myth is true. People are people, and living with a disability does not make a person over or under sexed.

I was asked to meet with a fifteen-year-old many years ago. Her special ed teachers feared she would have sex "promiscuously" (another word I dislike). In our first meeting, she was quiet for a long twenty minutes after I introduced myself, told her I taught sex ed, and would answer any of her questions. I told her I would meet with her weekly if she wanted me to. I told her I respected her. I assured her of my confidentiality. Then, silence, very little eye contact, and a lot of finger drumming and bouncing knees. I fought not to look at the clock as the silence dragged on! Finally, she asked me why I was there. I repeated I was there to answer her questions, but she interrupted me.

"My teachers think I'm gonna do it," she said matter-of-factly. "I know you teach about sex, but my class doesn't get to go."

I assured her I could fix that and she smiled, then said, "My daddy taught me how to do sex.

Red flags waved in my mind. "Your daddy did?" I asked. "Would you be okay telling me when he taught you?"

Five. She told me she was five and her father took her into the bathroom and taught her what good little girls did with the daddies. She said her daddy told her all little girls learned to make their daddies feel good. My heart hurt. One challenge of teaching with heart means you feel intensely when you learn of injustice and pain. I waited a moment. It didn't take long for her to continue.

"I can give really good blow jobs," she finished confidently, then sat back and stared at me.

When I explained I needed to report this to someone else, she didn't object. It was a rough afternoon. She ended up in foster care for a while. Dad was arrested, her mom didn't react well. When her father went to prison, she was sent to an aunt's home. She loved this aunt and was pleased.

I met with her weekly for over a year. Every session, she asked me the same thing, "Do you believe me?"

This young person of worth had disclosed her abuse repeatedly for ten years, but no one believed her because she was deemed not bright enough to know the truth. Her father was well thought of at church and in the community. It was easier not to believe.

Collaboration

In 2010, I embarked on an adventure with an organization in our local community called The Arc, which promotes community involvement, independence, and dignity for children and adults with intellectual and developmental disabilities. I was asked to teach their staff about sexuality. I didn't want to do a typical in-service. We set out to transform the culture surrounding sexuality education for people of different abilities. To do so, I took a systemic approach. I trained two groups of master teachers over the course of eighteen months. Those trained educators then taught the staff in group homes, the group home staff then taught residents.

We quickly moved into working with self-advocates. Self-advocates are individuals who represent the community of learners being targeted. My papa taught me to seek wisdom from the people I seek to reach. He often said, "If you want to know what an Italian-American needs, you need to listen to an Italian-American." Once more, his guidance prepared me. I believe it is presumptuous and disrespectful when a group of people meet to discuss the needs of another group without inclusion. I learned from the self-advocates at The Arc. We ultimately created a book about abuse prevention for disabled adults that was real. Photos of self-advocates make the book theirs, and their input was crucial. I listened. I learned.

Setting guidelines is part of every educational experience I facilitate. I set the stage for learning. When I train facilitators, be they peer educators or professionals or self-advocates, they are taught to set guidelines and create a safe place. Our self-advocates do very well with this concept. One self-advocate named Steve can be counted on to make the group smile. When his turn to set guidelines arrives, everyone waits in quiet anticipation as he leads a conversation on the meaning of respectful discussion, confidentiality, laughing together and not at one another, and other promises the group chooses. Then, with a twinkle in his eye, Steve inevitably adds, "One more. No one may fart."

Myths about sexuality and those living with disabilities are polarized. On one hand, such individuals are often considered asexual. They are dehumanized and desexualized as if they were child-like all their lives. Yet, an equally well-known myth claims an individual with different abilities is over-sexed, a potential predator, and out of control. The paradox is real. Like all people, each disabled individual is a unique person. Abilities are vastly different as well. Some individuals with intellectual disabilities want a sexual partner; some think of kissing as the ultimate act of sexual connection. People living on the autism spectrum may be romantic but asexual (not wanting to be sexually involved), or aromantic (not wanting dates or romance) but sexual.

Generalizing groups of humans is a mistake. Our first task was conveying the message that each person deserves information on sexual health.

My Me Too

The book that resulted from this partnership is called *Me Too*. One of my long-term students named it. Josh has a left-sided hemiparesis – a weakness in the left side of his body. Because of cerebral palsy, his speech is difficult to understand. He drools constantly. He's also bright and curious and one of my favorite students. We met when he was in eighth grade, and he was thrilled when his aide did not enter class with him. His mom and I became good friends. He's in his twenties now. In 2012, I visited Josh to discuss my work with the residents at The Arc. He was thrilled. We were eating pizza in his kitchen. When I asked Josh what I should call this program for people with different abilities, he was about to take a bite of pizza. He thrust the pizza into his chest in his enthusiasm and declared the words, "Me too." His mom smiled. She was truly his ally and advocate, pushing for inclusion and independence for her son. She asked him, "Tell us what you mean?" and he responded, "It's for me, too. Sex ed is for me, too."

I love doing trainings for *Me Too*, especially with self-advocates, who are my teachers as well. I did a training in Harrisburg, Pennsylvania right after the #MeToo movement began. The #MeToo movement focuses on individuals speaking out about sexual assault and harassment. One of my workshop participants asked me if I would change my program's name. I thought about it, and said no. Too many people know my work by the title *Me Too* to change it, and my support for the stories behind both versions of *Me Too* is lifelong.

They say any publicity is good. I don't know if retaining the Me Too name for our work with sexuality and disability is wise, but I do know one thing for certain. I won't disrespect Josh and the other self-advocates whose wisdom leads me. The reason for selecting Me Too to describe this program is important.

I can only pray that both missions – the #MeToo movement to support survivors and my *Me Too* program to help disabled individuals be visible and respected – thrive.

"Nothing about us without us" is a rallying cry for disability advocacy. Hear those words.

Step #23: Individuals with Disabilities are Worthy of Information on Sexual Health

Model respect for each person's sexuality.

Teach with respect.

Believe survivors.

Don't let bias towards disabled people assume a false accusation of abuse.

Protect while encouraging independence.

CHAPTER TWENTY-FIVE
Pain and Healing

We are all healers, if we open our hearts to the pain of another person. I remember when the pain scale was first developed. I was a young nurse at Children's Hospital. Prior to its use, health care providers struggled with assessing a person's impression of pain levels. *Knife-like, hot, intense, too much, like a sledgehammer in my chest...* words don't quantify pain. The pain scale isn't perfect. A teen dealing with osteogenic sarcoma once told me, "Ten isn't high enough!" John Green's *The Fault in Our Stars* describes its young protagonist saving her ten for a deeper pain. Still, quantifying pain as 1 – 10 can help healers.

When it ends, pain leaves us amnesic, with only memories of our distress but little to recall the actual intensity. In labor with our second child, a pregnancy I campaigned to conceive over five years, I told Rich, "This was all your idea," at eight centimeters dilated. I suddenly remembered the intensity of the pain! It took experience to bring the totality of it back to me.

Pain is complicated.

Emily Dickinson wrote:

Pain — has an Element of Blank —
It cannot recollect
When it begun — or if there were
A time when it was not —

It has no Future — but itself —
Its Infinite realms contain
Its Past — enlightened to perceive
New Periods — of Pain.

I learned to be a healer as a child. I didn't know what it meant to hold space with someone, but I spent many hours simply sitting in the dark with my mother, offering my presence. Even then, I knew the solidarity of my body beside hers was grounding. She was comforted. I didn't understand how, but I understood the need.

Evil Eye

Mama also taught me to remove the evil eye from someone. Her intelligence didn't override her superstition. In Mama's world, the evil eye or *malocchio* (pronounced in our family as *maloik*) was real. You may have seen a horn, called a *corno*, worn on a necklace. It's often gold and is thought to be a charm against the evil eye.

Mama fervently believed in this curse. Placed upon someone by a jealous person, she was convinced the malocchio had the ability to cause harm, especially headaches or stomachaches. At its worst, it could cause misfortune. She also felt the evil eye could be placed on someone inadvertently, without malice, just by expressing praise. If someone said, "Your baby is so beautiful," Mama would mumble

"Benedica," short for "God bless," under her breath. She taught me to roll my hand into a fist behind my back, placing my thumb between my first and second fingers, while mentally saying *Scatia malocchio*, or, "Go away, evil eye." (I've researched this phrase and it's not accurate Italian. Nevertheless, this is what I was taught.) In Italy, as an adult, I shared this bizarre ritual with a guide at Sorento. He laughed and quickly gestured for me to open my hand. "That means 'fuck you,'" he said, grinning. I was shocked! My little Italian mama, who never cursed, taught her daughter an obscene gesture!

Mama taught me how to remove malocchio. First, one must diagnose it. Sufferers are placed in a darkened room, asked to lie down and close their eyes. A shallow bowl is filled with holy water. Olive oil is then dripped into the bowl in three plops while the bowl is held over the person's head. The bowl is then moved in a circle over the head while prayers are mumbled. If the oil remains in firm circles in the water, the person is unaffected. If it dissipates, then more prayer must be offered, sometimes holding hands. The person has the evil eye. Mama would place her hands over where the pain lived and move her hands in circles over it, without touching, all the while breathing slowly and purposefully with her patient.

Even as a child, I was skeptical. Too much voodoo for my realistic soul. I did learn how much the quiet room, the soft mumblings of inarticulate prayers, the instruction to *breathe slow and deep,* and the laying on of hands calmed people. Left alone then, to allow the evil eye time to leave, people often fell asleep. Mama would play soft music on the stereo and tip-toe from the room.

I now realize I come by my desire to heal honestly, from my mama. It was the young people I serve, however, who taught me how to heal.

The Reality of Being There

When I first began working with young survivors of sexual abuse, it was overwhelming. I was young. I had no frame of reference for this pain. Even now, many years later, I cannot conceptualize the trauma, but I've learned how to ease the hurt and move the child towards healing.

My staff and I receive calls 24/7. We set boundaries, of course—we must to achieve work-life balance. Establishing a definition for emergency is key. Back when pagers were our primary communication, a teen paged me with a 911 emergency code. I rushed to find a pay phone. Her emergency? She needed a ride to the mall.

During my first China trip, my phone plan charged $2.99 for each text. I carefully set boundaries, giving each young person I served an alternative number from my staff, but assuring them they could connect to me directly if it was a true emergency. Some situations are tough to share with a stranger. I received fifteen texts while gone. No problem. I responded to each, reminding them that I was in China. There was only one wrinkle. Ten of them sent me another text, apologizing. One well-meaning teen apologized twice! At nearly three dollars a text, those were expensive apologies.

Long before my first China trip, a call came through on my home phone one Sunday morning as I prepared for church. This memory is from the days before cell phones, when even home phones were not portable. The caller was a fifteen-year-old sophomore at one of my schools. I'd taught her class only once, but I'd placed my phone number and name on the board and encouraged connection. Her voice was shaky, I could hear the tears. She told me she'd just been raped by a friend of her father's. Asleep in her room, she was awakened by his hand on her mouth and his erect penis penetrating her vagina. It was her first experience with anything sexual. When she told her father, he said, "What did you do to come on to him?"

I never made it to church that day. I made sure she was safe, calling her aunt, who took her to the ER for a rape kit. Despite helping her, her aunt also blamed her for the attack. After alerting the police and CYS, I connected with her again. We spent over an hour on the phone.

I had no idea who she was until I saw her at my office the next day. I testified at the trial, watched as her father brushed past her outside the courtroom, furious that his friend would go to jail.

A few days later, she dropped an envelope off at my office. It was her thank you. Her words were heartfelt and beautiful. She used phrases like, "Here for me," and, "The only person who heard me." I sank into a chair and re-read the handwritten note. My heart was heavy.

When I first began reaching out to young people, a note like hers would've made me feel good. I might have even congratulated myself on being at the right place at the right time to support her. I was wiser that day. All I felt was sorrow. *What type of world have we created?* This young woman had no real support. Even the aunt who took her to the hospital did so reluctantly, making comments under her breath about leading men on. I'd met this young woman once, in a classroom with twenty other sophomores. *How desperate was she to call a stranger for help?*

Healing took a long while. She needed to move past her family's hateful words as much as the rape. Her father and aunt's words assaulted her spirit just as the sexual assault violated her body.

A colleague in the Netherlands once told me her opinion on sexual abuse in America. "You damage young survivors twice," she said. Once when the assault occurs, and again when shame and guilt damage young people's spirits. This same colleague also summed up the difference in her nation's approach to sexuality education and ours: "In my country, we know our children will eventually have sex, and we teach them accordingly. In America, you pretend they never will."

Step #24: Offer Unconditional Love and Acceptance

Please don't base love or acceptance for a teen on their sexual experiences or their sexuality.

Being there means going above and beyond.

Connection needs time, trust, and commitment.

Respond to connection with honesty and humility.

When a young person discloses something, they honor us.

CHAPTER TWENTY-SIX

Forgiveness

I've believed in forgiveness since my parents modeled it for me. My mama said she was treated poorly by Papa's father before I was born, as if their problems with infertility were hers alone. She explained she loved her husband and his family and wanted me to love my grandfather. I watched her forgive. I learned from her.

My parents had sixty-four years together until they died four months apart. I loved their stories, especially of their meeting. My mama was a shy twenty-year-old, whose world - since she left school - was her home, where she cared for her younger siblings. My papa was an equally shy nineteen-year-old, who was placed in first grade when he arrived in America at fourteen. He told me that sitting in the tiny seats was mortifying. He respectfully waited until the class had recess and left. He walked until he found a coal mine, lied about his age (he had to be sixteen to work in the mine), and worked hard every day of his life.

They met at a wedding. My mama was a bridesmaid, my papa a grooms-man. According to the oft-repeated story, he noticed her right away and threw a grape at her during the reception to get her attention. Later, when I was an adult, he told me the full story: "Your mama was so beautiful, but I didn't know how to talk to her. So, I threw a grape right at her breast." My papa was real, down to earth, and deeply in love with my mama.

When he asked her to marry him, his father did not approve. Even though my mama was Italian, she was born in America and had no mother to raise her as a proper Italian girl. According to my mama's story, my grandfather gave my papa an ultimatum: Leave this "American" girl or lose any financial support. Mama told me they were in my grandparents' living room. My papa stood beside his father as he was told to abandon Mama. He didn't disrespect his father, nor did he speak. He simply walked over to my mama and put his arms around her.

Indeed, they were cut off. They worked hard and saved and made a life for themselves. Seventeen years later, after seeing doctors who knew little about fertility and praying unceasingly for a baby, I was born. Papa told me my arrival was the best thing to ever happen to them both. I only know they treated me as if I was the biggest source of their joy. I grew up with modest financial means, but with intense self-worth and self-esteem sprinkled into me daily with unconditional love. They treated my grandparents with great respect. I never knew the story of my father choosing my mother over his financial heritage until I was an adult.

Practicing Forgiveness

The support I receive from my community shores me up. It is consistent, it is affirming, and it makes my mission to young people possible. My good friend, Rev. Dr. Bert Campbell, a Presbyterian minister and mentor, told me once, "If people aren't angry at you, you're not pushing hard enough for change." Best of the best.

I've been attacked three times in my career. The first occurred when my father was dying. I missed two days of classes to be with him through test after test, as the doctors tried to diagnose his illness. When I returned, a school gave me all three days of students in one class period. The location they gave me was the ancillary gym – a large room with no chairs or tables. I knew better. I knew physical environment sets the tone for learning. I also knew chairs and tables provide order. I was very aware that teaching seventy-plus middle schoolers was a poor plan. I was also in deep emotional pain. Losing my papa was one of the hardest things I've ever had to go through. I arrived to teach, but my heart remained with him. It was May, he died in June. If I'd had a clear head, I would've walked out. I stayed. I did have the presence of mind to call one of my staff. She arrived quickly, so I had back up as well as a witness to all that transpired.

I was teaching boys that day. This school required my classes be gender split, even though I presented the same message to all students. I taught two classes of eighth graders without a hitch, followed by two classes of seventh graders. In retrospect, I think that was miraculous, but these young people knew me, they understood my guidelines, they knew how to be respectful in class. All went well.

After a brief lunch, my employee and I prepared for two groups of sixth-grade boys. Unlike their older classmates, this was my first meeting with them. The first group went well, although it took a little time to settle them down. The second group came in wild. Later, I discovered their health teachers had been deflecting any questions about sex to me. "When the Sex Lady arrives" had become a rallying cry for these curious young people.

Gaining control took at least five minutes. I was grateful another educator was with me. Then, class progressed normally. That evening, a teacher called to tell me a parent was incensed about the class content. I was confused. We covered puberty, nothing more. I was told a parent overheard his son discussing class topics over the phone with another student – topics I didn't sanction but were allegedly discussed in groups of students before I managed to gather everyone together.

I didn't think much of it, until the school pulled our programs. The attack on me personally came swiftly. I received calls and letters – this was 1996, before social media – and was called everything from a *child abuser* to a *daughter of Satan*. One of the strangest accusations stated I'd shared with the students the fact that I enjoyed using a dildo! I was dumbfounded. I would never, ever share something

220 SEX ED IS IN SESSION

personal with young people, and the topic of sex toys was not in my puberty lesson plan.

I weathered the storm. My papa was dying, and nothing approximated the stress of his illness. I let it roll over me. I forgave.

In October of that year, I went before the school board after hosting a standing-room-only parent meeting where I answered all questions about class content with transparency. The board voted unanimously to reinstate the program. One of the most bizarre interactions of that evening happened as one of my staff members and I approached our car to leave. A board member followed me and shared a personal anecdote of taking her dildo with her on an international trip, and her embarrassment when it began to vibrate in customs. One of my Guidelines Cards reads, "No personal stories about sexuality." I wished I could've waved that card that night!

Three days later, my mother died. Colleagues asked me why I dealt with the school crisis calmly. I couldn't really put it into words. Perspective is everything. *Was I angry?* I don't recall anger, but I do remember making a conscious choice to forgive.

During my absence, the school administration decided I was not to be referred to by the term "Sex Lady," since it was deemed disrespectful. The day I returned, the principal laughingly took me to a student bathroom. There, written in large letters on the wall, were the words, "Hurrah, the teacher formally known as the Sex Lady comes back today!"

Prayers for My Death

The second attack was deeply personal. A teacher at a public school accused one of my staff of demonstrating homosexual acts in her class. I wasn't with my employee while she taught, but I trusted her. Our program did not include any descriptions of any sexual acts. The teacher who made the accusation was never in the class with my staff member. I met with the principal and superintendent of the school, had a fruitful discussion, and our program continued without a hitch.

The teacher and I exchanged several emails, which I retain but will never share. What's told in confidence stays with me, no matter who told me. Our conversation was challenging. I was told I couldn't be a Christian if I talked about sexuality. In time, she began teaching at a local Christian school.

Teens attending this teacher's school told me many things she said about me. I took them with a grain of salt. They told me she said I turned teens gay. Quite a power, right? Identity is not something another person can create. To paraphrase Ellen, giving out toaster ovens doesn't make people LGB or even T.

I drew the line when three separate teens who attended our center told me the teacher instructed their class to pray for me to die so I would stop leading young people astray. I don't know if this was true, but I do know how volatile people can be. Rich was more than unhappy and asked an attorney friend to write a cease and desist letter. It seemed to work. I've never met this teacher, although I've tried to arrange a dialogue. I respect her right to believe as she does. She is a person of worth. I pray for the grace to continue serving all young people without judgement. They are all worthy. They are all glorious. Once more, I decided to forgive.

What's Up as You Grow Up?

The final attack came after I stopped sending staff into most of our schools. At one time, my staff taught sexuality education in forty-eight schools in four counties. The costs of keeping educators teaching became prohibitive. We lost significant funds in 2006, and I operated the sexuality education program in the red until 2011, when a superintendent asked if I could teach our curriculum to her faculty and I agreed. Over the next two years, I taught ten school districts how to teach sex ed. Consequently, none of my team taught in the third school when I was attacked, nor did I.

This attack was not only personal, it was harsh. The school had ordered copies of my book *What's Up as You Grow Up?* on puberty for each student. The book was created for use in my parent/youth program, where parents and young people could work at their child's pace. I'd used it since 1984 – nearly twenty years.

The school did not support the parents who attacked, but the parents were vocal and loud. I went to the school board meeting, where they addressed the curriculum. My husband, my staff, my education department chair from the college where I'm thrilled to be an adjunct professor, two staff from that department, nurses from the hospital, good friends, and four of my over twenty-five-year-old peer educator alumni attended. I didn't want to expose young people to the meeting, so I limited attendance to alumni. I did not speak.

One of my friends, a psychologist, told me the board meeting was the closest he ever wanted to come to a witch hunt. It was bizarre. Participants were told not to use my name, but everyone did, without correction. Speakers were limited to fifteen minutes, but no one monitored times. There was great anger over my training manual, which a temporary superintendent gave to the three parents, even though it was written for teachers and would never be shown to young people. They became fixated on the fact that I told educators to avoid teaching heteronormativity. Again, deep bias against LGBT young people rumbled through the attack.

A father spoke to his sixteen and eighteen-year-old sons' abstinence, stating that he was "sure they don't even masturbate because I've told them that's wrong."

What's Up as You Grow Up? focuses on respect, consent, communication, decision-making, and relationship skills, like all my curricula.

On the way home, Rich said, "I've never told you what to do, and I won't tell you now. If it were me, I'd walk away from that district."

I didn't. The district kept the program and I stayed on as a consultant for another eight months. One day, they asked me to revise the curriculum in ways I could not accept, by removing any reference to LGBT students and information on contraception. I severed our relationship then.

Perhaps the cruelest email of the many I received because of the publicity this attack created linked my 2005 breast cancer with an abortion I didn't have. The email said, "If you'd like to confess the abortion you had that caused your breast cancer, you should do so now." I've never had an abortion, but I didn't respond to the email. To respond would be to give credibility.

One of the strangest and saddest situations to come from that school board meeting was an email I received the next day from one of the women who spoke against me. She wrote to say she hadn't realized I was in the room during the meeting. She apologized for being so harsh. She said she'd heard wonderful things about me and wondered if I could meet with her to discuss her relationship with her husband. As with the email about breast cancer and abortion, I did not respond, but I did forgive.

I've always known teaching the sensitive subject of sexuality in a small, largely conservative community is dangerous. It takes courage to do this, one must be brave. I take pictures of all my sticky note questions so I have, in their own handwriting, the real questions students ask. I fear some parents would be shocked to see them. Children as old as ten and eleven watch porn on their phones. They need a trusted adult who can help them sort through their feelings at an age where sexuality education is under attack, but the world uses sexuality to sell everything from cars to liquor to fast food instead of providing medically accurate information on sexual health.

I won't stop what I consider a mission. Papa often called me a *testa duro*, a hard head. He said I was stubborn, which was good. I am. I will continue teaching until God tells me I'm done. I have no control over my length of days, but I do control how I spend them. I've never taught without praying first. I was taught to pray in secret. We don't pray for others to see, Papa told me. We talk to God.

I feel no anger to anyone who attacked me, even those for whom the need to try to personally hurt me drew them to use harsh words. Fear drove them. Fear is powerful. Once more, I forgave.

Families and Forgiveness

Despite my personal choices to forgive those who mean me harm, I refuse to tell young people to forgive those who hurt them. In many cases, forgiveness would ease the heaviness they feel connected to trauma, but the decision is theirs, not mine.

Families are not all healthy. Children are not all nurtured. Along with the obvious pain an abuser causes a child within a family, I've held space with numerous young people as they share – often haltingly – their childhood pain.

My own children were small when I went to a home to visit a young parent. Her baby was six months old. She was cooking dinner for her father and baby and herself. I washed my hands and helped her until her little one woke, then held the baby while she finished. I stayed through dinner at her request, but only had a few bites. My family's meal was in a crockpot at home, and I excused myself after clean up. She walked me to my car, said goodbye, then spontaneously turned and enveloped me in a huge hug.

Grinning, I said, "What was that for?"

She shrugged, "No one's ever cooked dinner with me – or for me – is all."

Sixteen years old and no one fed her! The Italian mama inside of me wanted to march back in and accuse her father, but I was silent. Even a mandated reporter cannot Childline indifference and apathetic parenting.

Often, the toughest families are those where LGBT kids come out – or are terrified to come out. Living a lie is horrible. I know of two suicides directly related to family rejection of a young person's sexuality. As a result of this tension, I am careful to meet with any family who wants me to connect because of LGBT issues. I meet with the young person first, then parents and adults in the family, then I bring everyone back together. My message is clear: This child is yours to love. Hating who your young person is will not ease pain. It will intensify it. I strive to guide parents to realize their child is worthy. It isn't always easy, but I will always try.

Sometimes, these parents are shocked when I don't charge for my time.

How could I? My role is to ease pain, my job is to mediate in tense situations, my hope is to help families connect. Confused, angry parents may attack me. I can handle it. I can even try to forgive a parent who says about her gay son, "He isn't my son anymore. He's dead to me."

Her son? I believe he has every right to withhold forgiveness. Someday, if and when he's ready, he may reconcile. It isn't my choice. It's his.

Our children grew in an environment like the one my parents gave me – of acceptance and respect. When they were high schoolers, other students in their school would ask me the same questions: "Mary Jo, what would you do if your daughter got pregnant in high school?" or, "Mary Jo, what would you do if your son was gay?"

I find it fascinating and a little disturbing that, over the twelve years I taught in their school district, not one person asked me what I would do if my son became a father as a teen. Not one.

No one ever asked what I'd do if my daughters were lesbians. Not one.

What does that say about our cultural judgement? Is it no big deal if a young man becomes a dad? Is coming out as a lesbian less a problem than coming out as gay?

How did I answer these frequent questions?

Simply, "If any of my children are in a situation where they're expecting a child, whether it's my daughters or my son, I will be there for them. I will support them. I will cry with them if they're sad. I will continue to love them, no matter what."

As to the "son" question, my response is equally terse: "If any of my children are LGBT, I'd want to know the same thing I'd want to know if they're straight. Are they good people? Are they happy?"

Power

The power to change a person's sexual identity is not mine. I'd never want such a power. I would love to have the power to bring each frightened parent into my classroom invisibly. I still teach sex ed, which means I teach consent and healthy relationships and communication and respect. I can guarantee you most parents would be happy with my message. Those few who deny their children any information about sexuality break my heart.

If I had power, I'd open each person's heart and help them develop empathy and compassion. I'd magically give parents the ability to love their children unconditionally. That would be a wonderful power, indeed.

Maya Angelou said, "You can't forgive without loving. And I don't mean sentimentality. I don't mean mush. I mean having enough courage to stand up and say, 'I forgive. I'm finished with it.'"

Teachers know which children go home each night to families where nurturing isn't available. Offer kindness, a listening ear, and your presence. Honor their forgiveness choices.

Step #25. Model Forgiveness
Only Love Can Conquer Hate

A child's forgiveness is not an adult's choice.

Model forgiveness if you can.

Hear and accept each young person's choice.

Remember, even a challenging family remains the child's first circle.

Become a trusted adult.

CHAPTER TWENTY-SEVEN

Boom Shaka Laka Laka

Pediatric oncology at Memorial Sloan Kettering Cancer Hospital wasn't all gloom and doom. Children bounce back faster than adults. Unless feeling ill, the unit was seldom full of somber kids. A huge playroom dominated the unit in the new hospital, and it was often filled with laughing children playing video games or air hockey, dancing, and listening to music.

As part of the staff, I participated in a feat of organizational skills when the entire hospital moved to a brand new building. The new hospital was adjacent to the old, and we took advantage of underground tunnels below both buildings. We carried babies, pushed beds, and maneuvered carts through passages lit as if we were in bright sun. The desperately ill patients were transported last. Each nurse was responsible for one of these little ones. I remember using a self-inflating bag to help my young patient breath, since we had no electricity in transit. A nurse's aid accompanied me to push the crib. A self-inflating bag or bag valve mask is used to provide pressure ventilation to patients who aren't breathing or who are breathing poorly. Once in our new digs, the children adapted swiftly. So did we.

One of my primary patients was a ten-year-old named Walter. He was feisty and full of spirit. Diagnosed with ALL (Acute Lymphoblastic Leukemia, the most common childhood leukemia), he knew as much about his cancer as most of our staff. He was smart, stubborn, prone to tantrums, and my absolute delight. I loved spending time with him.

Walter and I clicked, but he disliked most of the other nurses. He had names for them. Not particularly kind names. There was Big Nose, and Cold Hands, Smells Funny, and Always Late. He called a particularly preppy social worker Never Gets Dirty. One of his pediatric residents was a hit, the other Walter christened Can't Find My Vein. This little guy's face was as malleable as a mime. I've never known a child who could roll his eyes like Walter. He could level you with a look. When I wasn't on duty, and his secondary nurse was in charge, he gave her nothing but grief, refusing to eat or balking at treatments. He knew when his platelets were low. If she asked him to get in bed or eat something on his tray he disliked, he'd stomp one foot and say, "I know my platelets are eight. Keep this up! I'll slam my head on the wall and my death will be on you!"

I loved him.

For all his bluster, there was a frightened little boy inside of Walter. He liked to do sewing cards – the hard cardboard pages where you thread yarn through pre-cut holes. I brought him a new batch of cards once a week, and we'd do them together after my shift.

When Walter saw me coming, he'd shout out "Boom Shaka Laka Laka! You're here!" I still say it when I'm happy.

My young patients taught me about child development more than any college course. I learned little ones see life through their own lens, just as adults do, but most grown-ups can't conceptualize their perspective. A four-year-old named Tyler noticed everything, including how weary his nurses appeared. One day, after a long, grueling twelve-hour shift, I stopped at Tyler's room to bid him good night. "See ya tomorrow, Ty," I said.

"You look way tired, Miss Mary Jo," he said, looking around. "You want to take a nap under my bed?"

I thanked him for his kindness and said I needed to get home.

"At least get some platelets," he advised solemnly. "They'll perk you right up." In this sweet preschooler's eyes, we all had leukemia.

At Sloan Kettering, I was part of the team working in the innovative laminar flow room for pediatric bone marrow transplants. I remember the first patient I cared for in the room - a child with neuroblastoma who had an identical twin donor. I was astounded by the healthy twin's attitude. He knew harvesting the bone marrow would hurt, but this small preschooler was excited about helping his brother any way possible. My pediatric oncology patients taught me courage.

Parents of these sick little ones were my patients, too. At my first orientation into nursing at Children's Hospital of Pittsburgh, the orientation supervisor told us we always had more than one patient – the family mattered in all decisions. At Sloan Kettering, family members were involved in all treatment plans. I learned to communicate with parents openly, honestly, and with empathy.

My papa played a part in my early nursing career as well. My first Easter working, I'd decided I wouldn't be home for the holiday. My mama prepared our traditional foods of rice cake (rice pudding in a crust) and pizzagiana (literally, big pizza, stuffed with meats and cheese and eggs), shadoone (like a calzone, but filled with chopped pepperoni, eggs, and cheese and eaten cold), and tarale (a salt and pepper dough, boiled then baked) to send to me. Papa would have none of it. He was determined to pick me up after my shift on Saturday and bring me home, even if it was only for a few hours. I worked 7 a.m. – 3 p.m. Saturday, and 3 p.m. – 11 p.m. Sunday. He didn't care. It was worth it to him to have me in their kitchen, even though they lived an hour from Pittsburgh, where I was working at Children's. I reluctantly agreed.

Holy Saturday, the nurse who was supposed to work the 3 p.m. – 11 p.m. shift called off. I called my parents to tell them I was going to work a double shift, and for them to stay home. There was only one phone on the unit, and they couldn't call me (no cell phones).

A young patient arrested at 10 p.m. We were fortunate, he survived and was transferred to the ICU. Paperwork after a crisis is intense, and you're coming down from an epi high, so focusing on getting it done is a little anti-climactic.

A little after midnight, the overnight supervisor arrived on our unit. "Miss Cirelli," she said, holding back laughter. "There is a very irate man in my office. He'd like to know if I have any other nurses in this hospital besides his daughter. He would also like to take you home."

I was so embarrassed I could barely speak.

She grinned then, taking pity on me, "How much more do you need to do?"

"I'm just finishing charting," I said. I pictured my Papa in her office and my embarrassment renewed itself. "I'm sorry," I blurted out, looking down.

"Don't be," she said. "He's a very nice man. It's obvious you're important to him."

That was an understatement, I thought, annoyed with Papa. I was a grown woman. I'd just handled a life-threatening emergency. I could take care of myself. My head spun with the words I'd use to chastise him. I rounded the corner. There they were. Papa's grin was so wide, I could see his deep dimples. Mama was sparkling. She was barely five feet tall and stood pretty much under the wall of his arm. All I could do was smile.

The families at Sloan Kettering and Children's supported their children. I was an adult, but my family still supported me. My anger fled. What a fortunate person I was!

Families Who Fail

I pondered writing those words for a long time. Failure is part of life, we can learn from it. Was it harsh to refer to families who fail their own children?

I dislike the term "dysfunctional families" for one reason: it is said in front of children so much that they often report, "I'm from a dysfunctional family." I remind young people a reality of life – we do not choose our families. We are responsible for our own life choices, not those of our parents or grandparents.

I strive to avoid assuming a parenting role, even though many young people call me their "other mom" or, now that I'm older, their "nonnie." I embrace those terms. They're based in love. My staff and I do become significant adults for young people. What I avoid is putting down their parents or families. I listen, I nod, I use Rogerian therapy, but I try to respect families.

One of the most common stressors young people share deals with new adults in the family. A parent brings home a new partner who is a stranger. This stranger now has power in the family and lives with the young person in intimate situations, like sharing a bathroom or discussing finances. The change is intense and often complicated.

I fully support parent choices. I do suggest they talk with their young people to explain those choices, clear the air, and hear the young person's point of view. It's all about respect.

When we tell children their families don't work, they often judge themselves. They may think it is their fault. It's not.

Step #27: Take Off Your Adult Glasses and See the World Through a Young Person's Perspective

Don't fear being an important adult in a young person's life.

Don't try to take the place of a parent.

Honor each family.

Find the courage to serve as a mandated reporter.

Hold space with the child by being there if the family is disrupted.

CHAPTER TWENTY-EIGHT
Faith

Faith is a complicated concept. I need my church community. I enjoy the company of those who believe as I do. However, I honor all people in their belief – or lack of belief – in a power beyond themselves.

When I wrote *Nonnie Talks About Death*, my original storyboard included the two primary characters, Tamika and Alex, asking Nonnie what happens after someone dies. I planned to say, "No one knows for sure," and leave it there. I realized I was copping out. Instead, I connected with real friends and colleagues and asked them their thoughts on this important but volatile topic. I expanded my scope to include an illustration of each person, often with Tamika, Alex and Nonnie, and explore different beliefs. I start with agnosticism and move in ABC order through atheism, Buddhism, Christianity, Hinduism, Islam, Judaism, Mormonism, native belief, Paganism, Taoism, Unitarianism, and Wicca. The Nonnie books are meant to be read by children and parents. The death book guides children to discuss their family's beliefs. I'm happy with it.

Papa's favorite religious holiday was Easter. Every Holy Thursday, he spent in vigil at our small church. When I was old enough, he took me with him.

I'd grow restless quickly. The church was warm and there was no service, just a lot of people I then thought were very old, sitting in quiet contemplation. Papa said Good Friday honored the crucifixion, but the night before, Christ was abandoned by his friends. We needed to be there.

I tried. Sometimes, I fell asleep, waking with a start on the hard pew. Papa was patient. As I wiggled, he'd whisper softly, "Be still, honey. Be still and listen."

I listened. Nothing. I'd whisper back, "I don't hear anything."

Papa would smile, "It's not a voice. Listen. You will find peace. Be still."

Years later, at Sloan Kettering, we were taught mindfulness as a means of coping with our many young patients who were acutely ill and so often died. The importance of mindful meditation was reinforced for me yet again when I became Lamaze certified and trained to teach relaxation techniques during childbirth. Since my twenty-third year, I've done mindfulness exercises daily. My meditation is deeply spiritual to me and includes prayer, although not all mindfulness practice is prayerful. I am still. I listen. It gives me a foundation for my day.

I began finding fault with the church of my childhood as a teen. I was unhappy with the absence of women's roles. I spoke with my father, and he understood. "Churches are created by people," he said with confidence. "People make mistakes."

In college, I studied other religions beyond the Catholicism of my youth. I found so many reasons to doubt, but I never left my faith. Papa's faith was as deep as an ocean – *how could I abandon it?* I did move to a Presbyterian church after Papa's death. I couldn't leave his church while he lived - my respect for him was too strong. It took me four tries before I left. My friend Bert even challenged me to attend his church every Sunday in lent one year. I went to my church's mass and his service every week for six weeks. It was way too much! Every time I tried to leave, something would pull me back. I nearly left because of the church's reaction to long-term sexual abuse among its clergy, but I stayed. I continued to resent the lack of power for women, but I stayed. I liked Pope Francis, so I stayed. Then, the Pope came out against teaching sex ed. I'm not a hypocrite. I left.

I love my new church. Everyone is truly welcome there. It is a real safe place where all people are respected and honored. The congregation creates a community of believers. Everyone is warm and welcoming. I'm honored to be on session and serve as a liturgist. We recently baptized our youngest granddaughter. Coincidentally, I was scheduled to be liturgist that Sunday, so I was part of the baptism service. I was thrilled. Our pastor, Steve, is one of the wisest, kindest people I know.

Choices

Although my mama never received the therapy she needed, a relationship with a local chiropractor gave her peace. This fine man not only did house calls, he managed to connect with my mother on her worst days. He listened to her. He spent time with her. He eased her angst.

In fourth grade, I decided I'd be a chiropractor like him. I'd ease pain. Mama told me I couldn't be any kind of doctor. I was a girl. I mourned for a full week. I visited his office and longingly looked at his models of bones and posters of the spine. I wanted to unlock the body's mysteries and find my way to healing.

I turned to the library and took out books on healthcare. The first one talked about the role of the nurse. I knew then, at ten, I would be a nurse.

My next step was to become a missionary. I imagined myself helping with birth in faraway lands and teaching the gospel at the same time. Mama said this was too much - she had one child and I would never leave the country! Papa was calm. He helped me order magazines from missions and allowed me to send money to my favorite ones. Gently, he wove into my days the idea of "blooming where I was planted." I began to understand. I could learn to serve God by serving children no one loved. I didn't need to go across oceans. I've prayed to do just that for nearly sixty years.

In seventh grade, I thought I had a vocation, or calling, to be a nun. I begged to attend a weekend retreat at a convent. Papa wasn't happy – his expression was transparent. As he dropped me off for the weekend, he said one thing: "Notice how they treat each other."

Three days later, he picked me up. We rode home in silence for half of the ninety-minute trip, then he asked how I'd liked the retreat. I was honest. I told him the nuns talked about one another behind their backs. I said they were as cliquey as my middle school.

He nodded. "So," he said.

I remember laughing. "I'm gonna bloom where I'm planted," I said. "I'm not planted there."

He gave me a huge grin and a sigh of relief. "They give up a lot, honey," he said.

I knew a tiny bit about sex; it was enough to connect the dots. His grin continued as he glanced at me the rest of the trip.

When I was older, I asked him why he didn't just forbid me go. He shook his head. "Your life, your choice," he said confidently. "I knew you'd choose right."

Prayer

Prayer is part of my life. Like most people, I don't receive a bolt of lightning or hear voices telling me my prayer is heard. I don't usually pray for things; I pray for strength. One long night, caring for a very ill four-year-old, however, I felt grace. The little one was leukemic, and chemo had failed. She was in and out of consciousness, and her parents were exhausted. Her father was a pastor, her mother deeply religious. I asked them if they wanted to go to the adjacent parents' quarters to rest. They'd not stretched out on a bed for nearly a week. They reluctantly agreed, but were adamant I must call them if their daughter's condition worsened. I promised I would. As they started to leave the room, the father turned to me. "How will you know to call us?" he asked.

I'd been an RN for twelve years at this point, and my work with sick children had honed the skills Ruth gifted me with at the start of my career. I assured him I would know. He shook his head. I meant well, he could tell, but he couldn't leave this to chance. They needed to be with their daughter when she drew her last breath. He asked if he could pray with me. "Certainly," I said. The parents took my hands and the father said, "Lord, guide this young nurse. Help her know when to call us." They seemed comforted and left.

I monitored their daughter carefully that night, as I did all my young patients. Her signs were stable. At my 1 a.m. rounds, I stood by her bedside after assessing her and paused. My silent prayer echoed her father's. *Let me know*, I prayed. I sat beside her. Like with David years before, something felt off. I didn't hesitate. I called her parents. They were back in ten minutes. I apologized for bothering them, as we stood near this sweet child, listening to her labored breathing. It was unchanged. Time passed, her breathing halted a moment, then started again. Periodic apnea, I thought. Normal at end of life. Then, her breathing changed. I recognized Cheyne-Stokes respirations, an abnormal pattern of breathing where deeper, faster respirations are followed by temporary stops. The apnea, but with a difference.

I'm not sure why I asked, but I turned to the parents, "Would you like to hold her?" Tearful, they agreed with enthusiasm. The mother sat in a large rocking chair, and the father perched beside her on a smaller chair I'd brought from our treatment room. I carefully gathered the small body in my arms, gently placed her in her mother's arms, and stepped back. The father enveloped his family, his head on his wife's shoulder, the mother pressed her check against her child's head. I left them together in private, placing the call bell in the father's hand. I heard them murmuring to their precious daughter as I left. In less than fifteen minutes the bell rang. I joined them; they wanted company. We sat together in silence, watching the rise and fall of their child's chest. Less than forty-five minutes after I called them, she died.

LGBT and Christians

I know a man who was told to leave his church because he was gay. His pastor told him he couldn't be gay and a follower of Christ. He continued searching until he found a church where he was accepted. He lives a very giving life, and has been with one partner for nearly thirty years. I don't understand why he was shunned. I don't understand why so many people cherry pick the Bible and focus on only some passages for condemnation while other, more obvious ones are ignored.

I ponder those who say they are followers of Christ yet espouse so much hate for others. Like my papa, I believe people's lives are their own. Their actions are between them and God, not me and God. I love Matthew 25: 35-46, the *when did you see me* verses. My role model in faith lived those words. I asked Papa once why some Christians were angry and hurtful to others. *Why did they hate?* As you may guess, he had a ready answer. "It's okay," he soothed. "They're not your concern. Not everyone who says they are Christian lives a Christian life. They just don't understand. If you need to tell someone you're a Christian, you're not doing it right."

I think so, too.

Good deeds should be done quietly and with humility;
don't puff yourself up by saying, "Look what I've done!"

Step #27: Respect and Honor all Belief Systems

Connect sexual behavior to ethical and moral behavior, regardless of a person's belief.

Live your faith.

Honor the character of all people.

Do the right thing because it is the right thing to do, not for respect or accolades of praise.

Seek joy and peace.

CHAPTER TWENTY-NINE

Mentoring

Mentoring is a gift. If you've experienced a great
mentor, you know what I mean. If you've served as a mentor, you know how
wonderful it can be.

One of my fondest mentors was Elisabeth Bing, the mother of Lamaze
and childbirth education in America. When I was elected to the Lamaze International
Board of Directors, she invited me to her hotel suite at our national conference.
We spoke for over two hours. I rightly knew I was being vetted. When
I was elected board president a few years later, our friendship blossomed. She was
the wisest woman I've known.

Elisabeth welcomed me many times to her apartment in New York City's
upper west side. My daughter, Lisa, often accompanied me, establishing a relationship
that would blossom when my parents died. We enjoyed meals at Elisabeth's
favorite deli and took in Broadways shows – always drama, not musicals!
She played the cello for me and offered wisdom. When I started the Academy for
Adolescent Health, she cautioned me to hold on to my vision and not let it be
compromised. She held nothing back as she mentored me, offering counsel, listen-

ing to hear, sharing the wisdom of her experience. She was especially helpful when I was elected to be president of the Lamaze board. We dealt with issues surrounding our magazine and our brand. Elizabeth was deeply vested in the organization and consulted with me regularly. Her guidance resonates with me to this day.

The organization she co-founded was called ASPO/Lamaze in 1960; in the nineties, the board rightfully decided to change the name. ASPO stood for American Society for Psychoprophalaxis in Obstetrics. It was time to make the name reflect the organization's international focus. I spoke with Elisabeth privately to prepare her for the vote and discussion. She sat on the board as Emeritus Director. When I entered the room for the board meeting, I sat next to her. She said, "Have you selected this seat to provide me support?" I hadn't realized it, but yes, I had. The vote was unanimous, and she was pleased.

During one of my visits to her place, I told her I'd like her to write her memoirs. She padded into her back bedroom and returned with a densely typed manuscript. "Here," she said. "Do what you want with it!"

At the time, I thought this was the only copy. When Elisabeth died, her son Peter told me there were others. I only know my anxiety was high as we left. I turned to Lisa as our flight took off and said, "If this plane goes down, we'll lose Elisabeth's memoir!" My daughter laughed and said, "We'll lose a lot more than that, Mom." Lamaze International published her book, which would be her seventh. Its title is *A Life in Birth*.

My favorite story about this dynamic woman dealt with her past in England during The Blitz. Having fled Hitler's Germany as an eighteen-year-old, she lived in London as war heated up and bombings became regular. She told me, at first, she went to the shelters when the sirens split the air. Then, she decided she didn't want to die among strangers, huddled underground. "If I was eating when the sirens went off," she told me, "I ate my meal. If I was making love, I continued." Her attitude about life was feisty, passionate, and resilient. She reacted to 9/11 with equanimity.

When our daughter, Lisa, graduated high school as valedictorian, my parents' deaths were fresh. Elisabeth traveled to our small town and stood in as a grandparent. She lived to be almost 101. I miss her to this day. What a gift her mentorship was!

My grandmother was my mentor. I received the story of her journey to America from my papa. As her eldest child, he was privy to all that transpired. My nonna was a bright, strong woman, but never learned to read and write. Women in the late 1800s in Italy were not considered valuable enough to teach.

My grandfather traveled to America to make money, like many European men at the time. He was to send for his family when funds were enough. He left a wife and three children: Papa, who was six, my Uncle Mike, four, and my Aunt Christina, only two. Nonna lived with his family. She waited. And waited.

My papa wrote the letters his mother sent to America and read her husband's responses to her. He told me he knew when Nonna decided she'd had enough waiting. She began fabricating emergencies that would require money. My papa wanted to play guitar, lira was needed. Miquel broke his arm, please send money. Christina wanted to learn to make lace at the convent, the lessons weren't free. My grandfather dutifully sent cash.

Papa helped his mother dig a hole in the tomato garden. They lowered a small wooden box into the earth and added money when it arrived. Eight years later, when Nonna accumulated the cost of passage for her and her children, my papa wrote this note to his father in America: *Dear husband, I will not live through another war in this country. Your children and I will be in New York on (the date was lost to me). If you want a family, be there. If not, we're still coming. Love, your wife.*

Papa said his father was waiting when they arrived. Nonna went on to have two more births to her husband, one baby who was stillborn, and my Aunt Ann.

As an adult, I asked Nonna if she ever wondered if her husband took another woman during those long years apart. She shrugged her shoulders and her hands waved in an eloquent gesture of resignation. "Ah," she breathed. "Some things are better not known."

Nonna was a matriarch. She was illiterate. She was smart. When my grandfather died, he left five houses he rented to others. Nonna knew all the finances, who owed rent, which house needed repairs. She was my cheerleader. When report cards arrived, my mama believed I should receive no reward for getting As. "Your grades are your reward," she told me, "and your increased knowledge." Nonna asked to see my grades every time. Then, staring directly at my mama, she would take my hand, place five dollars in my palm, and roll my fingers over the money in a fist. Mama didn't dare object. Nonna would say, "You're smart. No one can take that from you. Spend the money on something that makes you happy."

In return, I've mentored many. My best mentoring involves young people who are able to fly on their own. Fostering independence means making oneself unnecessary. The connection remains, but young people can make their own choices.

Nothing gives me more happiness than stepping back and surrendering power to others. When our teens facilitate with skill and courage, when my staff takes on roles I pioneered and carried for years, when my college students do their internships and student teaching with grace and wisdom, I am full of joy.

Stepping down isn't a feeling of loss to me, but rather a feeling of completion. It's not about me, it's never been about me. It's about my students – the young people I serve, the young adults I help prepare to teach. Legacy is also about stepping back. I'm honored to be see my legacy evolving before my eyes.

It takes courage to teach with your heart and know when to step back.

Step #28: Encourage Peer Mentoring and Education

Nothing is more satisfying than watching young people succeed.

Surrender power and encourage their facilitation.

I love watching peer educators teach.

I'm never worried when they participate in a panel for adults. I know they're ready.

Believe in young people.

CHAPTER THIRTY

Ethics, Morals, & Integrity

We own one thing: our reputation. The elders in my family taught me to create a standard of ethical behavior. They taught me to respect others, but I've been tested, just like everyone else.

When I worked with adults in oncology, I cared for a woman whose life story rivaled fiction. When she was a teenager, she was sent to Auschwitz, where she was part of Mengele's infamous experiments. Many decades later, she still had nightmares that took her back to the camp. She was witty. She was kind, and I loved spending time with her.

Her abdominal tumor was external and extended from one side of her belly to another. One of my tasks was to apply sterile water to the site, to ease her pain. She did this herself for as long as she could. I'd sit with her in the bathroom, at her request. She was fearful of fainting. She worried the wound's odor was off-putting. I told her honestly, nothing about bodies bothered me, except for dentures. As a student nurse, an elderly man plopped his false teeth in my hand and said, "Here, sweetheart, hold these a minute." I fought to keep down breakfast. My story made my patient laugh. We often laughed together.

As she grew weaker, I took over her wound care. I'd talk of nothing while I worked, hoping to distract her. We discussed the other doctors and nurses in my unit and she told me who she thought was attractive. "I'm not dead yet," she'd say, grinning. She was interested in Watergate and entranced by the idea of a form of government that could remove someone from office without bloodshed.

Her family was very devoted to her. One day, as I left the hospital, I heard footsteps behind me, moving quickly. I turned. It was my patient's daughter. She caught up with me and thrust a fat envelope in my hands. Confused, I stared at her.

"For you," she said, catching her breath from running to meet me. "For taking such good care of my mother.

I explained I enjoyed caring for her mom and gently pressed the envelope back to her. I couldn't take money for doing my job, I said. She cajoled, I held my ground. She looked hurt, perhaps even insulted. I often wonder if I violated her trust in some way. I did what I thought was right, but it wasn't easy. As Albus Dumbledore tells Harry, "We all face the choice between what is right and what is easy."

Controlling Anger

Part of ethical behavior, for me, is holding back from my gut reaction of anger and respecting those who fail to respect me or the young people I serve. It's a struggle. My anger is slow to rise, but hot. I know this, and typically keep it in check. When I first began volunteering with young parents, my philosophy was tested.

I'm afraid I failed in the case of a young woman who gave birth in April of her senior year. She lived with a single mom who worked the 3 p.m. – 11 p.m. shift at a local factory. The new mother needed to be home by 2:45 p.m. so her mom could leave for work. She returned to school the first week of May and was on track to graduate. I arranged a fifteen-minute daily early dismissal for her since classes ended at 2:43 p.m. I secured administrative approval first, jumping through the appropriate hoops and making numerous phone calls over three weeks. All appeared to be going well.

I received a frantic phone call from her the first day back to school. She wasn't allowed to leave. I rushed to the school. The truancy officer made a unilateral decision that she could not be dismissed as planned. I went to her home and watched her baby while her mom left for work. The teen mom joined me at 3 p.m.

I returned to her school. I was incensed, but I intended to confront the officer respectfully, wrestling back my anger. So many phone calls, all the careful arrangements, useless, because of one man. Still, my responsibility is to teach, not chastise.

I approached him with deference. Before I could speak, he leveled a look of pure disdain at me. "I know you're a do-gooder," he said. "Hear me out. These kids shouldn't be having babies in the first place. You coddle them. If I let one girl have an early dismissal because she has a baby, they'll all get pregnant so they can get out of school early."

Dumbfounded, and accustomed to people judging young parents, I remained silent. Few people knew the antecedents to early childbearing: internal and external poverty, generational teen pregnancy, sexual abuse, foster placement or abandonment, and questioning sexuality. I try to educate our team. In my staff book club, we read Kristen Luker's *Dubious Conceptions: The Politics of Teen Pregnancy*. I knew this man was not alone in his bias.

However, I was weary that day. I slipped. Instead of nodding and explaining why these fifteen minutes, already approved by her teacher and principal and the superintendent, wouldn't make a difference in her education and would not impact other young women in her school, I said something else. Something unkind and sarcastic: "I'm so glad you shared your wisdom with me. Here I am, running all over the county trying to teach teens to delay childbearing, and you had the answer all along. All I need do is make an announcement every morning at every school: 'Attention, attention. There will be no early dismissals if you make a baby!' Then, I can retire."

I walked out. I'm not proud of my reaction, but it felt good. Thankfully, the school administration intervened to support our original plan. The young mother left school fifteen minutes early until the end of the year and graduated with her class.

Burning in Hell

I've only "lost it" one other time. I was preparing to do the keynote for a large conference in Seattle. As I approached the auditorium, a woman got in my face - truly, inches away. She asked, "Are you one of us?" I was confused. She pointed to the cross on the necklace my papa gifted me with on my last birthday. I said, "Depends on what you mean."

She frowned, "I mean, you don't talk about condoms to teenagers, do you?"

I offered a tentative smile, "I teach many things, like consent and communication and refusal and problem-solving skills. Relationships and…"

"Do you or do you not discuss condoms?" she demanded, cutting me off.

"I do," I said. I genuinely believe I was not defensive. "Perhaps we could talk about…"

She cut me off again. "You'll burn in hell for all eternity," she said, and stormed off.

She didn't bother attending my keynote to hear my message. If she had, she would have heard me reflect my parents' wisdom and talk about respecting young people. She would have played the interactive games I created to connect with teens. She would have heard and seen me. She did not hear. She did not see. I was not a person to her.

If I'd been kinder, I would have let it go, but I was annoyed. I found her at lunch, staffing a booth for abstinence until marriage education. Her handouts were shame and fear-based. They were not only heteronormative, they described the sin of homosexuality in great detail.

I didn't do the right thing in Seattle, at least not by my personal standards.

I approached the woman who condemned me to an eternity in hell and opened my purse. I removed a condom and unrolled it from its package. "Look at this," I said. "It's smelly and weird. Young people don't have sex because they see a condom or know how to use one correctly. They have sex for a multitude of reasons."

She looked ready to spit, so I laid down my final words. "I'd like to ask you a question," I said. "Have you ever served as a doula for a teen mother who had no support, staying with her for over twenty-four hours, never leaving her side, and received no payment for your time?"

She shook her head, no.

"I have," I said, "more times than I can count. We'll see which one of us burns in hell."

Developing a Moral Compass

Teaching Ed Psych (Educational Psychology) at Washington and Jefferson College is one of my favorite teaching experiences. Our Education Department students are eager to learn and excited to teach one day. Theorists may sound boring, but they present a depth of awareness and discussion that opens doors to critical thinking. On the first day of class, I state unequivocally we will not only explore "old white dead guy" theories, but the theories of women, people of color, non-Americans, and LGBT thinkers get equal time.

Even as a young teen, I was intrigued by the development of a moral compass. Two theorists on morality are Lawrence Kohlberg and Carol Gilligan. Both have their critics.

Kohlberg looked beyond the work of Jean Piaget on child development to try to determine how moral development happened in children. He's been criticized because his work was culturally and gender biased towards white, upper class men and boys.

He theorized three levels or stages: preconventional, conventional, and postconventional. The preconventional stage is when a child's sense of morality is controlled externally, by authority figures like parents or teachers. At this level, children do the right thing for fear of consequences. They don't eat forbidden snacks for fear of punishment if they're caught. In my opinion, many adults remain in this stage.

An individual during the conventional stage ties a sense of morality to personal and societal relationships. Authority figures' rules are still accepted, but now because rules are necessary for relationships and societal order.

Postconventional morality defines morals in abstract principles and values. At this stage, my papa's maxim of doing the right thing because it is the right thing is key. Unjust laws are questioned and may be protested.

While Kohlberg's theory is, justifiably, challenged, I've occasionally used it to teach. In the early 2000s, I took thirty-six peer educators to Disney. I knew supervising them in the Magic Kingdom would be like herding cats. At one of the many prep meetings held before our trip, I facilitated a discussion on Kohlberg and morality. I needed them to jump quickly to doing the right thing because it was the right thing!

Carol Gilligan was Kohlberg's research assistant at Harvard. She felt Kohlberg's theory was male-oriented. She wrote the book *In a Different Voice* in 1982 to examine women's ways of thinking about morality. She is credited with inspiring the passage of the 1994 Gender in Education Equity Act.

Gilligan believed women approach ethical dilemmas differently than men by centering their moral decisions around relationships. Women, she said, see moral issues as a problem of conflicting responsibilities without relationships. Her concept of this "ethics of care" is incompatible with the male-focused "ethics of justice," focused on rules.

Morally Objectionable Part for All

As a teen, I think I was quite an annoying person. I questioned. I tested. I wanted to understand the *why* for rules and behavior and morality.

The Catholic church ratings on movies presented a conflict when I was young. Before Hollywood created their own movie ratings, the church established the Legion of Decency in 1933 to review and recommend acceptable viewing. The Legion was reorganized in 1965 as the National Catholic Office for Motion Pictures. I was fifteen, discovering I loved movies, and pushing the parental envelope regularly (not that I ever won my arguments!).

Current CNS (Catholic News Service) classifications are:

- A-I — general patronage

- A-II — adults and adolescents

- A-III — adults

- A-IV — adults, with reservations (this indicates films that, while not morally offensive in themselves, are not for casual viewing because they require some analysis and explanation in order to avoid false impressions and interpretations)

- L — limited adult audiences, films whose problematic content many adults would find troubling (replaced A-IV classification Nov. 1, 2003)

- O — morally offensive

I recall a C for Condemned rating (it was used from 1933 to 1978). If condemned, a movie was completely off limits.

I argued to be able to watch anything I wanted, with the caveat that I would discuss the movie with my parents and find my own moral compass. In 1967, I was asked on a date to watch the movie *Bonnie and Clyde*. It was condemned. I approached my argument like an attorney – I was well prepared, respectful, and articulate. My argument fell flat until my papa's moral compass was suddenly at odds with his strong feelings of empowering my independence and my own moral development. He knew nothing of education or psychology theories; he only knew he trusted my judgement.

What turned him around? I posited that the people who reviewed these movies needed to watch them in order to assign a rating. *Why was it okay for priests view them?*

Mama was not moved. These holy people received a dispensation to suffer through horrible movies for the good of the whole. Papa smiled at me. "True," he acknowledged. "You are no better or worse than a priest. I see no reason you can't review movies as well, as long as we talk about the movie's plot and discuss it."

My victory was truly moot. I seldom went to the movies as a teen, so I had little chance to review anything. I savored my win, nonetheless. I did see *Bonnie and Clyde*. My strongest memory of the movie was the realization that I did not really enjoy the company of the young man who accompanied me. It was our first and last date.

Early Steps to Moral Development

Early lessons on empowerment and responsibility set the stage for a child's personal development of a moral compass and integrity.

I was president of my fourth grade class. My teacher gave me the task of calling the courthouse to arrange a field trip. She gave me the number for the judge's office. I was terrified. I don't know what my ten-year-old mind thought I'd encounter, but I asked my papa to make the call for me.

Says Papa, "I'm not the class president."

I whined. I cajoled. I pulled out all the stops. "If you loved me, you'd call for me."

His response, "I do love you. That's why I won't call for you."

I was embarrassed the next day when my teacher asked if I'd made the call. I mumbled something about doing it that night.

I can see myself with my hand hovering over the black rotary phone. Glaring at my papa, I dialed the number. Guess what? A person answered. Just a person!

I stopped glaring at my papa. It was hard to glare at him at that point, because his grin was so wide and his dimples were darting in and out.

"It was just a person," I said to him.

"I know," he said, nodding. And he told me that I was just as good as any person and I should never fear talking to anyone. He paused, then added, "When you take on a job, you need to follow through. You, not someone else."

When we do for others, we stop them from making mistakes. We all learn from mistakes. When we do for others, especially for young people, our message is loud and clear: *You need me to do things. You can't do things on your own.*

I encountered an extreme parental reaction to empowering their own teen many years ago. I was teaching a training for parents at a high school. A mother in the training called out, "I object to the idea of teaching decision-making."

I respectfully asked why.

Her response? She alleged her son had never made a decision "independent from me," and she saw no reason to encourage such independence.

I pondered a kind response. "How old is your son?" I asked.

"Sixteen."

I cringed mentally as I considered all the independent decisions sixteen-year-olds make. Then I was inspired! I asked her, "Did you feed him strained beets or strained squash as a baby?"

Confused, she said, "Of course."

I smiled and said gently, "If he spit it out, he made a decision independent of you."

I've been criticized because I hire teens to run our Teen Center. I know they can do it. I know they're worthy. I set clear, high standards and they reach for them, achieving them. It's THEIR center. They need to make it work.

I learned the importance of healthy relationships by watching my parents. Some of those lessons were unconventional. My mama worried about my future when I was a child. She gave up eating cake when I was a preschooler. I thought she just didn't like it. Birthdays, anniversaries, weddings, she said, "No, thank you," to cake. When my Rich and I became engaged, she grinned at me and said, "Pick a great wedding cake. I can't wait to eat it!"

Confused, I asked her why. She responded by telling me she'd stopped eating cake when I was three as a sacrifice, with the petition that I would have a good relationship in life. Her half superstitious, half religious belief system made her feel this was a quid pro quo. It saddened me on one hand, and underscored her deep love for me on the other.

She was right. He is a good match.

Laying Blame

In 1999, we started an Adolescent Advisory Board. Seventy-plus students from our county schools meet monthly at the Washington Health System's community room to share their perspectives on adolescent culture. As I said before, each encounter with a young person is a cross-cultural experience, akin to traveling to China or Russia. Adults must tread with care and respect.

Advisory Board members write curricula, create learning games, and critique existing activities. Teens are honest and direct. Adults in a workshop may appear content but write negative comments anonymously. Young people will simply say, "This sucks," right out loud!

These young people are our ambassadors for respect. Each year, we select a theme to guide us. Last year, as the American election made debate increasingly divisive, we selected Respect for Civil Discourse as our theme.

We had a great deal of fun with this theme. Each school district created their own sovereign nation, complete with a system of government, flag, song, philosophy, budget (based on the district's actual budget), and policy. I wasn't surprised when these young people's choices reflected today's complicated world. Only two of the districts selected a democratic government. Oligarchy was the most common choice. Monarchy was second.

Our year ends with our county-wide youth conference at Washington and Jefferson College. The final meeting prior to the conference, each school created two questions to ask the panel of adult leaders I created. We spent the first hour of the conference in introductions since each nation invited citizens (ninth graders) to attend. The Advisory Board members sang their national songs, unfurled their flags, and sent a delegate to our United Nations (we also had a refugee camp and a Red Cross).

Our panel consisted of our mayor, the county commissioners, our state senator, our state congressperson, the Education Department chair of the college, a superintendent of schools, the vice president of the health system, a retired Army colonel, the vice president of the NAACP, the chief of police, the owner of the local newspaper, and a faith leader. The panel was diverse in race, age, and gender. Each nation's press secretary asked their questions of the panel. The questions were incisive.

- "At what point does free speech become hate speech? And is hate speech still free speech?"
- "How difficult is it to remain neutral when reporting the news?"
- "If you are old enough to work and have a job, do you feel you should be able to vote?"
- "Do you think racism is a problem in our county?"
- "What challenges do you foresee for healthcare in the future?"

While the young people enjoyed lunch with our panel, my staff and I created a mock disaster. Using yellow police tape, we roped off one of the nations. The students were handed an envelope of instructions as they filed back into the ballroom. One of the nations experienced a devastating earthquake. Adjacent nations were affected. Leaders were missing or dead. The epicenter of the earthquake left a school district called Chartown without leadership. In the scenario we created, Chartown was rich in oil. A neighboring nation, HillerNation, coveted this oil. Another nation, PrexieNation, was an ally to HillerNation, but wanted peace. Which nations would go to war? Which nations would accept refugees? How would nations align? If a broad conflict arose, would some nations choose diplomacy? How would nations without leadership govern?

It was like playing the game of Risk with 150 teens!

When we processed, at the end of the conference, the representative from HillerNation, who was also one of our peer educators, took the microphone and said, "Well, we considered nuking Chartown and Macadelic, but decided to strive for peace." He looked at me and laughed, "War seemed like it would be more fun, but we knew what Mary Jo was trying to achieve."

Model Humanity

What was I trying to achieve? I had no political goals, but I readily admit I sought to encourage being human. I know colleagues who worry we're losing basic human decency. I stand on the shoulders of giants, learning from wisdom passed on from wise humans. My parents. My nonna. My students. Simple people and renowned. Mahatma Ghandi said, "You must not lose faith in humanity. Humanity is an ocean; if a few drops of the ocean are dirty, the ocean does not become dirty."

I strive to avoid political comments on social media, yet I spoke strongly about the psychological damage separation from parents/caregivers causes children. I use social media as a teaching tool, and my silence, unlike the silence of non-educators, sends a strong message to the young people I serve. I must speak. Childhood trauma is real. Childhood adversity has life-long consequences. I'm speechless when I find people who genuinely oppose interventions that will spare children trauma. Which politics matter when young people are suffering? I've also seen some of my Facebook friends post angrily that they are finished with those who don't agree with them on this issue. That's tempting. I know unfriending is always a possibility, but it is not in my nature to turn my back on anyone. My papa told me there is the potential for good in each of us. He also advised me that there is the potential for evil. A human wrote Tchaikovsky's overtures and concertos. A human designed Auschwitz. Which will we choose?

I am my father's daughter. I don't give up on people!

So, at this point in our culture, if you:

1. Believe the children being separated from their parents/guardians at our border are child actors

2. Believe they are being kept in summer camps

3. Believe they are being separated because of a law from the past, not a recent zero-tolerance policy

4. Believe these children are less worthy than other children because they are brown or Black

5. Believe they are less worthy because they don't speak English

6. Believe that the term "illegal" takes away a person's humanity

If you believe any of these things, I am not angry with you. I am an imperfect soul. I cannot judge another. I can share how very sad this makes me. I can also do the one thing my papa said was my best arsenal - the tool no one can take from me. I will pray, with all my heart, for wisdom for us all - for eyes to be opened, for people to see the truth. And for those who do not pray, I honor you. Each person's path is their own.

I know it's easy to lay blame for negativity,
but it's better to model respect.

Step #29: Respecting Those Who Disrespect Us is Not Easy
Ethics isn't Easy
Doing the Right Thing isn't Easy
Model it Anyway

No one has the power to change our individual responses to hatred.

Gift one another with respect.

Teach empathy.

Make moral choices.

Mentor young people.

CHAPTER THIRTY-ONE

Grief

Losing a beloved family member isn't easy; losing my parents hurt. I am left with their lessons and wonderful memories, but it's been twenty-one years and I still feel like picking up the phone and sharing with them. I wish they knew how well their grandchildren are living life. I wish they could see their great-grandchildren.

My father believed in prayer, but he prayed for strength and grace, not to receive material goods. If he wanted something, he worked to get it. There was one exception. I know he prayed to be a father. When I was born on March 24th, my mother told me Papa considered naming me *Annunciata*. The Annunciation of Mary is March 25th, the day Catholics celebrate to commemorate the angel Gabriel telling Mary about her baby.

My nonna, thankfully, thought such a name was *not merigan*. To stop him, she told him she'd call me "Lancy" – Nancy – for short, as if she couldn't pronounce the 'N.' She could. No one pulled one over on my nonna. When I was an adult, she laughingly told me the story. Papa was so troubled by his baby girl being labeled with the name Lancy that he changed his mind. He named me Mary for the Annunciation and Jo for St. Joseph, whose Saint Day is March 19th.

Before you imagine my papa as a quiet, soft-spoken man, let me share the way he explained my name. He would say, "I named you for Mary and St. Joseph, because your birthday fell in between their feast days. I thought it would be good to get their protection. Besides, I didn't want to piss either of them off!" Papa had a rough exterior and a core of solid love.

Life, of course, goes on. As they prepared me all my life, they got me ready for their deaths. Papa's faith never faltered. I hosted a party for him on their anniversary, June 14th. His church's priest said mass, I had his favorite foods, and their porch was full of his friends and family. His brother, my Uncle Mike, said to him, "Let's pray for God to heal you." I heard Papa respond, "The Lord's will is the Lord's will. I bow down before the Lord's will."

I pray to have his courage. Lung cancer doesn't provide a gentle passing. As an "old" hospice nurse, I often gave report to his hospice RN, telling her about fluids and drains and levels of pain. One day she stopped me. "You're dealing with this clinically," she said. "You need to feel this." Good advice, but difficult.

Papa cried once in the months before he died. Seeing my father cry wasn't an aberration to me. Unlike many strong men, he had no problem showing emotion. He didn't cry often, but he showed no shame when he did. I'd seen tears when he and my mother fought one Easter Sunday when I was a child, and he escaped to his garden to calm down. I saw him cry when his parents died and when my babies were born. The May before his death, I was at his bedside at the hospital. We were taking him home that day. He was anxious to be in his own house; he walked so quickly from our car to his front door that we could barely keep up with him!

This day, I'd just gotten my mother a snack, and she was sitting beside me, eating a peeled and sliced apple. Her legs were short and didn't touch the floor; they swung to and fro. She was humming. She was happy. Papa looked at her and then at me. The tears came. I glanced at Mama. She appeared oblivious. I rose to stand by my father. I didn't offer platitudes. Lessons learned at his side kept me silent. I held his hand, holding space with him. After a few minutes, he wiped his eyes and sighed. "I'm leaving you with a mess," he said, looking fondly at his wife.

"I'm okay, Papa," I said. "I can handle it. I'm forty-six and I run my own business. I have a supportive husband and great kids. I won't be alone."

He shook his head. "I know all that," he said, squeezing my hand firmly. "It's just… you're my baby." This good man's drive to protect me continued until his last breath.

At Papa's funeral, I said the words he blessed me with nightly. When I began serving young sexual abuse survivors, I couldn't wrap my head around their reality. How horrible it must be to lie in bed, waiting to be assaulted by someone who is supposed to honor you and respect you? Papa said the same thing every night when he tucked me in. He gave me a light kiss on my forehead and said, "Buona notte al più bella figlia in tutto il mondo. Ti amo." (Good night to the most beautiful daughter in all the world. I love you.) I would respond with "Buona notte al più bella papa in tutto il mondo. Ti amo." (Good night to the most beautiful Papa in all the world. I love you.) It was years after his death before I could say those words without crying; tears threaten me now as I write them.

In his last weeks, when I said, "I love you," he always responded with, "I love you more." As a parent, I know he did. Little in life approximates the love we feel for our children.

Papa died June 18th, four days after his anniversary celebration. He prayed for a good death his entire life, and I believe his prayer was answered. He was mobile up until his last moments, he never slipped into a coma. His last words were to my mother, "Eat your snack," he told her. "You're tired. Then go to sleep."

Mama's Alzheimer's was a challenge after his death. I quickly realized how much Papa covered for her. With his absence, she lost her grasp on reality. Mama died of a heart attack on October 31st, four months after him. It was fitting. She loved Halloween.

In the months between their deaths, I was gifted one incredible experience, for which I have no explanation. I was sleeping in Mama's bed. She wandered during the night, and I wanted to keep her safe. I woke to the feeling of someone staring at me. My children did that when they were young. It's a bizarre feeling. You sense someone's eyes on you and wake with a little person's face only inches from your own! I woke one night, at my parent's house, to my mother's face that close to mine. She was peering at me, her expression grave.

"You're my baby, aren't you?" she asked solemnly. Just that evening, she hadn't known me. It had been years since she recognized anyone.

I found my voice and told her yes, I was her child. We talked for over an hour. She asked of my husband and children. She discussed my work and expressed pride in me. She shared meal ideas, laughing when I told her it was tough to follow the handwritten family recipes she gave me at my wedding, because she so seldom measured any ingredients. "The instruction on some," I said, "is tough to quantify." My adult children now tell me I do the same. "Knead the dough," I say, "until it feels right."

We talked about my first apartment in New York, and the call I made to her to clarify an amount in a meal I was cooking. "How much broth?" I asked. "Just fill it to the first screw on the pot," she responded. "I don't have your pot," I countered, and she giggled. She loved that story.

She told me, again, how the rules in the obstetric unit in 1950 said if a baby was born after 9 p.m. a new mother could not see her newborn until 7 a.m. I was born, she reminded me, at 9:36 p.m. She got out of bed and marched to the nursery. "I waited seventeen years for you, honey," she said. "I wasn't waiting one more minute to hold you." Her doctor intervened, and she triumphed and swaddled me in her arms. "I'd like to have seen them stop me," she announced with glee.

I was transfixed. I don't know how, and I don't care why, but for that short hour in the middle of the night, I had my mama back.

Despite my comfort with my own mortality, becoming a parent made my survival urgent in my mind. Like my parents, I took on the role of parenting as my biggest joy and greatest job. I simply needed to raise my children.

Grief has no timetable. Each person reacts differently to each loss. The pain of losing a loved one is often acute at first – as if one is in the ocean, being tossed about by huge waves, treading water, struggling for breath. In time, the waves lesson in intensity, but they never really stop. Grief hits at obvious times, like a loved one's birthday or a holiday, but also when we're in the supermarket and we spy our lost loved one's favorite food, or when a smell reminds us of them. A full twenty years after Mama died, a recipe in a cookbook brought me to my emotional knees. Grief gets better, but it carves us into different people—resilient people, who, if we're fortunate, find joy again. Nonetheless, different.

Teen Grief

Teens, like adults, grieve in their own way.

A relationship break-up can be devastating. Support teens, even if the relationship didn't appear serious, or if the partner was an online connection only. Online friends/relationships are real to young people.

I've heard teens mourn the loss of a parent from cancer or in an accident and also feel the grief of change. Moving to another home or school district only adds to pain. One grieving teen's calls were frequent after her mother died, saying repeatedly, "I just want to be a kid, a fifteen-year-old kid. I'm tired of people looking at me with pity. I'm tired of being the girl whose mom had cancer and died."

Some might thing her words self-serving, but they're developmentally accurate. Erik Erikson's Theory of Psychosocial Development tells us that the major developmental task during ages twelve to eighteen is Identity vs Role Confusion. Finding one's identity is enough of a challenge without adding the social ramifications of being "the new teen" in school or "that girl." If parents could only think of their children's lives as steps to adulthood, where they need to walk through steps to arrive there healthy and strong, perhaps they'd be less judgmental.

Remember my words to my Rich – children go through critical stages of

266 ❀ SEX ED IS IN SESSION

development! I've been with teen parents when their babies were born stillborn (perinatal loss), I've comforted them during a miscarriage (spontaneous abortion). In both situations, unfeeling adults may say horrible, hurtful things like, "You're better off. You weren't ready to be a parent anyway."

I keep a file on my computer of three types of pregnancy outcomes: miscarriages, perinatal losses, and adoptions. I try to connect when the due date arrives after a miscarriage, on the dead baby's birthday, and on the birthday of an infant given for adoption. When I taught in Canada, a lovely nurse and doula told me the term her community used for choosing adoption was "surrendering the baby." It sounds harsh, but I think it exemplifies the grief and loss these young mothers feel. There is pain in all those life experiences, and young people feel that pain no less than an adult.

Dreadful Images in Parents' Minds

When our youngest was in fifth grade, I was doing a training in St. Louis. My maternal anxiety was so high, Rich finally quipped, "Why don't you tell the pilot you're a mother. If there's a problem with the plane, you can just stand in the aisle and hold it up. Your tension is that high."

I'm not sure why that trip freaked me out. My partner is a great dad, but I was panicked at the thought of him raising our kids without me. The day before my trip, I was given a life lesson. A fellow teacher and friend got up to go to school, fell in the shower, and died of an aneurism. In her house, in a safe place. I realized I didn't need to be in an airplane to die. I could be anywhere.

Grief is part of life, as is death. It's the journey that matters most. My mama was fond of Psalm 30: 5: *Weeping may endure for a night but joy cometh in the morning.*

I choose to look for joy.

Step #30: Validate Emotional Pain

Provide support.

Young people may grieve over the loss of a friendship or the end of a relationship.

Acknowledge grief.

Strive to avoid judgement.

Don't limit grief with positive platitudes and clichés.

CHAPTER THIRTY-TWO

Cancer is Just a Word

Tattoos

I have a tat. It's a yellow rosebud, it symbolizes both women's right to vote and the flowers my Rich gifts me at every major event in our lives. I got my tattoo after I healed from breast cancer surgery and radiation in 2005. Radiation sites were marked with ink and small, round tattooed dots. I didn't resent the tattoos I needed for treatment, but decided I wanted my own. It's on the healthy breast, discreetly placed above my bra line. I made the tattoo artist laugh when I asked him to draw the design, with my bra on, and then allow me time to go to the restroom. I wanted to remove the bra and make certain the tattoo was strategically placed, so it didn't become a long stem rose as I aged! Our peer educators were sure I'd get another tat, and then another. They were wrong. Just the one.

Some young people are covered in tats. I knew a teen who got a tattoo of Michael Jackson on his ankle the same day he received a larger one of a rainbow on his calf. I said, "I didn't know you were such a Michael Jackson fan." His reply? "I'm not. The artist threw it in for free." Tats are part of youth culture. Each tattoo has a story. Asking for that story is a great conversation starter.

Contrasts

In 2000, I attended an AASECT (American Association for Sexuality Educators, Counselors, and Therapists) conference in Las Vegas and presented on sexual abuse. The hotel booked three groups: AASECT, consisting of sexuality educators, counselors, and therapists, a National Rifle Association regional meeting, and the International Body Piercing and Tattooing Association. I'm surprised there wasn't bloodshed.

Yet Another Lesson Learned

When Rich and I married in March of 1973, jobs were scarce. My fiancé found work in New York City with American Airlines. I followed, of course. I applied for the pediatric/adolescent unit and was given that post, but, to my sorrow, needed to do a three-month stint on an adult experimental unit before I could transfer to peds. I didn't know then, but the experience prepared me for the hospice nursing I'd do a decade later. Chemo was tested on this unit. I was familiar with research studies from Children's and comfortable with keeping exacting data, but I was unprepared for what I would see patients endure in the name of living longer. One therapy regimen that never reached beyond our unit was MBV, mixed bacterial vaccine. Patients were given a cocktail of bacteria in the hope that malignant cells would die under the assault. I remember how ill my patients became. I remember the fire of their fevers and the intensity of their tremors. I held innumerable shoulders while people cried and cleaned more emesis basins than I could count.

It was in New York City, on that pediatric/adolescent oncology unit, that a true spiritual moment was given to me. A mentor there, a middle-aged woman from mainland China, who was trained as a nurse in her homeland but worked as an aide in America, guided me through a difficult death. Like my Chinese guide Mabel, she selected the English name of Daisy. One of my primary patients, an eight-year-old Puerto Rican child whose mom was a teen, died after a long struggle with leukemia. I loved her, but I thought my job was to support her mom and be stoic. As I cleaned the medical devices we used in her last days of life, I finally let the tears come. Daisy found me in the treatment room, blubbering over the sink.

"Cry," she said. "It's good. Cry with the family, too."

"I'm supposed to be professional," I muttered, angry at myself for losing control.

Daisy shook her head, "No. You're supposed to be human." Wrapping her arms around me, she directed me to the table and chairs. She held me while I finished crying, then said, "It all comes together, Mary Jo. These children you love and care for now will not forget you. When you die, they'll be waiting for you, and they'll say, 'Mary Jo, what took you so long?'"

That evening, I sat my new husband down. "We're gonna die," I said without preamble.

He laughed, "I know. What shall we do for dinner?"

I growled at him, "Honey, I'm serious. We're gonna die."

When we returned to Western Pennsylvania to be near my parents and Rich's parents, I wrote to one of my nurse friends from our pediatric oncology unit. She was a nun who lived with three other sisters in an independent convent. I inquired of the children I cared for and left behind. Her response came swiftly. She ended her note with the words, "All the children you asked about have died. They'll be waiting for you." Daisy influenced more than me.

Later, in our lives together, Rich has shared he wishes he experienced what I did at Sloan Kettering. Have I let slip my conviction that each day is a gift to be treasured? Sure, I'm human. I think of it more than most. I tell my family each holiday, each birthday, each day is the best day ever. I mean it. Mortality is real to me.

Welcome Back, Cancer

In January 2019, a suspicious growth was seen on my annual mammogram. One biopsy and one phone call later, I was once more a cancer patient. As a survivor for fourteen years, this was unexpected. I was confident, however. I'm strong, I've survived six surgeries in my life, and I went back to teach two days after my lumpectomy for my first cancer in 2005. I wanted to model that cancer isn't a death sentence and doesn't define a person. It was one of my dumbest decisions. I had surgery on a Tuesday, taught on Thursday, and took Friday off!

Two weeks, I thought, *in 2019. This time I'll be up and running in two weeks.*

Wow, was I wrong!

What I call the "2019 cancer" was unrelated to my first one; a primary cancer, it was not a recurrence, but a brand new, genetically different malignancy. It was also more aggressive.

I decided I would be as aggressive as the tumor. My decision to have a bilateral mastectomy and remove both breasts was immediate, and I've not looked back. I don't believe in doing "what ifs" in life… you know, the second-guessing so many of us do after a decision. Move forward.

The surgery was tougher than the one in 2005 and it was compounded by sudden hemorrhaging at 4:30 a.m., less than ten hours post-op. A PCT (patient care technician or nursing assistant) saved my life. She checked the drain on my right incision and said, "That's a lot of blood!" I agreed, waking quickly. She removed 90cc of bright red clotting blood from the drain and ran for an RN. Another 90cc, and only five minutes had passed.

The nursing staff moved quickly. I remember being very clinical about it. I said to the nurse, "I'm going into shock. I'm really nauseated, and my head is spinning. I can't feel my extremities and my heart is tachycardic. If you take my blood pressure, it's gonna be low." It was, at 80/40.

I remember being very calm. Before they wheeled me to the OR for emergency surgery, I texted Rich and our three children, told then I loved them, and I was fine.

I remember praying a simple prayer: "If you're done with my service, I'm ready. If you'd like me to keep on with my mission, I'll stay." My papa's words echoed in my head. *The Lord's will is the Lord's will.*

What a busy day that was! Our family was with me the night before, when I had surgery (I was last on the schedule), and when I woke after the emergency surgery, Rich was there, Lisa moments later. She was on staff at the hospital that day, since she's a palliative care MD. She brought her laptop and never left my side the rest of the day. Our daughter, Amy, and her family arrived as soon as they could. Nate was there as well. I was surrounded by love and support.

I remember taking three texts from teens while still groggy from anesthesia. I think I was tired, because I told a teen I'd lost 1.5 liters of blood. The young man gasped and said, "That's almost a 2-liter bottle of Mt. Dew!"

Word spread. Soon, teens were texting to make sure I was alive. When I returned to our teen center, the same young man told me, "I Googled it. If you'd lost a full two liters, you'd be dead." Only young people!

Our family, friends, and community wove a tapestry of love around me. I don't think we needed to create a meal for a full month! A dear friend crocheted me a beautiful shawl, a thirty-something peer educator alumnus made me a blanket for chemo. Flowers and gifts and cards (I love cards) came daily for weeks. I sat back and let love help me heal.

I was wrong about being up to teaching in two weeks. It was a full month before I could sleep lying down in a bed. My Rich was everything to me during this time, taking our relationship to a new level of intimacy.

Chemo started in March, but after only one dose at five weeks post-op, our family made a much-anticipated trip to Disney in Florida. I'd planned the trip for a year, and I refused to miss it. The memories of our grandchildren there will be my February memories for years. (What's a February memory? It's term I use for a memory that brings so much joy that one takes it out and treasures it on dark days.)

Knowledge and Experience are Different

My 2005 breast cancer was easy. Returning to school so quickly wasn't my wisest decision. Still, even after taking Tamoxifen and then Arimidex for five years post-op, this was an "easy" cancer.

As I shared, I responded to the 2019 cancer with a bilateral mastectomy in January and began chemo that March. I finish chemo in February, 2020.

Cancer doesn't bring me down. It's not fun – it does, as the t-shirts say, "suck," but I see it as part of life. I'd been an oncology nurse, so I knew what would happen. Knowledge and experience are two different things, though. Walking through surgery and treatment was a whole other dimension to nursing someone through it.

I cried two times in the last six months – once when I needed to cancel my sexuality class at W & J College, and the second time when I realized I didn't have the strength to teach a full day of classes. Everything else, I just took in stride.

When I returned to school, many young people seemed glad to see me. A ninth grader I'd taught since sixth grade took me aside and blurted, "Thank God you're back. You're the only person I can talk to about my dick." (He was frightened he wasn't physically "okay" when we first met because it seemed – to him - that his penis slanted to the right).

My favorite student reaction to my return came from a senior. Let me give you a visual. This young person is tall, think six-foot-five or higher. He always dresses as if he's ready to go hunting. We met in his sixth grade year, when a teacher warned me of him before our first class together. "Be careful with that one," she said in a firm tone. "He's a bad kid."

There are no bad kids. I called him to me. "Would you like to sit here?" I asked.

He snorted. He'd heard the teacher's words. "Cuz I'm a bad kid?" he grunted, glaring at me.

"I don't believe in bad kids," I said. "I'm interested in you. Sometimes kids who are full of energy are called 'bad kids.' I like people with energy. We're going to play a dice game. Would you please be captain of one of the teams? That means you'll listen to your team's answer and then tell me it. Your voice is the only voice that will count from your team."

Curious, he glared a little less, then said, "You don't want me."

Non-plussed, I confirmed, "I do. You'll say the answer. If you say the right answer and everyone on your team is yelling the wrong one, your team will get the point. If you say the wrong answer and your team is telling me the right answer, your team will lose a point. So, you'll need to talk with your team before you answer."

"And you think I can do this?" he looked disdainfully at me, then glanced at the teacher's back as she left the room.

"I know you can," I said, projecting confidence.

He did well. Six years later, we're friends. He doesn't hang out at our Teen Center and he's not a peer educator, but he never fails to participate in class and he's shared many relationship stories over the years.

On my third day back teaching in his high school, he saw me for the first time since I'd gotten sick. His joy was palpable. He shouted at the top of his voice, "I thought you were dead!"

His peers tried to shush him, but he reached me in four long strides, picked me up, and carried me around the foyer. When he put me down, he whispered, "Don't die, hear?"

It's such a gift to teach.

Heartbreaking...

As much as I seek joy and believe a day without a smile and laughter is wasted, I cannot be casual about some things.

I'm unable to be casual about the attacks on women's health and repro-ductive health in our nation. I cannot fathom how the same people who are so vehemently against abortion are also against contraception or family planning. It makes me think these attacks are on women, period.

I'm unable to be casual about our maternal death rate. More American women are dying of pregnancy-related complications than any other developed country. The only one of these nations where the maternal mortality rate is rising is the U.S.

I'm unable to be casual about the reality that Black mothers in the U.S. are three times more likely to die in childbirth than white mothers.

I'm unable to be casual about the rise in racism and hate crimes in our nation, or the modeling of "us vs them" attitudes among people in power.

I am truly unable to be casual about the traumatic conditions of children at our southern border.

I cannot bear the reports of children denied basic human needs. The words of these children haunt me. I hear their pain and it breaks my heart.

A friend posted on social media that we are now two Americas - one that supports white nationalist philosophy and wants America to be white, and the other that hopes for a multi-cultural republic representing all people.

I hope this is not true. I pray it is not. If it is, then we are sliding back in time.

Going Back?

I remember my fourth grade Jewish friend who was openly mocked - in front of teachers - for honoring Yom Kippur. No adult spoke up. When she returned from taking a day off to honor her faith, there were swastikas carved into her desk. No one removed them. They were small, so she often positioned her books to cover them.

I remember a fifth grade transfer student - a Black girl who became the only child of color in my room. When I went up to her during recess to welcome her, she gently told me, "Thanks, but you should stay with 'your own kind,' so you don't lose friends." I heard her mocked for her color. I heard the N-word said, with no adults intervening. We were friends, but I couldn't truly know her pain.

Small memories of the fifties. As a white child, I was only an observer. I didn't really know. I was troubled, though, so, of course, I went to Papa. I wanted an explanation for hate. He sat me down, as he always did, and told me of his treatment as a fourteen-year-old worker. Yes, he said, he was called horrible names. Yes, he was treated poorly, but did I know how much he was embraced and loved at church? In his community? There are good people, he said. Reminiscent of Mr. Rogers, he told me to look for the good people.

Papa loved America. He also told me what made America great was our right to vote. He had, he said, the same vote as a rich man. He didn't understand people who would not vote. "I would die for America," he would say, shaking his head, "yet some people do not vote."

If Papa disliked a politician, he talked about it at home. Publicly, he supported all elected officials, because he said his fellow Americans' votes for these people needed honored. He respected regardless of party or policy. The concept of hating a member of another political party was alien to him. The party system was key, he said. Too much power in one party wasn't okay. Except... if an elected official was not ethical or fair. If an elected official did not uphold his high standards of morality. If an elected official hurt children – like me, he loved and protected children.

He believed elected officials needed to put aside party lines to work together for the good of all people. Only in these negative situations did I see him work at polling spaces and distributing literature. All people, he said. What sets America apart is our belief in all types of people.

How good, he'd tell me, that we are of so many. He talked about this a lot. The doctor who cared for him during his final days was a Jewish oncologist. He asked him about his faith (after telling him Jewish doctors were smart, which made me cringe, but the MD was terrific, smiled at me over Papa's head, and agreed. Yes, he said, he was indeed smart). One of the caregivers who came to him through hospice was a person of color. He asked about her culture. Even dying, he was intensely interested in people. He loved learning about difference.

Papa modeled my belief that each person is a person of worth. I know how he would feel about these children's trauma. I know how he would feel about death in childbirth. I know how he would feel about women's health. I wish everyone was raised by my papa. The world would be kinder.

Words of Love

Try to escape fear of death. It is universal and part of life.

Please trust in your own strength and goodness.

Please remember each day is a gift.

Talk and teach about death. It is, after all, universal to us all.

Wake each morning grateful. If you are called to work with children and teens, do all you can to love and serve them.

May today be your best day ever.

Teaching death education is just as controversial
as sex education – have courage and face it.

Step #31: Knowledge and Experience are Two Different Things

Young people are watching. Show them you can deal with whatever life brings.

Stand for those who have no voice.

Teach what is true and right.

Live with joy.

Model peace.

CHAPTER THIRTY-THREE

Thirty Years

❀

In 2018, our outreach held its thirtieth anniversary. I know it sounds cliché, but I don't know where the time fled. I ponder how much I've learned since 1988. I had little experience serving LGBTQIA youth, but I learned. My best teachers were young people.

Some outstanding trans youth guided me to a realization of their unique needs. They also taught me they were simply human beings who wanted the same rights as other humans. I've been subpoenaed to speak on the behalf of trans youth in foster placement. I've given more copies of *Nonnie Talks About Gender* away than I've sold. I've watched parents of gender non-conforming or gender fluid youth become amazing advocates for their children, letting them lead. I've seen parents deny their children's selfhood and lose them emotionally as soon as the young person is legally an adult.

One of Our Best!

I want to speak to my pride in one of my former peer educators. Emmett gave permission for his inclusion here. I cannot imagine this book without him.

At twenty-four, Emmett is a dedicated professional, teaching and training on his own. Just last December, he presented at the National Sex Ed Conference. The year before, I was conference co-chair. After his proposal was accepted, he told me he'd submitted three times before. He knew I was able to open doors for him, but he sought no favors. He did it on his own. He and his educational partner, Lex, presented a workshop called *Not Your Average Sex Talk.* They focus on peer to peer sex education in college communities and offer unique sex ed for people who are often ignored – trans and disabled individuals. I was bursting with joy as I watched them present. The 2018 National Sex Ed Conference was a bookend experience for me. I did a pre-conference session called Nonnie Talks About Life: Presenting Challenging Topics to Children and was part of a panel called Past to Future: Creating a Life-Long Career in Sexuality Education with three of my esteemed colleagues and friends, Michael McGee, Debra Haffner, and Pam Wilson.

I'll quote part of an article written by the Observer-Reporter about the conference, where Emmett spoke freely. "Mary Jo is part of my history," said Emmett Patterson. "She is the person who showed me that this is something people can do and I'm good at – talking to people about things that are not easy to talk about. She trusts young people, with such an open heart, to lead. I was one of the first openly transgender people to come out. It shook the community a bit, in not such a fun way all the time," he said. "Even before I came out to others, I came out to her. She was so supportive. I started working for her at the Common Ground Teen Center with young LGBT people like me... she saved me. She gave me a job when no one would give me one. She trusted me as a seventeen-year-old. The most important thing she really did was encourage me to trust my own knowledge. Lived experience is critical knowledge. You might not get a certificate but trust your gut. Provide context someone on the outside can't offer. She practices what she preaches and showed me that this work is possible and can be monumental."

Why I Won't Stop Teaching

I continue teaching sex ed in schools. I continue serving as a sexuality counselor to adults in need, although less than I once did. I continue to take calls and emails from young people, parents, and grandparents. Not long ago, a mother called me to ask me to help her son. I listened as she described his long showers. He was fourteen. I asked how she reacted to his time alone in the bathroom. She said, "I pound on the door and yell, 'Stop sinning in there.'" For a flash, I thought of my 1905 sex ed books.

I engaged this mom in conversation for a while, talking about anything except her son. I ascertained she lived with his father. Finally, I gave her my opinion. *Her son was typical. He was no longer a child.* By this point, we'd established a little trust, so I asked her if she understood the messages she gave when she pounded on that bathroom door.

"That he should stop," she said,

"Sure," I paused. "You're also telling him his body is shameful."

"I don't want that," she mumbled.

"One thing more," I said, "You're teaching him to hurry up."

Silence.

She asked if I really was a sexuality counselor. I said I was. She made an appointment with me, where she revealed she'd been in a long relationship with a man but had never been orgasmic. She shared a greater understanding of her son's emerging sexuality as well.

I repeatedly receive the question, "What does an orgasm feel like?" in my Curiosity Bag. I answer it by using an analogy to pain. "What if," I say, "I caught my finger in the door and the bone fractured?" I point to the heavy classroom door, holding up my finger. "Would you know what I felt?"

My students eventually acknowledge they could have empathy for my pain, but they'd only know what it felt like if they too experienced a broken finger. Pain, I tell them, is difficult to put into words. Is it sharp, dull, piercing? Is it the worst pain of one's life or a small discomfort? Pleasure is equally challenging

284 ❀ SEX ED IS IN SESSION

to describe. "Suppose," I say, "you are from an alien planet. In your culture, the words 'chocolate,' 'sweet,' and 'cold' don't exist. You have no perspective for those concepts. I offer you chocolate ice cream and tell you it's pleasant to eat. How can you possibly know what to expect?"

I can and do teach what happens physiologically during orgasm. I can describe ejaculation and clitoral stimulation. Describing the feeling of sexual pleasure is more challenging. Each person is unique.

One never knows where a life in sexuality education and sexuality counseling will bring you. I'm blessed to continue to find out!

Plan for sustainability in agencies or businesses
or schools. In a family, discuss the future.

Step #32: It's Not About Us

Train a successor.

This work doesn't stop because we do.

Leave a legacy.

Write clear instructions and directions to password protected files.

Plan for your absence.

CHAPTER THIRTY-FOUR

Level Sixty-Seven

❁

I'm at the age where you tell someone how old you are and they don't argue with you. No one says, "Oh, no, you're not that old!" Instead, people pause, smile, and nod, as if to say, *Oh yes, I thought so.*

At one point, I taught childbirth education four times a week. That's a lot of babies! Four years ago, I decided I needed a pillow for our sofa. The cashier at the store said, "You taught me when I had my baby."

I said, "How nice to be remembered. How old is your baby?"

"Thirty-nine," she said.

I was so shocked, I walked out without the pillow.

Growing older doesn't usually bother me. My only concern is having time to accomplish my dreams. It's rumored that Alexander the Great's last words were, "…so much to do." I'm certainly not a conquering hero, but I've had a five-year plan since my eighteenth year. The to-dos never stop, they just change.

My primary dream in my current life is passing on knowledge. I want to take everything in my head and share it. I know the techniques we've used to connect with young people work and I want them to go on beyond me. I know what it means to teach with heart. In a very real way, this dream is why I wrote this book.

This work, serving young people, is not about me. It's not about any adult. I believe this work is a mission, a vocation, an honor. It exists for and through young people; my passion for using peer education is predicated on the reality of teen wisdom. They get it, they truly do.

I love my birthday. When the first of March rolls around every year, the joy starts. I seek joy daily, but my birthday month is special to me. I don't recall birthday parties as a child, but each March 24th, I was told the story of my parents' years without children - how sad they'd been, and how happy they were when I arrived. How could I not love my birthday with such an annual marketing campaign on its behalf?

Our community is generous during Christmas holidays. I am deeply grateful. Young people's birthdays are less celebrated than Christmas. We try to make up for that. I know many teens whose birthdays are grim. How much does it hurt to be told, "Today is the day you ruined my life," by a parent? We acknowledge each young person's worth. Kin is not always the people to whom one is related by blood. We often host a day for each teen in our program, filling in for adults who fail to honor them. There is great joy in teaching that each person is a person of worth.

Last year, in honor of my birthday, I ordered Chinese food for our peer educators at our teen center. Nothing makes teens happier than food. We were having a lovely, casual conversation (in our usual circle, with twenty-four young people). A young man asked me my age. I said honestly, sixty-seven. His face fell. Later, I discovered his grandmother died at sixty-eight. To him, my age was a scary number. He looked simultaneously shocked and dismayed. I didn't think twice about his reaction, and the dialogue continued. We were talking about music and movies and books, as we often do. When we hold peer educator meetings, the young people often select a topic to share during introductions. One infamous evening, each person was asked to share their favorite song. Over the next half hour, twenty-seven teens sang out twenty-seven songs, and I didn't recognize one! That did make me feel old!

Later that night, the incredulous young man texted me. "I feel bad," his text read. "I don't think I reacted well to your age." I assured him it was not a problem. I knew my age and I was quite okay with it. He went on to text, "Don't think of it in years. Think of it as if you're playing a video game and you've achieved Level 67. Not everyone gets that far. It's quite an accomplishment."

Young people are wise. Level 67. Not bad.

This year, I was teaching eighth graders a week before my birthday when one of my students remembered the date was near. I was touched. I mentioned I was getting up there.

"How old will you be?" he asked.

"Sixty-eight."

He nodded, pensive.

After class, a young man lingered. In a tone of gravitas, he said, "I need a promise from you." I listened. He hit his chest over his heart and said, "Promise you'll do this through my twelfth grade year. I need you to help me get there." I said I'd do my best. He nodded, still solemn, as if he'd given me a mandate!

Even if I wanted to retire, how could I? Age is a gift not every person receives. I'm grateful. Boom shaka laka laka!

Aging is a gift not everyone receives.

Step 33: Model Respect for Older Adults

It's tough to see oneself aging.

Age with grace.

Older adults are steeped in life's wisdom.

Advocate against ageism at any of life's levels.

Connect young adults with older ones. Their connections are priceless.

Closing

❀

When I teach, I prepare an opening and a closing. The opening sets the stage, the closing leaves the group with food for thought.

I thank you for the priceless gift of your time. When I teach professional trainings or speak at a conference, this poem is often part of my closing. I leave it with you as a gift and a guide. We do not know what other people know. Empathy and compassion will lead us, if we let them. If you teach – and we all teach – teach with your heart.

Knots by r.d. laing (1972)

There is something I don't know
that I am supposed to know.
I don't know *what* it is I don't know and
yet am supposed to know,
and I feel I look stupid if

I seem both not to know it
and not know *what* it is I don't know.
Therefore, I pretend I know it.
This is nerve-wracking since I don't know
what I must pretend to know.
Therefore, I pretend to know everything.
I feel you know what I am supposed to know,
but you can't tell me what it is because
you don't know that I don't know what it is.
You may know what I don't know, but
not that I don't know it, and I can't tell you.
So, you will have to tell me everything.

We don't know what a young person doesn't know.

Step 34: Teach What Young People Need, Not What You Think They Should Need

A Final Gift

I began Chapter One by hoping my words would bring you joy. In the spirit of my parents, I'd like to offer you a final parting gift.

If I knew you personally, I would feed you. I once overheard one of our Common Ground Teen Center teen staff tell a new attendee, "That's Mary Jo. One thing's for sure, she'll feed you!"

Since I cannot break bread with you, I offer you the next best thing. The recipe below is from my mama. My papa also cooked. I learned early what a true partnership was like by watching my parents pull together to share household tasks and parent me. Such a beautiful lesson!

This, then, is my final Step for you:
If you truly want to connect with young people, feed them!

Mama Cirelli's Minestrone
(adapted for real life by her daughter!)

Make this soup your own. I'm convinced the first minestrone soup was made in a busy family where money was tight and the parents threw everything in their garden into the soup!

You'll need the following ingredients
(leave out any veggies you or your family don't like):
- **4 cups chicken broth.** Canned is fine. As I've gotten older, I use low salt versions. If you can tolerate salt, I recommend using the typical kind! I reserve an extra cup of broth in case the soup is too thick. (Yes, mama made it from stock. I did that one time!) Vegetarians can use vegetable broth.
- **1 small can tomato paste** (Italian seasoned is a plus). Use from ½ can to a whole can, depending on how tomato-y you want the soup to taste.
- **One 20oz can of chopped or diced Italian seasoned tomatoes (use the juice)**
- **Medium bulk sausage,** sautéed in small pieces and drained. If you use the same pot for the soup as the sautéing, wash the pot before you add the other ingredients. (Leave out the sausage for vegetarian soup, but it's not as tasty!)
- **3 cloves garlic,** minced
- **½ medium onion,** chopped
- **1 tsp – 1 tbsp olive oil** for sautéing (Depending on how much fat you want to use, but please use olive oil. It makes a difference.)
- **2 fresh basil leaves,** chopped.
- **The following fresh vegetables, diced or chopped,** as you like. You can also use chopped frozen veggies (again, not as good, but works in an pinch):
    - **small zuchinni, skin on**
    - **½ green pepper**
    - **½ red pepper**
    - **3 white potatoes**

- 1 small sweet potato
- 6 -10 small carrots
- 3/4 cup fresh green beans
- ½ cup fresh broccoli
- ½ cup fresh cauliflower
- ½ cup corn
- 3/4 cup mushrooms
- Small cans of the following (all drained):
  - **Northern beans**
  - **kidney beans**
  - **cannellini beans**
  - **ceci beans**
- **Pasta** (pre-cooked, drained, and then added to the soup): ditalini or acini de pepe. You could use a thin spaghetti or vermicelli, but then the pasta must be cut into small pieces. The ditalini and acini de pepe are easier to eat. If you boil the pasta in the soup, it soaks up all the broth.

To fix: Brown the sausage well and drain. Sauté the garlic and onion (use the olive oil to sauté), add the broth, canned tomatoes and tomato paste, bring to slow boil. Add chopped fresh veggies, stir, bring to boil, lower heat and cook slowly for one hour. Add the canned beans, heat. Boil the pasta separately, drain and add. Heat. Serve with grated mozzarella and parmesan cheeses as toppings, and fresh bread. Add a salad and you've got a great meal.

Mangia, bello (eat, beautiful). I wish you joy.

Acknowledgements

No effort of merit is accomplished alone.

My gratitude goes out to six:
First, I am grateful for my family: my parents, my grandparents, my cousins, and my aunts and uncles – all of whom helped raise me.

My immediate family means more to me than words can say. My husband and partner, Rich, shores me up, is my best cheerleader, the father of our children, my lover, and my best friend. When my grandmother died, my grandfather cried out at the cemetery, "Il mio compagno" (my companion). What will I do without my companion?" My Rich is my companion, in every sense of the word.

Our children bring me joy daily.

Our eldest daughter is Amy. Amy teaches with me, which gives me not only the comfort of family at work, but the security of knowing my mission is in the capable hands of someone who "gets" my philosophy and is dedicated to young people. Watching her mentor young parents as I once did is one of the high points of my life. Amy created our only fundraiser in 2009 and continues to make it real. Amy and her husband, Paul, are parents of our oldest grandbabies: Jai, Lily, and Evan.

Our second daughter is Lisa. Lisa is a palliative care physician. I ponder if my days as a hospice nurse influenced her calm, empathetic, caring attitude about death, since she was a preschooler then. She comforts me with her expert diagnosis and love during my cancer treatment. Lisa creates programs on mindfulness for medical residents. She, too, is a teacher.

Lisa and her husband, Evan, are parents of Andy. As I write this, we await the arrival of his baby sister.

Our son is Nathan. Of all our children, Nate spent the most time connected to my peer education group. He took on many roles with our Real Talk Performers and was an excellent peer educator. He was truly the SLS (Sex Lady's Son); he's served as a role model and mentor all his life. He's an engineer and a great cook and daddy, but I know he could teach if asked.

Nate and his wife, Erin, are the parents of Joelle.

Second, my memory and my heart sings with anecdotes of the young people I've served. I appreciate you all. You are people of great worth.

Third, I am deeply cognizant of how much the Washington Health System's decades-long support has shored up my programs and made teaching a quarter-million young people a reality. Without this outstanding community system and the fine group of excellent professionals who lead it, starting with Helen Bartus and Telford Thomas, through Gary Weinstein and Brook Ward, the Teen Outreach would not exist.

Fourth, I am grateful to Lindsey Smith and Amanda Filippelli of One Idea Press. I'd self-published for decades before connecting with these two excellent professionals. They embraced my words, supported my mission, and made this book come alive. Without them, it would not exist.

Fifth, I am grateful for my dear friend Anastasia Higginbotham, the author of the book series for young children called Ordinary Terrible Things, which complements my Nonnie Series of books. Anastasia took time from her own busy schedule to read the book and write the introduction. How blessed we are with our friendship!

Sixth, like my Papa before me, I stand on my faith. As a fourth grader, I thought I wanted to be a missionary to a far away land. My parents gently taught me to bloom where I was planted. I remember the day I changed my mind. It was my tenth birthday. I prayed a lot in those days; I was being raised by deeply faithful parents. I was reading Thomas à Kempis' Immitation of Christ. I wrote this prayer in my journal:

> *Lord, help me to love and serve Your children, especially those who have no one to love them, so through them I may learn to love and serve You.*

Nearly 60 years later, I pray the same words every day.

Finally, I want to thank you for reading. Sex Ed is in Session is a deeply personal manuscript.

I'm seventy in March, 2020. I find myself thinking of legacies.

My true legacy is my own children – three babies we raised to be good humans, who parent well, and who work for good.

My second legacy are the young people I've taught, many of whom teach in their own lives. My amazing staff are part of my legacy as well – they are people who follow in my philosophical footsteps.

This book is a way for me to teach beyond the end of this life – a tangible treatise of my life mission. I hope it encourages and empowers others to respect young people and validate their worthiness.

CPSIA information can be obtained
at www.ICGtesting.com
Printed in the USA
LVHW031722210220
647794LV00003B/520

9 781944 134266